CATHOLIC POLITICAL THOUGHT

Catholic Political Thought

1789 - 1848

*Texts selected, with an Introduction and
biographical notes, by*

BÉLA MENCZER

LONDON
BURNS OATES

PRINTED IN GREAT BRITAIN BY THE GARDEN CITY PRESS LTD
FOR BURNS OATES AND WASHBOURNE LTD
28 ASHLEY PLACE
LONDON, S.W.1
First published 1952

Quia membra sumus corporis eius, de carne eius,
et de ossibus eius.

TO MARJORIE

IN MEMORY OF ANOTHER DEDICATION

CONTENTS

vii

INTRODUCTION

1. AUTHORITY AND LIBERTY IN THE WESTERN CONSCIENCE

Our Faith is of the stuff of history. The Old Testament differs from all other sacred books venerated by the nations because it is history—an account of events full of mystical significance. Christian history differs from all other history because it comprises an era, because it is an account of a fundamental change in the order of the world, and the consequences of that change.

Man alone of all created beings has a history. Of all the records of human actions and events, the Old Testament is the first to be fully related to society, and to be in full relationship with the essential nature of man. Other civilisations have had their annals and chronicles, but these were never intended to reveal the essential. The names of Pharaohs have been recorded, and those of the rulers of China; their virtues were praised, and some of their actions made known and transmitted to posterity. Nearer to us in time, the historians of Greece and Rome—Herodotus, Tacitus—tell the story of events with a fuller and more personal characterisation of the actors; indeed they describe national characteristics with such penetrating observation that in the field of literature they remain unsurpassed. But what makes the Bible unique, and different in essence from all other venerated books of those distant centuries, is its focus. The biblical story moves visibly to a climax. Changes in institutions, the transition from the rule of prophets to that of kings, forced migrations, catastrophes and conquests, victories and defeats—all these occur because they have to occur. Nothing happens by mere chance. Everything has a discernible cause. Events have their context on a divine plane, the essentials of which are revealed. Reason and power were revealed in the act of Creation; love and sacrifice, as the essential relation of God to Man, were revealed on the Cross; justice and judgement are foretold for the end of the centuries.

Established on this threefold basis of will, sacrifice, and preparation for final judgement, life derives from Christianity a wholly new significance. Of all living things created, only man can voluntarily destroy himself; and only man can accept life voluntarily, in the full and certain knowledge of coming to a material end. Christ condemned self-destruction, and proclaimed the relativity of the material end, but by no means the insignificance of that end. He proclaimed its relation to the three fundamental bases of will, love and judgement, these three aspects of Divinity, faculties of supreme Reason.

Once the full truth has been revealed, a chosen people is no longer needed to serve as an example; mankind itself becomes the example. Survival after death, sensed in the cult of the Egyptians, stated in Buddhism, and pondered by the Greeks, is now demonstrated and defined. It is given a complete sense and a precise meaning, with no room left for either obscurity or indifference. Christ revealed the mystery. He conquered the world, and its conquest is final. History, the science of human actions, becomes the science of the definite, the science of accomplished finalities.

It was only a generation earlier that the poet Virgil, singing the glories of the age of Augustus, had foretold fulfilment, the coming fullness of time. Again, there is no place here for speculation or change. The meeting of Christ and Rome was a providential necessity; it was a message in action, a story with no episode of secondary importance. All is precision, like the Latin language itself, which as the common language of the Church was to unite the Christian peoples of the West.

Thenceforward they live in Time, the time between Creation and final Judgement. What is but a longing, a vague divination, in others, is for them a certainty; God conquers chaos and sets an aim to history. Before conquering space, European mankind recognised Time. It saw the dividing moment in Time, the presence of God on earth. Now that limits had been set to human time and history, it was to go out and conquer space. European mankind carried history into space by carrying Christ to distant peoples living in closed realms, who had never had any notion of time and whose history had therefore remained static. This achievement, which has altered the whole image of the world in such a tremendous way during the last few centuries, cannot be explained otherwise than by the fact that the European nations had a different notion of history—the Roman and Christian concept of history as a progress from

Creation, through Redemption, to Judgement. " Discovery "
is a word peculiar to the vocabulary of a civilisation that is
founded on Revelation. Other nations may conquer, but the
Christian nations " discover ": they open closed realms to the
Light, and static realms to Time.

The evil inherent in the world becomes transitory. In the
words of Tertullian, the Teacher of the Church who coined the
expression *unum necessarium*: " God suffers, or the world breaks
into pieces." God's suffering is not only a plausible explanation
of the continued existence of the world, it is the only possible
explanation: *Aut dissolvitur machina mundi, aut mundi creator
patitur.* And St Augustine, otherwise so completely different
from Tertullian in his appreciation of pre-Christian learning,
says that this necessary belief is the necessary explanation of
the unity of human history, and of the survival of an Empire
in the throes of invasion and devastation.

To Christianity, and Christianity alone, we owe the historical
conscience of Europe. And it is to Christianity alone that we
owe the full meaning of both order and liberty.

The sense of order is an acceptance of Creation, the rational
acceptance of necessity. Liberty is the moral acceptance of
order, a voluntary action subject to final judgement. Liberty
means choice: the choice of voluntary sacrifice, the means
whereby a final and for ever undisturbed harmony of Order
and Liberty can be established; it means the offering of a
sacrifice made freely for the proclamation and explanation of
the law of Order—the death on the Cross—and our personal
participation in this supreme act of Liberty through the Mass.
Christ has set us free for all time. Liberty is as final as the
order of Creation: " The truth shall set you free."

The historical conscience which Christianity gave us is a
recognition of the eternal in what is passing and ephemeral, a
recognition of something which is not subject to change amidst
the infinity of material changes. This principle of eternity is
found in the very nature of an unchanging Creator. " All that
He ever created," says St Augustine, the father of a Christian
philosophy of history, " was in Him, in His unchanged fixed
Will eternally one and the same."

Thus everything within Creation, within Order, appertains
to the category of the necessary, and necessity is clearly
defined and demonstrated. Yet Creation itself was a voluntary
action, a gift, an effect of Liberty. Authority was established,
not for the sake of the Creator, but for the sake of the

creature: its establishment and acceptance should be equally final.

This divine finality in History, this acceptance of the final and definite in Revelation, of an authority freely given and accepted, became the quintessence of the Western Christian political doctrine. The elaboration and evolution of this doctrine was bound up with the fate of Charlemagne's Western Empire. Paris was the centre of the scholastic philosophy of Scotus Erigena; it saw within its walls St Albert the Great and St Thomas; there Duns Scotus taught, the Franciscan Doctor of the freedom of the will as the principal attribute of man, which had been created by the free sovereignty of the divine Will. Paris was also the capital of the monarchy of the heirs of Charlemagne, the capital of the kingdom of chivalry. All that survived the barbarian invasions of St Augustine's century in the south and east of the pagan Empire of Rome, survived because of its Christian baptism.

But this survival was not accomplished without pain and difficulty; it involved a temporary surrender of Caesarism to Christ, followed by attempts to create a Church subservient to Caesarism. It was in the West that the new Monarchy, entirely Christian in its origin, came into being, the monarchy of a Caesar who took the style and name of David, anointed by the Pope as David had been anointed by the high priest—the realm of voluntary obedience, sustained only by the tie of Faith, *Fides*, which is the derivation of the feudal idea.

" Frank," the name of the people who accepted authority in freedom, became synonymous in current language with sincerity and loyalty. Privilege, freedom and personal right was given the name " franchise "; the granting of freedom became known in Western languages as " affranchisement." From the time of the *Song of Roland*, the first epic poem of Christian Chivalry, through the Franciscan spirituality of the era of the Crusades and Duns Scotus's elaboration of the doctrine of voluntary creation, down to the very recent French spiritual revival on the eve of the First World War—to the poetry of Charles Péguy—we meet the same concept of free and voluntary sacrifice as the very essence of Christianity:

> *Comme j'ai créé l'homme à mon image et à ma ressemblance,*
> *Ainsi j'ai créé la liberté de l'homme à l'image et à la ressemblance*
> *De ma propre, de mon originelle liberté.*[1]

[1] *Prières*, Charles Péguy, Gallimard, Paris, 1934, p. 66.

2. THE RELIGIOUS CHARACTER OF THE FRENCH MONARCHY

THE Kingdom of the Franks, the Western Monarchy, was the first modern nation, just as St Augustine, the teacher of the West, was the first modern man. It was a nation with a history which was not simply recorded, but was above all related by all its laws, institutions and actions to the spiritual and moral focal point of History. This notion of the focal point in History replaced in the Western mind the idea of a geographical centre of the world. Since the time of St Augustine, who postulated the perfect unity of individual life with the universal and omnipresent life of the Divinity, the government of the World—of the City of God—had become known as " temporal," or " secular," adjectives which relate to Time and not to space; the Western Empire meant temporal power, secular government, related to the *saecula saeculorum* of the Western liturgy, a temporal power which was related to Eternity. Thus the people of the Western realm considered themselves to be the chosen people of the New Testament, whose actions were manifestations of the Divine—*gesta Dei per Francos*. Charlemagne's name became synonymous with a dignity, just as Caesar's had been in the Empire of antiquity, and the Slav and the Magyar titles for the new East European Royal dignity were taken from the name Charlemagne, or Karl—*Kralj, Király*.[1]

Yet, at the same time that the Kingdom of the Franks was becoming the norm of Christian society the heritage of Charlemagne suffered a division, and the imperial heritage of Charlemagne ceased to be in the same hands as the royal sceptre of France. To tell the story of this division, and to relate all that followed upon it, would be nothing short of writing the European history of eight full centuries. We are not engaged here on such a tremendous task. Ours is infinitely more modest in scope; we are dealing with the historical background to the crisis of Authority and Liberty, which culminated in the French Revolutions of the eighteenth and nineteenth centuries, and the new direction of religious thought which originated in this crisis and transformed every concept of the " profane " order of Europe—we use the word in the sense underlined by Jacques

[1] Important new research material, and for the first time a full historical survey of the relations between the Kingdom of the Franks and East and Central Europe, is given in *The Making of Central and Eastern Europe*, by Fr. Francis Dvornik, Polish Research Centre, London, 1949.

Maritain in his *Humanisme intégral*, as a contrast to " sacred "—
the crisis of Authority and Liberty in France, which is not yet
at an end in Europe or the world today.

We can thus only touch slightly upon the centuries of struggle
between the two branches of Charlemagne's Monarchy and
the Papacy, and just mention in passing that there were conflicts between France and the Papacy in the reigns of Philippe-
Auguste and Louis XII, as well as conflicts between the Papacy
and the Empire. It must however be said that Charlemagne's
quality as defender of the Papal sovereignty, his title of " eldest
son of the Church " and of *Rex Christianissimus*—a title which
sovereigns imitated at the time of the great dynastic rivalries,
when the successors of Ferdinand of Aragon called themselves
Catholic Kings of Spain, and the successors of Maria-Theresa
called themselves Apostolic Kings of Hungary—gave the
French Monarchy a religious character of the first importance,
a claim of primacy over the secular rulers of Christendom, a
consciousness of that primacy which was sometimes questioned,
but which was the unalterable basis of French policy, and of
the whole political doctrine of the nation for centuries.

The unity of the Kingdom and the unity of Christendom
became, in a way which must be considered providential, one
and the same cause. The two greatest religious events of the
Latin West, the scholastic movement of the twelfth and
thirteenth centuries and the Counter-Reformation of the
seventeenth century, evolved in the context of French national
history. Neither of them was an exclusively French historical
phenomenon, and neither was restricted in scope to France
alone, but they were replies to heresies which threatened to
disrupt the unity of the French Crown, as well as the unity of
Christendom and the Church. They were replies to the
Albigensian and the Calvinist heresies and to the Jansenist
aberrations, the controversy in each case centring round the
freedom of the human will.

This is a paradox which needs emphasising in this century,
because it was often overlooked in the nineteenth century.
Modern historians, writing with a more or less conscious, or
even virulent, anti-Catholic bias and intention, have completely reversed this phenomenon and affirmed the exact opposite of the truth, by interpreting the various revolts in the
history of French Christianity as so many steps towards
" emancipation," an aim which was, according to them,
ultimately achieved with the triumph of the Great

Revolution, after several minor ones had proved abortive.[1]

This modern opinion, commonly held because it has been spread by historians, omitted to bear in mind the theological essence of the Albigensian, Calvinist and Jansenist movements, although the doctrinal documents are easily accessible, especially those concerning the two latter. They all challenged the authority of the Church, and at the same time, the doctrine of the freedom of the will; the relation between the two trends is obvious. The Crown and the Church recognised that they were a peril to moral responsibility, this indispensable basis of every legal and social order. To be free means to be responsible, and any doubt cast on this free, responsible and voluntary action is a danger to Church and State alike, whether it is a doctrine of predestination, or one which casts doubts on the sufficiency and efficacy of Grace.

The Revolution, which made Liberty the first of its catchwords, thus confessed its spiritual ancestry in all the negations of freedom.[2] The most memorable link in the chain from the

[1] The French Liberal historians, the grave and philosophical Guizot, the often attractive and epic Michelet, the frequently original and sometimes absurd Edgar Quinet and, somewhat platitudinous in their conclusions, but on account of the bulk of their researches and their output, the important Henri Martin and Ernest Lavisse, as well as Seignobos—more scientific in his method—have all attempted to show us that the movements which aimed at the disintegration of Christian unity were steps on the road of Progress, that these Western heresies were the precursors of the ideas of 1789. In the opinion of Jean Jaurès, the intellectual leader of French Socialism during the period when this movement had given up all idea of a new revolution, and postulated the thesis that all its aims had been realised with the " natural " development of the ideas of 1789, the unity of the Reformation and the Revolution was a foremost axiom of modern times. He devoted the thesis he wrote for the Sorbonne (one of the last ever to be written in Latin and almost certainly the only Latin contribution to the literature on Marx, his doctrine and his German precursors) to a demonstration of this unity. The postulate of a close Franco-German friendship, based on the affinity of the Reformation and the Revolution, became such a favourite rhetorical formula in Jaurès' public activities, that many of his followers left him on that account. This happened with the young Péguy—as we know from his own *Souvenirs* and from the books which some of Péguy's closest companions, such as Jean-Jérôme Tharaud and Henri Massis, devoted to his memory and the spiritual legacy he left behind. It also happened in the case of Charles Andler, Professor of German at the Collège de France, who took a less optimistic view of the " Germany of the Reformation " and its natural love for liberty and peace, which Jaurès saw in every historical phenomenon " emancipated " from Catholic authority.

[2] In the works of all its apologists, Michelet, Quinet and Jaurès. A possible exception is Alphonse Aulard, in whose analysis the Revolution is not so much the continuation of those older religious phenomena, but a new phenomenon, a rational, agnostic philosophy put into practice. But Aulard would admit that this theory only holds good in that aspect of the Revolution represented by Danton and Condorcet, and not in the one represented by Robespierre, who is the central figure of the revolutionary history—or shall we say apologetics?—of the late M. Albert Mathiez, Aulard's successor in the Chair of Revolutionary History at the Sorbonne.

Reformation to the Revolution was the thinker Jean-Jacques Rousseau, who relegated freedom and personal responsibility to the realm of his imaginary natural life, which was prior to a civilisation in which man's action was corrupted by social rules and regulations, his good intentions were frustrated by his surroundings, and by the institutions of society and the State. Inconsistent as it seems, the same determinist tendencies common, in various degrees, to the three great heretical movements which in three different centuries shook the Christian Monarchy in France to its foundations, proclaimed free and individual judgement as the only criterion in matters of Faith. Yet, this contradiction is more apparent than real: Christian ethical rule cannot be separated from Authority, a word which, in the vocabulary of the Christian, can only be derived from the *auctoritas* of God, manifested in Creation by His free and sovereign Will.

Any challenge to the notion of Authority must necessarily and logically lead to a denial, or at least to some major restriction, of the attributes which Man derives from Authority. Like everything, or almost everything in spiritual matters, this is largely a question of emphasis. We need not go so far as to accuse Calvinists and Jansenists of a flat denial of the free, voluntary action of God in Creation. This would assimilate them to a more remote heresy, that of the Manicheans, in whose theology God's own freedom becomes problematic, so that He acts in rivalry with an equally powerful force of evil, and acts by an inevitable necessity in an *undecided* struggle between Good and Evil. Yet by removing the Church, which is Authority incarnate, and the visible depository of the divine guidance of men, as the link between God and Man, the relationship between them necessarily becomes more remote, so that Man is a less perfect being, enlightened only by his own intellect, and ultimately faced, as the Teachers of the Church are unanimous in underlining—St Augustine against the Manicheans, St Thomas against the Albigenses, the early Jesuits and Bossuet against the Reformation, and St Alphonsus Liguori against the Jansenists—by the alternative of despotism or anarchy. Nearer to our own day, the Spanish theologian Jaime Balmes shows, in the analysis of Protestantism which he makes from the point of view of historical progress and secular civilisation, that this alternative has been the hallmark of modern times since the sixteenth century.

3. THE CATHOLIC INTERPRETATION OF THE SECULAR ORDER: BOSSUET AND PASCAL

FRANCE is, on the historical plane, the centre of Western Christianity. The contribution which other countries have made is certainly not negligible; St Albert the Great, St Thomas, Duns Scotus and other masters of the scholastic era of Paris came from countries other than France. They came from Orders founded by St Dominic and St Francis outside France, although these Orders were largely founded to combat heresies which in France herself were the causes of real civil wars. From the extreme west of the Iberian Peninsula to the Sarmatian steppes of Poland and Russia, there were Christian Kingdoms and realms all over the European Continent. All were rivals for the common glory of Christendom.

Hegemony was a new term which grew out of the rivalry of the dynastic powers; thus in the political vocabulary of Europe, it is not older than the sixteenth century. There was no question in any modern sense of a French " hegemony " in the Middle Ages. France could however claim seniority through the succession of Charlemagne. Right up to the Revolution and the Restoration of the Bourbon dynasty in the early nineteenth century, we shall meet the argument—for the last time in Bonald's *Théorie de Pouvoir* and in his *Réflexions sur l'intérêt général de l'Europe* and in Joseph de Maistre's comments on topical events from St Petersburg—that the Empire east of the Rhine was a sort of political schism from the foundation of Charlemagne, just as the Church of Byzantium was a religious schism from Rome. The most monumental antagonist of this argument in the political literature of Europe was Dante, a keen enemy of the French kings and a supporter of the Imperial power. Yet it was only in the nineteenth century, when the Empire finally became Austrian and Danubian and withdrew from the West,[1] that the " seniority of Charlemagne's heritage " disappeared as a fundamental thesis of French policy.[2]

[1] A consequence and result of the Napoleonic wars, which the subsequent defeat of Napoleon (though largely due to Austrian participation in the " War of the Nations ") did not alter. Metternich preferred his monarchy to play the part of the centre of a " European " system, and wisely renounced all western claims (which in his position as one of the victors he could possibly have claimed from his allies).

[2] Bonald's comments on the Vienna Congress in *L'intérêt général de l'Europe* (like much of his philosophy) are a distant echo of Leibnitz' political theories, which aimed at a reconciliation between France and the Empire. They must be seen against the background of the time of Louis XIV in France and of Eugene of Savoy's liberation of the Christian Eastern Empire from Turkish rule and the re-integration of the latter into the Habsburg dominions.

B

This is but a part, although an indispensable part, of the
central issue with which we deal in these pages, which is the
evolution, from the Christian foundations of European politics
and the European state-system, of the political conscience of
the West. We have to bear in mind the primacy of France, in
order to understand the central importance of the French
Revolution for modern times, and the significant part it played
in the dissolution of the European state-system. We cannot yet
see the end of the crisis, although we can already discern—as
even the best political intelligences of the generation of Bonald,
de Maistre and Friedrich von Schlegel could not know—that
in the twentieth century it means the growth and expansion of
the deeper European problems to other civilisations and continents.

The ultimate meaning of this expansion of systems and
institutions, which are themselves in a state of dissolution, may
be, as we can already see, the implication of the whole world
in concerns which are, for all those who are not satisfied with
the most superficial appearances, the concerns of Christendom.
A historical conjecture is that in a distant future the vocation
of the Church may be the consecration and consolidation of a
new world order and unity, which the European order failed
to create, but which may slowly come into being through the
spreading of a European chaos to distant parts of the globe.

We have previously indicated that each of the great steps
taken to consolidate the Western Monarchy coincided—provi-
dentially—with the end of a great crisis in Christendom. The
elevation of Clovis to the Kingdom of the Franks marked the
end of the barbarian invasions of the West, and the triumphant
emergence of Latin and Western Christianity, of the Catholicity
of Rome, from the Manichean and Arian confusions of the
East. The coronation of Charlemagne followed upon the first
decisive victory of Christian Europe over Asia, although as far
as the West was concerned, it was not a final victory. Its
significance lay in the creation by the Papacy of a secular
Christian order, or a monarchy which was spiritually dependent
upon the prior existence of the Papacy, as David's monarchy
was on Samuel's priesthood. French unity was achieved (apart
from some conflicts over the frontiers of the north-east, which
remained an open question until the wars of Louis XIV) by
the victory over the Albigenses. The final consolidation and
unity of the central monarchical power came about through
the civil wars of the sixteenth century—in other words, the

Reformation was responsible for the unity of the French monarchy.

For many centuries, France enjoyed primacy, even in a more strictly geographical sense. The diplomatic thought, language and action which governed Europe for three centuries, and of which Metternich was the last classic master and depositary, used the expression " Central Europe " in the sense that the central powers in Europe were those which bordered the Rhine and the Alps, and were made the centre of Christendom by Charlemagne.

In the closing chapters of his *Lectures on the Philosophy of History*, Friedrich von Schlegel defined the key to German history as a strong German participation in the European system (an argument which was fairly general among the Austrian and Prussian-inspired publicists between Napoleon and Bismarck)[1] by pointing out that the German crises—the Lutheran Reformation and the Thirty Years' War—were bound to affect the whole of Europe, that order or chaos inside Germany were symptoms of the order or chaos of Europe; for Germany is, for good or ill, a sort of miniature Europe, with her naturally federal structure and local diversity, so that socially and historically, as well as geographically, she is the central nation.

France could also claim to be the " central nation " and that is one of the reasons why a Franco-German controversy has dominated the European scene for so long. The similarity between these claims hardly hides the differences between them, which make them ultimately irreconcilable. In France, the outcome of religious crises meant consolidation and unity, whereas in Germany similar crises led to disintegration, and an almost complete dissolution and absence of power in the seventeenth and eighteenth centuries; with the result that only Austria and Prussia, which were not purely Germanic powers, remained in the German East, and only Holland and Switzerland, which again were not purely Germanic societies, in the West.

One of the reasons for this evolution was certainly the sympathy France received from the Papacy, whose constant preoccupation was to keep the Emperor out of Italy. Richelieu

[1] This argument was taken up by F. W. Foerster in his analysis of the Germany between the two World Wars, *The German Question and Europe*, published in America, and also by the French scholar Edmond Vermeil, *Les doctrinaires de la Révolution Allemande*, 1938, and in *L'Allemagne: Une tentative d'explication*, 1940.

had the approval of Rome, not only because he safeguarded French unity by subduing the Huguenots at La Rochelle, but also because he opposed the Imperial power in the Thirty Years' War, an opposition which went to the extent of supporting Gustavus Adolphus and Protestant Sweden.

The preservation, restoration and the final triumph of French unity under Henry IV, Richelieu and Louis XIV, became one of the most significant events in Christendom, one of the greatest periods in the annals of European mankind. It was a secular event, but one which Bossuet—the mouthpiece of his century and nation, and by no means an isolated man of genius—interpreted as of the greatest religious significance. To him we owe the vision of History as the working-out of the designs of Providence. Bossuet had a mystical insight into History (as later on Joseph de Maistre was to have after the Revolution) and at the same time, in theology, he marked a return to St Augustine from the formal logic of medieval schoolmen, and a return to Revelation as a vision and a fact from a philosophy of the Absolute, which approached Revelation through syllogism. Bossuet's *Discours sur l'Histoire universelle* is an analogical synthesis. Religious and spiritual truth are seen here in the analogy between the Divine and the human. There are two histories for Bossuet: the universal history of immutable truth, foreshadowed in Eternity, and gradually and progressively revealed by action in time; and a history of " variations," a history of human errors and aberrations, of no final and definite significance, except that they prefigure what will be rejected on the day of final Judgement.

The importance of Bossuet in his own century, and in the whole of the intervening time between his day and ours, can hardly be over-estimated. For some people, his name may evoke the memory of stormy Gallican controversies which were intense in the seventeenth century, and still more so in the following one, not finally subsiding, indeed, till the Vatican Council of 1869.[1] How far Bossuet was the master-mind of the Gallican theories, which claimed special privileges for the French hierarchy and the French Crown—though neither he, nor any other thinker of his time, considered it as a purely secular government—and how far his theories encouraged the

[1] Heralded in the French Church by Louis Veuillot's lively "ultramontane " polemics against Mgr. Dupanloup and other " Gallicans " of the hierarchy, and against secular political leaders of the Liberal-Catholic variety such as Falloux and Montalembert.

Gallicans who favoured a restriction of direct Roman interference in the Church of France, could be made the subject
of a special study. The question has been examined by many
writers on Bossuet; it is of no great concern here. All that need
be said is that Bossuet's *Correspondance* and the published documents concerning his diocesan archives of Meaux, show him to
have been a bishop of moderately Gallican tendencies. Such
was the opinion of many of his contemporaries. But the
Gallican controversy is dead. It never contained any actual
threat of schism, still less of heresy. It was an ephemeral
political symptom, which disappeared, as such symptoms do,
with the transformation of the whole historical context—with
the Vatican Council of Pius IX and his Bull of Infallibility.

The Gallican controversy was not of primary importance in
Bossuet's achievement. To assert the contrary is to belittle this
monumental landmark which stands at the beginning of modern
French Christian thought.

In the spiritual history of Europe, the influence of Bossuet
can be discerned in the religious thought of Leibnitz. The
great German philosopher's plan for a reunion of Christendom
and for a European " Harmony " through restoration of peace
between France and the Empire—a more profound political
synthesis, and one that was more aware of historical reality
than Spinoza's abstract conception of an " equilibrium," or
balance of powers, to be established *more geometrico*—were
largely the fruits of Leibnitz's long and extensive exchange of
ideas with the Bishop of Meaux.

In theology, as we have already indicated, Bossuet signified
a great step forward from formal logic to historical understanding and—in a cultural sense, this was of equal importance—a step forward from the scholastic formula to that
perfect artistry of personal style, which is the main feature of
the French *grand siècle*. The *siglo de oro* in Spain saw God and
His work in the colours of passion and glory; the *grand siècle* in
France saw God and His work in the perfection of proportion
and form and language. It was the century of style—the style
of Boileau and La Fontaine, of Corneille, Racine and Molière,
of La Bruyère and Madame de Sévigné—which Bossuet
epitomised on the plane of divine knowledge. The French
style became the vehicle for all the dignified secular and
profane concerns of modern Europe; it occupied the third
place in Christendom, after the Greek of the Revelation which
united Jew and Gentile, and the Latin of the monastic rule,

of the liturgy and of the scholastics who spiritualised the Barbarian.

Bossuet made this triumph of style and artistic form a new triumph for the Church in the *grand siècle*. He was the foremost master of the unique and personal expression and the concise word, the power of which lay in allusion, in the concise manifestation of the deeper, hidden truth of the sign, the image and the symbol—in other words, the incarnation and fulfilment of the Word, *natum ante omnia saecula*, the fulfilment of that time which is contained within, and prefigured in, Eternity.

The French *grand siècle* changed the European vision by its idea of style, by the directness of its images, by its presentation of Truth, not in abstraction and reasoning, but in figure, image and word, which, in Bossuet's hands, became apologetic weapons wherewith to combat the heresy of a purely abstract, intellectual and rational Christianity, such as Calvin and his sect claimed to establish.

We are obliged to linger over Bossuet and his century, so important is he as a landmark in the spiritual progress of modern Europe. Indeed, without the *grand siècle* and Bossuet in particular, there would have been no Vico or Hegel to speculate on the unity of the spirit, as it is seen in its works and manifestations amidst the variety of the temporal and material order. A still greater loss, there would have been no Goethe, at any rate we should not have had the best of Goethe, who pushed rational effort to the extreme limit of the humanly possible, in order to recognise in the end the symbolic transcendence of all things created, *Alles Vergangliche ist nur ein Gleichniss*, the inexpressible which has been accomplished, *Das Unbeschreibliche, hier ist's getan*, and transcendent purity, *Das ewig weibliche. . . .*[1]

---

[1] Hardly anyone who has seriously attempted to understand Goethe could avoid quoting and analysing these lines. The latest comer is the French philosopher and poet Jean Guitton, in *La Pensée moderne et le Catholicisme*, in which he states that Goethe's concept of purity and his " eternal feminine " are expressions of a devotion, which is only a half conscious one, to the Blessed Virgin. Generally distrustful as we ought to be when well-meaning Catholic attempts are made to " annex " great thoughts from a strange or hostile camp to the Church—such attempts are dangerous because they minimise gigantic errors which we should face courageously—we feel that M. Guitton has probably said the last word on Goethe's Christianity, a controversial subject now fully resolved by a remarkable Catholic thinker of our own day.

An inevitable rapprochement of Goethe's *Alles Vergangliche* with the *Luce intellectual, pieno d'amore*, with the light of the " Paradiso," *ché transcende ogni dolciore* seems to contradict what we said above on the relation of Goethe to the French style of the seventeenth century and points to a still nobler origin of his transcendentalism. But between Dante and Goethe, there were the numerous attempts

The French *grand siècle* was misunderstood in the subsequent century, and has often been misunderstood since, as one which worshipped style and form, these two words being used in a pejorative sense to indicate an absence of " depth "; this was unfortunate, because it prevented any true appreciation, and even was an obstacle to any true understanding, of more recent French Catholic thought of the highest significance, the thought of Joseph de Maistre, Barbey d'Aurevilly, Ernest Hello and Léon Bloy, to which we shall come back later on in these pages.

It was not a century which worshipped style and form as an external ornament, but one in which the Faith acquired its modern style and expression. For Joseph de Maistre and the young Chateaubriand (of the *Génie du Christianisme* and the *Essai sur les Révolutions*) the Revolution meant a destruction of style, an interpretation which the former gave with irony and polemical wit, and the latter with melancholy. Chateaubriand, however, was perhaps the first French author to see style as a matter which only concerned aesthetics; unfortunately, this lowered the metaphysical, historical and religious level of his whole argument, so that the author of the *Génie du Christianisme* ranks below Joseph de Maistre or Bonald among the classics of modern apologetics. What de Maistre or Bonald considered to be an expression of Order, in accordance with the correct hierarchy of spiritual and social values which the Revolution had overthrown and cast into confusion, was for Chateaubriand an expression of subjective imagination and beauty. Therefore, what de Maistre saw as incredible human presumption, a substitution of human judgement and human creation for the divine, Chateaubriand was inclined to see as a mere rationalisation and levelling down of the poetic variety of imagination. In Barbey d'Aurevilly's view, the whole post-revolutionary period was marked by the decline of style, in a deeper sense

to separate the ideal *nomina* from created reality by abstractions which over-spiritualised and over-rationalised the former. This unity was restored by the French *grand siècle*, by " style," which, in other words, is unity in essence. It is a unity between the supernatural and the natural, visible in the harmony and the perfection of form and proportion. It was a unity that was restored above all by Bossuet, who as a theologian never ceased to be a historian, and as a master of prose never ceased to be a priest and bishop. The restoration of the unity between the supernatural and the natural by means of style followed upon the two parodies and caricatures of genius in France—that of the " purely natural " of Rabelais, and of the " purely spiritual " which Montaigne gave in his *Apologie de Raymond Sébond*—those parodies of genius which began the whole of modern French literature.

than was imagined by the English aesthetics of the nineteenth
century (whom Barbey d'Aurevilly admired during his early
days when he wrote his *Dandyisme* in the 1830's) from Byron to
Wilde and from Carlyle to Ruskin, who considered theirs to
be the century of utilitarian ugliness. Style declined during
this time because human personality, of which it is the expression, was no longer a reflection of the personal reality of God
in the current philosophies. It was a pantheist century, which
believed in the difformity of the masses, and either praised
difformity, or postulated uniformity under some future tyrant
which Democracy would one day produce; the pantheism of
Victor Hugo and of Michelet were the chief targets of Barbey
d'Aurevilly's critical genius.

For Léon Bloy, " *les événements historiques sont le style de la
Parole,*" the Word that was in the beginning and the full
meaning of which has been gradually unfolded in the dimen-
sion of time throughout the centuries, the Word born *ante omnia
saecula* and valid for Eternity. This philosophy, which under-
lies the whole of Léon Bloy's historical writing—his *Révélateur du
Globe*, his *Byzance*, *Marie-Antoinette*, *L'Ame de Napoléon*, *Jeanne
d'Arc*—gave him his whole vision of history: " *Il n'y a que les
saints, ou les antagonistes des saints, capables de délimiter l'histoire.*"[1]
Ernest Hello, that remarkable French mystic who was a monumental figure in modern Catholic thought between Barbey
d'Aurevilly and Léon Bloy, and to whom some belated justice
is rendered by admirers in our day,[2] thought that the century
of style was Catholic and French in the truest sense: the
Catholic Faith and French style have nothing in common with
vagueness—Faith is affirmation and style is precision.[3] Essence
and form cannot be separated; the appearance of Divinity in
form was the Word humanly incarnate. God spoke when He
made the Word incarnate. The vague, purely subjective value
given to words is the great aberration of romantic sensitiveness,
which characterised the century following Rousseau: " *Quand
un homme s'égare, soyez sûr qu'il vient de se chercher.*"[4]

The commonplace in language is a fallen and debased fragment of the Word, with nothing left of its mystic origin, as the
human beings who speak it are, so to say, fallen fragments
of the Divine Person. Yet true style in poetry and prose

---

[1] *La Femme Pauvre*, Ch. XXII, p. 156 of the first edition. Paris. 1886.
[2] Stanilas Fumet: *Ernest Hello. Le drame de la lumière*. Paris. Egloff, 1946.
[3] Ernest Hello: *Le Style : Sa théorie et son histoire*. Paris. 1879.
[4] Ernest Hello: Ibid. p. 216.

can approach the divine and bring us back to the Word.[1]

We shall return later to this century of violent crises and national catastrophes. Meanwhile we must come back to the *grand siècle* of style, in order to consider it from another angle.

This is provided by someone who was perhaps as far removed from Bossuet as it was possible for a French thinker of the same century to be—by Pascal.

Pascal was the first lay apologist of the Church who developed a theological argument, not against the " Variations " of the heretical theologies, but against an enemy who never varies: Worldliness. Pascal refuted, and, in his own wisdom, surpassed worldly wisdom, even such wisdom " of this world " as can feel comfortable inside the Church and can conform perfectly to a secular order of Catholic inspiration. Pascal gave the full Christian answer to Montaigne and Descartes, and it is mainly for this reason that we are concerned with him here. His espousal of the Jansenist cause in *Lettres à un Provincial* remains a controversial subject. His attitude can be explained by his misunderstanding of the Jesuit case against the Jansenists, by his excessive austerity—perhaps even it was the result of insufficient knowledge concerning the Spanish Jesuit casuists, who were only known to him at second hand. As he himself admitted, they were read for him by Jansenist friends, who may well have been biassed. We may leave aside this, for some time the most widely discussed aspect of Pascal's work, as we left on one side the question of Bossuet's Gallicanism. Pascal's defence of Jansenism consisted of the argument that there was no such thing as " Jansenism," for the group who were known under that name did not accept the propositions which were condemned by the Sorbonne (and later by Pope Innocent X), as issuing from Jansenius's book on St Augustine, and that it was even doubtful if Jansenius, who died a Bishop of the Church, ever really meant to propose a doctrine on free will which was incompatible with that of the Church.

If Bossuet had only been a " Gallican," and Pascal only a " Jansenist," how would their reputation have survived ? Who takes any interest today in the Abbé Noailles, who engaged

---

[1] Léon Bloy commented on these thoughts of Hello in his *Exégèse des lieux communs*. We may allude here to an important parallel: the critical approach to contemporary German writing of two German masters of aphorism, Theodor Haecker in *Satire und Polemik*, and Karl Kraus in the whole of his work.

We may also call attention here to Barbey d'Aurevilly's and Hello's analysis of the romantic subjectivism which began with Rousseau, reflected in the critical work of a later generation, in Pierre Laserre's *Les Romantiques* (1908) and in the various books of Ernest de Seillières.

in the Gallican controversy at the Sorbonne ? And who reads
Pascal's friends Arnauld or Nicole, except perhaps to find some
references to Pascal ?

Pascal, however, is one of the thinkers who did more perhaps
than anyone else to make his century great. He was, in his
various aspects, the highest expression of his time and of
religious thought.

He was, above all, in that broader and more complex sense
which we have explained, a master of style, and it was he who
defined style better than any other writer:

*Quand on voit le style naturel, on est tout étonné et ravi, car on
s'attendait de voir un auteur et on trouve un homme. . . . Ceux-là
honorent bien la nature, qui lui apprennent qu'elle parle de tout et même
de théologie.*[1]

*Un même sens change selon les paroles qui l'expriment. Les sens
reçoivent des paroles leur dignité, au lieu de la leur donner.*[2]

Eloquence qui persuade par douceur, non par empire, en tyran, non en roi.[3]

For Pascal, and for all those who have ever meditated like
him on this particular problem, the full religious truth is also
the full social truth. If not the first, Pascal is at any rate the
most powerful master of the religious argument in defence of
the social order. His unerring sense of precision, his geometrical
sense of perfect proportion, his mathematical experience of the
extreme limits of rational and intellectual truth, make him a
major figure in the history of modern apologetics. Right up to
the twentieth century, a great deal of French thought was to be
a comment and a gloss on those unique fragments, providen-
tially left unfinished, which we know as the *Pensées*. As a
secular defender of the Faith, he is the spiritual ancestor of
Joseph de Maistre. His social doctrine on Order, which he
considers to be preserved by the sound sense of the common
people, who always instinctively prefer Order to anarchy, was
to be the social doctrine of Bonald. It was also to encounter the
criticism of Voltaire (for whom Pascal's relativism went too
far) and, more recently, that of Jacques Maritain, who, in his
attempt to define the Christian attitude to the *Things that are
not Caesar's*, and the Christian task in the *Rédemption du Temps*,
accuses Pascal of a " Christian cynicism " which, in his view,
the Angelic Doctor would never have approved. We shall
return to this debate.

[1] *Pensées:* Section I, 29, in the version edited by Léon Brunschvicg. Paris. 1904.
[2] Ibid. Section I, 225.   [3] Ibid. Section I, 130.

From the diametrically opposite philosophical camp, Henri Poincaré's *Science et Hypothèse* and Boutroux's whole system form something of a belated commentary on (and confirmation of) Pascal's fundamental thesis of the primacy of belief, which he preferred to that primacy of thought formulated by Descartes.

Cartesian philosophy attempted to jettison Aristotelian and medieval scholastics. In the end, it confronted man with the Absolute, in a world of pure syllogism and lofty abstraction. Pascal returned man to his natural level, he put human ethics back into the social and historical context, gave a more natural expression to notions of philosophy and gave Reason and Will back their natural direction: *La raison croit naturellement et la volonté aime naturellement* . . . a surprising and paradoxical statement at first sight, but it shows Pascal's wisdom at its deepest. It comprises his whole philosophy in one short formula, which can be meditated upon and commented on almost indefinitely. It gives us perhaps the final word in the controversy on the relation between Reason and Will, which has been familiar in the Church since the days of St Thomas and Duns Scotus. Pascal saw both Divinity and Humanity, the attributes of God and the faculties of Man, in the fullness of their nature. He fought two errors, two exaggerations: the Cartesian separation of the Absolute from the complex nature of Man, whose nature includes some of the attributes of the Creator, and at the same time, the exaggeration of Montaigne, who saw nothing but relativity, uncertainty and passing futility in the human world. Man is *ni ange, ni bête*, a warning against the exaggeration[1] of Descartes and against the sensualist dangers of Montaigne. These two dangers, in the following century—the fatal eighteenth, preceding the Revolution and the whole contemporary catharsis—marked the beginning, and were the cause, of all the aberrations of the French mind and of French-speaking Europe, since the *grand siècle*, the century of style, had made Europe French-speaking.

Yet before we attempt a survey of the eighteenth century, the period of the Revolution and the religious rejuvenation which followed it, let us hint at a few more aspects of the enormously extensive and rich inheritance which Pascal left us.

We often find an echo of Pascal in unexpected quarters. We

---

[1] Jacques Maritain in *Trois Réformateurs*—Luther, Descartes and Rousseau, Paris, 1929, gives perhaps the fullest analysis of this " *angelisme* " in Descartes' philosophy, the most systematic Catholic criticism of the postulate of knowledge separated from human nature and from society. Already in Barbey d'Aurevilly's *Les Prophètes du Passé*, we see this criticism of Descartes.

find one in Theodor Haecker's passionate polemics against the
" neo-Manichean "[1] tendencies of our time, present in all his
books, against the modern primacy of Liberty over Order
which the nineteenth century tried to establish and which
denied a divine quality to Order and to Power, thus decrying
Power as an evil which men, formed in this mental atmosphere—Communists, Nazis and Fascists—passionately embraced
as the means to achieve their evil ends. It was Pascal who
defined Power, and the right place of Power, and who thus
defined Tyranny as power used in the wrong place; Force,
which claims love and affection instead of obedience; beauty
and loveliness which claim not love, but obedience; eloquence
which tries to persuade not by strong and conclusive, but by
ingratiating argument; and above all, the human presumption
which assumes the force of absolute Justice, while the whole
condemned nature of Man can only hope to render that Power
and Force just, instead of transforming justice into Power—all
this signified for Pascal the various forms of tyranny. A contemporary of the English Revolution, Pascal had a foreboding of
the French Revolution and judged it one hundred and forty
years before it happened.

This is perhaps a somewhat neglected aspect of a much-
explored and much-commented-upon genius. There may even
be readers who are astonished to be told that Pascal was a
defender of Order. There are often indications to the contrary.
Many are inclined to see the author of the *Pensées* as the opposite
to Bossuet in every respect, and to class the latter as the spiritual
ancestor of more recent *bien-pensants*, of traditionalists, who
conform complacently; some of these—unfortunately the least
attractive makers and defenders of platitudes, such as a Henry
Bordeaux or a Ferdinand Brunetière—have often enough
attempted to cover their thin theories and thinner style with
Bossuet's great name and authority. In the face of all this,
does not Pascal represent a " revolutionary " sort of Catholicism, an unconventional style in defence of conservative values,
an unorthodox system of reasoning which concluded in orthodox
truth; is he not the spiritual ancestor of all great Catholic
writers who, in an unorthodox way, have defended orthodox
truth—Barbey d'Aurevilly and Hello, Bloy and Péguy, and

---

[1] " Neo-Manichean " is Theodor Haecker's own coinage. It originates in the
Manichean conclusion that the struggle between good and evil has no decisive
outcome, that God's power, not being the stronger of the two, does not give the
final word on the issue.

outside France, of Chesterton, and in a less direct and conscious line, even of Kierkegaard and Dostoievsky ?

We have made an effort in the preceding pages to elucidate the sense, and to ascertain the value of Bossuet's heritage, and we have taken up our position in a recurring controversy about classification. Bossuet and Pascal certainly form a contrast to each other. The author of the *Pensées* is undoubtedly also the spiritual ancestor of all those who defended orthodox truth in an unorthodox style, those whom we have already named and many more besides. Pascal's work is above all a demonstration. The mathematician which he always remained began his *Pensées* by distinguishing strictly between the *esprit de géometrie* and the *esprit de finesse*. His work is a demonstration, made with geometric precision, that Reason cannot exist without belief, the Will without Love, or human life without God. Pascal relegated all godless science to the chaos of the unthinkable, all godless ethics to the chaos of the unlivable; he it was who put Jacques Maritain on the right track when he coined the phrase *l'invivable athéisme*. The *Pensées*, despite its fragmentary character, is the first fully elaborated study of fallen nature, a study to which Pascal was after all brought by his opponents the Jesuits, casuists of the school of Escobar, and not by his Jansenist friends. It was the study which Balzac was to take up later in his novels, Léon Bloy in his volumes of spiritual autobiography—and far away from France and outside Catholicism—Dostoievsky and Kierkegaard. Pascal was the foremost teacher of a *vital* Christianity, of an " existentialist " Christianity, as it has lately been fashionable to say, although he would probably be the last to take part in any *querelle d'Allemands* on a possible separation of Essence and Existence, and fortunately the last author whose support can be claimed for any " ism."

Like most great spiritual figures, Pascal rejected worldliness and easy conformity. He rejected and condemned acceptance of the riches of this world by those who did so with an easy conscience. He even went further; he rejected that wisdom which, by serving the necessities of this world, or human concerns only, provides an easy moral satisfaction here below.

The primacy of Order over Liberty was Pascal's final conclusion. This primacy was manifest in the chronological sense in the Bible, it was obvious on the level of theology and clear in logic. It was a primacy established by a " revolutionary "—if we care to apply this term to any man who feels a passionate detachment from the world, which we do not dare to call holiness, but which we feel cannot be far removed from it—but a " revolutionary " who consciously judged in advance, and more sternly, all the revolutions which were to come than he judged the conventions and the platitudes of this world and of his century. Pascal realised this primacy of Order better than anyone else, better than those weaker minds and hearts who came after him, and attempted to challenge and destroy it by postulating an imaginary order which reflected Man's liberty and free will alone. That was why he loved Liberty, the Liberty of Man to know God and to love Him, the Liberty to follow the dictates of his heart and to act accordingly. *Dieu incline le coeur*. . . .

4. DECADENCE AND CRISIS: THE EIGHTEENTH AND NINETEENTH CENTURIES

FOR about a century, Europe spoke French. Her princes were brought up on Fénelon's *Télémaque*; the taste of the educated classes was formed on La Fontaine from their earliest years; La Bruyère and La Rochefoucauld were the masters of every conversation; passion spoke the language of Corneille, sentiment the language of Racine, good sense spoke the language of Molière and abstraction the language of Descartes. All cathedral pulpits echoed the eloquence of Bossuet and Bourdaloue, and few letters were written without a delicate and charming touch of Mme. de Sévigné. Italy stood for colour, rhyme and sound; Spain had once meant romance and imagination; now France epitomised thought, speech and style, and as infinitely more people speak and write in prose than in the language of colour, sound or image, France dominated more minds and assimilated an infinitely greater number of people, who, to think and write in French, needed not much more than a few brief stays in Paris. We must cast our imagination back to this French-speaking Europe, before we can understand why and how the French Revolution excited so many foreign passions, and why so many foreign thinkers produced their best work on French issues, without in the least feeling strangers to the quarrel—Burke and Horace Walpole in England, de Maistre in Italy, young Metternich and Friedrich von Gentz in Germany, Karl-Ludwig Haller and Johannes von Müller in Switzerland. There were great

French writers in the " French century of Europe " (which in the strict calendar sense began earlier than the eighteenth, and lasted on longer) who were leading men in their own countries: Joseph de Maistre, Ambassador and Minister of the Kingdom of Piedmont-Sardinia, and Prince de Ligne, Field-Marshal and Ambassador of Austria. They represented French thought, style and wit wherever they were, even when de Maistre was planning the downfall of Napoleon in St Petersburg, and even when de Ligne asked for a last opportunity to practise the principle of his life—*tonner et étonner*—at the head of an army composed of Walloons, Hungarians and Croats *pour décharlemagniser Bonaparte*. Right up to our own day, French has been the intellectual language of Egypt and of modern Greece, and hardly a generation has elapsed since José-Maria de Hérédia from Latin America and Jean Moréas from Greece were considered French, or at any rate, Parisian poets.

This is a unique case of the extension of a civilisation which is only equalled by the Hellenism of antiquity; never since the Oriental Philo and the Roman Marcus Aurelius wrote Greek has there been a case of a universal language being adopted voluntarily, for no other reason than love of style and intellectual delight. Yet this enormous and almost unprecedented peaceful conquest of a continent, based only on refinement of thought, taste and style, has not been altogether a blessing for France herself. The cause of the decay—the cause of all decay—is facility, the easily acquired technique of imitation and reproduction.[1] In the second part of his *Faust*, this is Goethe's vision of the Witches' Sabbath: an almost universal devaluation, through easy reproduction, of everything noble, even of everything sacred; the debasement of gold and of honour—of everything except the cross on the hilt of the Imperial sword, which pseudo-Field Marshals, as not truly consecrated men, were incapable of using. If we accept the proposed formula of facility as a warning of doom to come,[2] we cannot do otherwise than discern the signs of approaching catastrophe in the period of the French intellectual conquest

[1] Perhaps this one formula will dispense us from recapitulating the volumes of speculation on the decay of civilisations, which Vico, Hegel and Spengler, to mention only the dead, spent their whole lives in producing.

[2] This certainly offers us no happy augury for our own century of mechanical reproduction, although Catholics cannot fall into the aimless, unredeemed pessimism and confessed emptiness of the representative voices of the century, from the massive technician H. G. Wells to the refined intellectualist Paul Valéry, from the grave André Gide to the lucid cynic Jean-Paul Sartre.

of Europe. The Revolution itself, in all its consequences and variations, the Revolution considered *en bloc*—as Georges Clemenceau, a belated heir of Jacobinism, wanted to consider it, that is, from 1789 to the Third Republic—must have appeared to those who were still near enough to the old ideal of greatness and of style as facile imitation run riot. The Revolution invented its Deity and its cult, it re-enacted its own version of Sparta, Athens and Rome—rather than an innovation, it was a vast imitation of models. Almost a whole century of hybrid facility preceded it and another century of regret followed. As an anonymous and, for that reason, probably widespread criticism of Voltaire put it—*il a fait de l'esprit pour ceux qui n'en ont pas.* The whole century which followed him, and the Revolution which quoted him so often, but which would probably have guillotined him had he lived to see it, was one of undoubted intellectual expansion, although it may be doubted whether this expansion brought us any nearer to real greatness—to the greatness of form and style of Bossuet. In the seventeenth century, greatness was within the reach of a man whose thought did not aim higher than La Fontaine's; in the nineteenth century, the love of greatness, of form and beauty, took the form of desperate protests against their time on the part of Flaubert and Baudelaire in France, of Carlyle and Ruskin in England, of Jacob Burckhardt and his pupil Nietzsche in the German-speaking world; we leave aside for the time being those who found in God and the Church a remedy to this aesthetic despair, as we have dealt with them in another context, and shall have to return to them.

Decadence, a decay of greatness in style, began what has grown into one of the greatest and most significant spiritual and moral crises of modern mankind. Just as, in the mechanical sphere, most mortal accidents occur because machines get out of control, so in the sphere of human history and the history of human thought all catastrophes can be traced back to words and values which have lost their original meaning, and have passed beyond the control of those minds which once fully possessed their original sense. Three figures divided the intellectual atmosphere of the *grand siècle* from the Revolution and from the whole trend which began with the principles of 1789, that crucial trend which is not yet at an end. They are Voltaire, Montesquieu and Rousseau.

The change was gradual with Voltaire; it was hardly noticeable at the beginning of his literary output and only became final when, at a mature age and with a considerable achievement behind him, he made a prolonged stay in England, and received the influence of English thought and literature. This was the only foreign thought which came to full maturity later than the French, for the golden age of Dante and Petrarch, Tasso and Ariosto, the *siglo de oro* of Cervantes and of the great spiritual teachers of Spain preceded the full maturity of French thought and expression. Voltaire interpreted, in a language which the whole of intellectual Europe spoke and read, English thought from Hobbes to Locke. Even before *Candide*, which was a challenge to the French-inspired European thought of Leibnitz, political and social "Voltairianism" hardly existed.

Voltaire had style, and according to the lights of his century (the taste of which was largely formed by him) even poetry. But unlike Corneille and Racine, in whom poetry and style were the natural accompaniment to dramatic action, style in Voltaire became merely decorative and moralising was the chief aim of poetry.[1] But rhyme and drama were accidental forms of Voltaire's philosophy and do not concern us here. We are not writing a French, or even a West European literary history, but an analysis of the evolution of the theme of Authority and Liberty in the Western, and above all in the French mind, since the religious and moral crisis arising from these two notions first broke over France, and by French intellect was propagated throughout the world.

To decry Voltaire as an "atheist" is a simplification. Some of his contemporaries applied this term to him: with a true woman's instinct, Maria-Theresa detested him and his whole sect of "philosophers," and Mozart frankly rejoiced at the end of this "hideous atheist" whose dry reasoning was in such contrast to his own simplicity and angelic purity as a musician.[2] Since his own time, Voltaire has found a champion, surprisingly enough, in Jacques Maritain, who, in his *Humanisme Intégral*, is

[1] A similar evolution of English literary style, a transformation of poetry and style under the influence of the English philosophical movement of the eighteenth century, which was the decisive influence on Voltaire's mind, is described in *The Life of Reason—Hobbes, Locke and Bolingbroke* by D. G. James. London. Longmans, Green & Co., 1949.

[2] For the influence which conflicting opinions on Voltaire played on the politics of the eighteenth century, it is useful to read Capefigue's *Marie-Thérèse et Frédéric II* and his *Madame Pompadour*, although prudence and caution must be exercised before accepting the views of this very enjoyable, but strongly anti-revolutionary historian, who judged Voltaire and the Revolution from the perspective of Louis-Philippe's time and from his own loyalist feelings.

C

" grateful to him for his idea of civic tolerance," and in the English Catholic poet Alfred Noyes, who (censored, it is true, in Rome for so doing) saw in Voltaire a critic of the Church who was imbued with a truly Catholic spirituality, and was thus superior to all Protestant heresiarchs.

Voltaire is a very complex case indeed. He did not simply open up a wrong path, as many others did, but he summed up (so to speak) aberrations from the right path of Faith and Reason: he *epitomised* the aberrations of all those who had stopped half way before him on some wrong path. He was a " Gallican " with Bossuet in his *Siècle de Louis XIV*, and in the *Essai sur les moeurs* he was far more Jansenist than Pascal.[1] A believer in God, this champion of logic denied most of the logical implications of Divine omnipotence, such as the possibility of miracles and revelation.

Human wisdom was the only authority he accepted, yet—like Berkeley, Hume, and Kant after him—he denied that the human mind could ever know final certainty. That his passion for justice was genuine and that he attacked real abuses and scandals of his time, we do not want to deny. There was compassion and even charity in Voltaire; but a total lack of humility spoiled even this, the highest of his gifts. Indignant over the abuse of power, he proposed (again illogically enough for a champion of Reason) that philosopher princes should enjoy absolute power; yet, at the same time, this keen moralist, in his *Lettres sur l'Angleterre*, was ready to pay the heavy price of oligarchical and aristocratic corruption, for the sake of " Liberty." To sum up his importance in the field which is our present concern, Voltaire secularised both Authority and Liberty, not admitting that either had any other foundation than human reason and human need. In this sense alone, he is the father of Revolutions, yet no writer, thinker, or critic of public affairs was more at home in a Catholic, monarchical and aristocratic society. And nobody has felt more uprooted in a secularist and democratic Republic than belated Voltairians such as Charles Maurras and Anatole France. The first made a desperate attempt, in the early part of our century, to reconstruct mentally a monarchical and aristocratic society without a religion, but founded on merely pragmatic necessities, recognised by Reason; he even tried to construct a Church which

[1] When it suited his purpose: when he wanted to argue the immediate presence of divinity in the soul, which does not therefore need the mediation of Church or priesthood.

would teach doctrines that were admittedly problematic in the light of Reason, but which were needed for the social discipline of the masses. The second belated Voltairian clung desperately, under cover of a self-imposed and permanent ironical smile, to what remained of monarchical, clerical and aristocratic France, to all the red robes of Cardinals, gala swords of Academicians and tiaras of great ladies that survived in the drawing-rooms of the Faubourg St Germain, until the eve of the twentieth century and the First World War.

Opportet ut fiant scandala. . . . Voltaire was the scandal of a narrow world which was disguised in the solemn robes of Authority; but it sinned in its Liberty, for the substance of Authority, the primacy of Order, was no longer present in its mind and heart. He was the minor, very minor, scandal of a world which had lost every Cartesian perspective of the Absolute, every Pascalian sense of the Infinite, every sense of the unity of essence taught by Bossuet, and thus even of every measure of true human greatness. Even when this world, a little more than a century after Voltaire had shaken it with laughter rather than indignation, took " lessons in energy " from Maurice Barrès, or listened to the pious, complacent reassurances of Paul Bourget, it will not deceive us. This was just " the world," the one rejected by Pascal. The greatest glory and the culminating point of French letters, as we said before, came when Pascal, a man not of the Church but of the world, rejected worldly wisdom, and at the same time made it quite clear that the primacy of Order was the first principle on which society was based, and when human society, a unit in the natural order, received from a thinker in its own ranks a declaration of its own supernatural nature. As the Abbé Brémond[1] said, the true history of literature, like the true history of a nation, is the religious history of the people, and this is more so in the case of France than of any other nation.

The Gospel tells us to judge people by their fruits. We may weigh the fruits of Voltaire, Charles Maurras and Anatole France, and we may taste them. They are not very substantial or very sweet. The first of them adopted the pose of intransigent affirmation and of strict doctrine: he assumed the attitude of the depositary of a great classic, monarchical

---

[1] Henri Brémond: *Histoire du sentiment religieux dans la littérature française depuis le XVIIe siècle jusqu'à nos jours:* a work whose chief trend may be described as religious and Catholic romanticism, a religious history based on the study of profane texts.

doctrine, dignified by the scarlet robe of Richelieu; yet he was nothing more than the teacher of rabid semi-literates, worthy of the black shirt rather than of the scarlet robe. Maurras, recognising a fellow-Voltairian in Anatole France, singled him out as the great writer of his generation, despite the revolutionary sympathies of this latter, arguing that his aesthetic preference for every sort of intransigence was more favourable to the anarchist worker than to the moderate bourgeois of the Third Republic. The fact is that Anatole France's whole message and style died with the moderate bourgeois of the Third Republic, and in any case were no more worthy of survival than this era itself. The said bourgeois felt that Balzac, the " reactionary," execrated them; felt offended by the impotent ill-humour of Flaubert; was shocked, not by the opium-smoking of Baudelaire, or the absinthe-drinking of Verlaine, but by the final conversion of both *poètes maudits*. He was delighted and pleased, on the other hand, by Anatole France, the " revolutionary " sophist; flattered rather than disquietened by Maurras, the " monarchical " sophist, who offered him plenty of justification for a comfortable social immorality, and a comfortable escape from serious affirmation into an easy and pleasant position of prolonged and unperturbed scepticism—a position which was compatible with the external cult of those ancestors of the *bourgeoisie*, the Athenians (much beloved by both Maurras and Anatole France) who put Socrates to death.

A fruit of Voltaire, outside France, was Heinrich Heine. Many critics on both sides of the Rhine have dwelt on the Plutarchian parallel between this German who served the French king, and Voltaire who served the King of Prussia. The parallel goes further than that; but, unfortunately for Voltaire, what was really noble in Heine was not his wit or his persiflage, still less his grim and presumptuous laughter and his facile sentiment, but the infinite regret, behind all this, at the slow approach of a terrible end, the tragic collapse under what he felt to be the double curse of Germany and Juda, his break with atheism " not only out of disgust," but through " a fear " which he admitted—the fear of a sensitive artist in the face of Revolutions that were yet to come in an apostate Germany, and a faithless modern Israel which had denied Jehovah.

Perhaps the best spiritual descendant of Voltaire was Stendhal. Practically ignored during his life-time, he was the last writer to belong to the eighteenth century, although he wrote exclusively in the nineteenth.[1] Stendhal was undoubtedly of the family of Voltaire. In him there was no melancholy regret, none of the nostalgia for a more beautiful past, which began with Chateaubriand, the German romantics, young Victor Hugo and Walter Scott, and continued throughout the whole of the nineteenth century. This melancholy and nostalgia sounded a more sincere note than all the artificial paroxysms concerning the "future," all the semi-scientific, optimistic philosophies which, in most cases, were nothing but retrospective Utopias, transferred to the future from some imaginary past. Stendhal, like Voltaire and the eighteenth century as a whole, believed in the power of the senses, and in almost nothing else. Curiosity concerning the sensual nature of man comprised almost his only philosophy. His was an exceptional case of a narrow and insufficient philosophy which did not spoil the greatness of his art. He was fortunate in that he inherited sensualism, rather than dry rationalism, from Voltaire; and he nourished it with Italian impressions and ample subjects for meditation drawn from history and politics, especially in the *Chartreuse de Parme*. But Balzac, Stendhal's pupil, who was greater than his master and who virtually discovered him, saw in the author of the *Chartreuse de Parme* more of Machiavelli than of Voltaire. He recognised in Stendhal's *Conte Mosca* a portrait of his much-admired Metternich, a homage to superior statesman-like principles and intelligence, and he deplored the fact that only some fifteen hundred men who formed the brain of Europe would be able to understand Stendhal and the book which a nineteenth-century Machiavelli would have written.[2]

Voltaire's heirs did not therefore always choose the side of Liberty in the great debate between Authority and Liberty, despite the blessing their master gave to Benjamin Franklin's grandson in the name of " God and Liberty." We have already pointed out that it would be very difficult indeed to make a modern democrat out of the very loyal chronicler of *Le siècle de Louis XIV* and *Le siècle de Louis XV*, the man who at one moment sought and obtained the favours of Madame de Pompadour and her circle, and who, before his disgrace at Potsdam, was

[1] Just as Chateaubriand was the first writer of the nineteenth century, although his early period belonged to the eighteenth.

[2] *Etude sur M. Beyle*, par Honoré de Balzac. Epilogue to an 1846 Paris edition of *La Chartreuse de Parme*, p. 484 sq.

at any rate a devoted friend of the King of Prussia. He admired tyranny in Peter the Great, he admired the absolute philosophy of China, he reproved Leibnitz for not making the new Alexander, Charles XII of Sweden, his pupil, as Aristotle made Alexander of Macedon his pupil. But when it comes to Charles XII sending the royal boots to preside over the Stockholm Senate, Voltaire expressed little democratic objection, just as his much praised humanitarian tolerance did not go so far as to make him a friend of the Jews—as Bonald remarked in *La Question Juive*[1] (1806).

The secularisation of Liberty by Voltaire, which we have analysed above, required a full and complete Catholic answer, which he did not live to receive, and which could not perhaps even have been given without the practical experience of an integral Voltairianism which mankind received with the French Revolution. This answer was given by Joseph de Maistre. It cannot be repeated too often that Christian thought has always triumphed when it possessed the knowledge and the spiritual weapons of its opponent. The Redeemer and His Apostles knew the Scriptures better than did the Synagogue; St Augustine knew Greek thought better than any of the pagan philosophers, and the force of evil better than the Manicheans; St Thomas was more unprejudiced and tolerant towards the thought of those who did not possess the full measure of Christian grace than any of the Albigenses; St Ignatius was superior both in independence of mind and self-discipline to any Protestant; St Alphonsus Liguori was stricter and more austere in his submission to Authority than any Jansenist, who rejected it for allegedly purer forms of Liberty and austerity. Pascal was superior to Montaigne in *esprit de finesse* and to Descartes in *esprit de géométrie*.[2] Joseph de Maistre had a finer

---

[1] *Oeuvres complètes de M. le Vicomte de Bonald, Pair de France.* Paris, 1859. Vol. 2, p. 934:
   " *Quand je dis que les Juifs sont objet de la bienveillance des philosophes, il faut en excepter le chef de l'école philosophique Voltaire, qui toute sa vie a montré une aversion decidée contre ce peuple infortuné.*
   " *Il est probable que cet homme célèbre ne haïssait dans les Juifs que les dépositaires et les témoins de la vérité et de la révélation qu'il a juré d'anéantir.*"
   Thus Bonald discerned in Voltaire the beginnings of a more recent anti-Christianism, disguised as hatred of the Jews, that anti-Semitism which moved Léon Bloy to write *Le salut par les Juifs.*

[2] We mean naturally *esprit de géométrie* in philosophical thought and style. The respective greatness of Pascal and Descartes in geometry and mathematics proper is not our province, although creditable sources inform us that no scientific authority questions that Pascal is entitled to the very highest rank. We have done our best to study his scientific work as far as it is relevant for his philosophy and theology.

love of history than Voltaire and did not mind appearing, when the necessity of the argument required, even pedantic. He was fully prepared to appear as a " philosopher " in order to refute the bad, eighteenth-century meaning of the word, which no longer bore any relationship to the *philosophia perennis*, but followed Descartes in purely individual reasoning, or Berkeley, Hume and Kant in considering the consciously and confessedly doubtful individual judgement as the final authority. When he had to play this rôle, it was in order to establish a common ground for discussion; then, after demolishing his opponent's arguments, he appeared in his true colours as a man of the *philosophia perennis*, as a Christian whose concern it was to believe, rather than to be omniscient, for—this is the noblest aspect of de Maistre's thought—he admitted fully that it is more difficult to believe than to know, but he insisted that the effort to believe, and the sacrifice which acceptance of belief entails, is in itself heroic, and an act of moral greatness.

The primacy of morals is the subject of Joseph de Maistre's great dialogues called *Les Soirées de St Pétersbourg*. Taking part in these conversations, in the first year of the century, were an Imperial Russian Senator, a young French *émigré* nobleman in the Czar's service, and de Maistre himself. He waited almost twenty years before he wrote them down. The argument in the dialogues, however, is not addressed to the elderly Russian and the young Frenchman, but to the whole of the eighteenth century, in which Joseph de Maistre spent the greater part of his life, forty-seven out of his sixty-eight years. Voltaire separated morals from faith and dogma and put the accent on morality. When Voltaire challenged Pascal by coining aphorisms in opposition to the *Pensées*, he challenged him on moral and intellectual sidelines, not indeed on real fundamentals: belief in God and in Christ. Joseph de Maistre replied to Voltaire. Voltaire said in essence that he was not concerned with a man's beliefs, as long as his actions were moral. De Maistre replied that, as a rational sceptic, he was unable to trust anybody's morals, unless they were prepared for the first and most difficult sacrifice of all, the effort to believe. Voltaire and his whole century dismissed the Catholic position by saying that it was easy to believe, that any child could do so, whereas to know demanded a serious and manly effort. Joseph de Maistre replied that it was quite easy to know, but that it was a gift and a grace to believe; that it required a heroic effort on the part of all the human faculties, purity,

imagination and emotion.[1] And he illustrated his point with
his habitual sense of paradox: it was easy enough, he said, to
know the Theses of Wittenberg, the Thirty-nine Articles
of the Church of England, the Confession of Augsburg,
or the Helvetic Confession, whereas a man needed rhythm,
musical sense and deep emotions to sing the Nicene
Creed.

Joseph de Maistre created new matter and a new style for
apologetics, although there is no doubt that he owed much to
Pascal and to Bossuet.

He was indebted to Pascal for his sense of paradox and for
his wit, which defeated Voltaire and disconcerted the Voltairians for ever. Wit, satire, jokes, these terrible arms which
Voltaire used against the Church, were mastered in the *Soirées*,
and turned against him. Only a few Voltairians in later years
dared to try to use them again after de Maistre: Paul-Louis
Courier, in whose hands the Voltairian weapons became either
vulgar or heavy and pedantic, like his German-inspired
Hellenic science, and Victor Hugo, when he wrote *Les
Châtiments*. Yet ever since Péguy's brilliant exposure and
unmasking of Hugo's pseudo-democracy and pseudo-pacifism,[2]
we can never again believe, to Hugo's credit, that this grandiose
bard of military glories, this rhetorical but genuine mystic, was
ever a Voltairian. After all it was not the Church, but the
Liberal bourgeoisie, who rallied round the flag of conformity
waved by Napoleon III, which was the target of *Les Châtiments*;
and we must not forget that, as we are told in the *Memoirs of
Granier de Cassagnac*, Hugo wished his disciples *de dire franchement
que Voltaire est bête*, many years before committing the blasphemy
in *Actes et Paroles* of comparing the tears of Jesus with the smile
of Voltaire, as the two most powerful weapons against the
evils of this world. Anatole France tried to make Voltairian
jokes; he was at best an unconscious humorist when he created

---

[1] We may quote here a few echoes, only partly conscious and direct ones, of
Joseph de Maistre and the *Soirées*: When Balzac declared so emphatically in the
Preface to the *Comédie Humaine* that he was on the same side as Bossuet and Bonald,
he certainly echoed de Maistre; also when he said that human society did not
need masters to teach it how to doubt, but masters who knew how to affirm and
how to believe, i.e. Authority, which, in the thought of this great inventor of an
imaginary society, was the keystone of social justice and happiness. Chesterton
found truth in the irresistible paradoxes of the Faith, and not in logical but
unimaginative reasoning. The whole life-work of Kierkegaard was an auto-
biographical comment on the moral value of the effort to believe. For Romano
Guardini, real knowledge begins " beyond the self-evident," in the mystical
sphere which can only be entered at the cost of sacrifice.

[2] In *Notre Jeunesse et Victor-Marie, comte Hugo*.

Professor Bergeret, and only succeeded in making us smile
happily in small masterpieces like *Le Jongleur de Notre Dame*, at
stories of child-like devotion. Joseph de Maistre banished the
enemies of the Church into that " Sorbonne-esque " and
pedantic gravity which they assumed in the nineteenth and
early twentieth centuries, amidst the scorn and the laughter—
and what laughter!—of Veuillot, Barbey d'Aurevilly, Charles
Péguy, Chesterton, and Theodor Haecker. He laughs longest
who laughs last, and thanks to Joseph de Maistre, the
Church laughed last on all the topics raised by the
eighteenth and early nineteenth centuries. But let us
rather quote de Maistre, the superior protagonist of paradox, before we show him as the spiritual son of Bossuet in
his graver, but not necessarily more mystical or greater
moments:

> *Rien n'égale la patience de ce peuple qui se dit libre. En cinq ans*
> *on lui a fait accepter trois constitutions et le gouvernement révolution-*
> *naire. Les tyrans se succèdent et toujours le peuple obéit. Jamais on*
> *n'a vu réussir un seul pour se tirer de la nullité. Ses maîtres ont réussi à*
> *le foudroyer en se moquant de lui. Ils lui ont dit: Vous croyez ne pas*
> *vouloir cette loi, mais soyez sûrs que vous la voulez. Si vous osez la*
> *refuser, nous tirerons sur vous pour vous punir de ne pas vouloir ce que*
> *vous voulez.*[1]

He could show the party who believed in the primacy of
Liberty, fellow-exiles of his in Lausanne before his St. Petersburg period—Mme. de Staël and Benjamin Constant—those
who were later to be answered more fully by Bonald than de
Maistre ever cared to do, that he, the Piedmontese whose
mother-tongue was French, knew his Europe, and did not
suffer from any sort of French " provincialism," which Mme.
de Staël tried to overcome by recommending English politics
to France in her political writing, German learning and sentiment in *De l'Allemagne*, and Italian emotions in *Corinne*. Not
only did he know his Machiavelli to such a degree that he could
be fair and just to this ardent republican, from whom he took
most striking arguments against attempts made to replace with
paper constitutions the natural conditions consecrated by
history and experience; but he knew his Kant and Lutheran
Germany, whose intellectual influence he saw spreading to
schismatic Russia, where the secular authority confined itself
to resisting the true authority of the unbroken tradition of

[1] *Considérations sur la France.* Lausanne. 1797. Ch. VIII.

Rome, instead of resisting the intrusion of wild intellectual liberties from heretical Germany.[1] He knew English philosophy and the English language well enough to conclude his famous polemics against Locke with the half-serious, half-comic lament: " *L'esprit européen est emprisonné.* . . . It is locked in."

When she was in Lausanne, Mme. de Staël delighted in the frankness and naturalness of great military style, personified in Prince de Ligne, for the publication of whose aphorisms and recollections she was responsible.[2] We share in this delight, and are almost inclined to like Mme. de Staël better because of it. But only Joseph de Maistre could show in *Les Soirées de St Pétersbourg* the essence of military style and morals, in a way which established a relationship between all dedicated lives, and showed that all manifestations of purity come from a sense of dedication and sacrament:

Le spectacle épouvantable du carnage n'endurcit pas le véritable guerrier. Au milieu du sang qu'il fait couler, il est humain comme l'épouse est chaste dans les transports de l'amour.

And only he could explain so pleasantly, a little further on in the *Soirées*, that it is love of liberty and love of humanity that may make a man reject popular revolutions and pacifist utopias, which are inhuman and only possible at the price of tyranny, and more cruel " wars to end war."

It is rather an echo of Bossuet that we hear in the early de Maistre of the *Considérations sur la France*. It is the belief in the providential mission of Charlemagne's monarchy. For de Maistre, it was the hand of Providence which had prevented the destruction of France, the country which had been given the mission of unifying Europe, not under a sceptre or a sword, but in Christian civilisation and liberty. This devotion to France—Joseph de Maistre was Piedmontese by citizenship, and if he had a second country it was Russia—this devotion was such

---

[1] Joseph de Maistre: *Quatre chapitres inédits sur la Russie*. Paris, 1859. The volume was edited by Admiral Count Robert de Maistre, who during his father's term of office at St Petersburg served as an officer under Czar Alexander I, and who, with his uncle General Xavier de Maistre, the author of *Voyage autour de ma chambre*, *La jeune Sibérienne*, etc., had an immense and intimate knowledge of the Empire of the Czars.

[2] Cf. M. Louis Witmer's most interesting study of the anti-revolutionary and anti-Napoleonic party in Europe: *Le Prince de Ligne, Frédéric de Gentz et Jean de Müller. Leur correspondence inédite*. Paris, 1925.

a constant factor in everything that he wrote,[1] from the
Considérations in 1797 to *Du Pape*, composed at the time of the
fall of Napoleon, that it is understandable that Friedrich von
Schlegel, or Joseph Görres, reproached him for misunderstanding the Germanic *sacrum Imperium*, concerning which de
Maistre was hardly less critical than Voltaire, and never far
removed from the views of the author of *Essai sur les mœurs*, who
sided with the traditional French concept of European primacy,
but without the religious content and the significance of this
concept.

Joseph de Maistre is the great lay Doctor of Christian
Authority. He gave the various enemies of the Church a
nostalgia for a supreme religious authority. From the queer
sect of Saint-Simon, to the still queerer philosophical school of
Auguste Comte, called "positivist," from Mazzini and his
Young Europe down to Charles Maurras and his sect, this
nostalgia for a spiritual authority, for a social theology without
the Church, was to appear on every page, and in almost every
manifestation of the coming century of secular sects. This
applies even to the most highly organised and the most powerful of these sects, the only one among them to achieve material
power, the Communist International of Moscow. Theoretically
it even denies what the earlier sects had still affirmed—the
primacy of the spiritual—and replaces it by a crude and rough
materialism, apparently daring and intransigent, but in reality

[1] Much of de Maistre's work remained in fragments during his life-time, and
the final picture of his intellectual evolution and a final analysis of his work in the
light of his biography is a fairly recent achievement. The best contributions have
been made by the Savoyard historian F. Vermale, who reconstructed his youth
and early life in Chambéry and Turin; Georges Goyau: *La pensée religieuse de
Joseph de Maistre*, Paris, 1921, whose study was based on material which had
remained unpublished for a hundred years. For de Maistre's influence on German
romantic thought, we are indebted to Hermann von Grauert's *Görres und de Maistre*,
in the *Jahrbücher der Görres-Gesellschaft*, Köln, 1922; and Richard von Kralik's
Das Neunzehnte Jahrhundert, in *Zeitgemässe Broschuren*, Frankfurt, 1905; and in the
same author's analysis of the romantic period *Oesterreichische Geschichte*, Wien, 1913,
p. 320 sq. On de Maistre's action in Russia, see the biography of Madame de
Swetchine by Alfred de Falloux, 1860. C. Ostrogorsky: *Joseph de Maistre und
seine Lehre von der höchsten Macht*, Helsinki, 1932; M. Jugie: *Joseph de Maistre et
l'église greco-russe*, 1922, and the publications—in Russian—by M. Makoshin and
M. Stepanov, under the auspices of the Russian Cultural Centre in Paris, 1937.
See also Frederic Holdsworth: *Joseph de Maistre et l'Angleterre*, Paris, 1935. The
most intuitive critical survey on de Maistre is to be found in Barbey d'Aurevilly's
Les Prophètes du Passé, 1850. Among the serious and appreciative, although hostile,
students of de Maistre's thought, the first place goes to Sainte-Beuve. Among the
most recent studies, we may mention an analytical anthology with comments:
La politique expérimentale de Joseph de Maistre, by M. Bernard de Vaulx, Paris,
Fayard, 1940.

shameful and cowardly, calling itself " dialectical " to imply
the independence of the spiritual element, which it otherwise
denies. This usurpation of authority does not hesitate to condemn miscreants, brands " deviations " from the doctrine
without ever stating what it is that sets that doctrine above the
human level, and by what means that doctrine has been
authentically transmitted or can possibly be proved.

We have already shown that, challenged by Voltaire's
laughter, Joseph de Maistre drove the enemies of the Church
into an attitude of ridiculous gravity and imitation. He it was
whom even intelligent opponents like Sainte-Beuve tried to
decry as a mind preoccupied with praise of the past, who made
the clearest guess as to the future; we can be more sure of this
than even Barbey d'Aurevilly was in 1850, when he first called
him a prophet. His central thesis was that Man is essentially
unfit to " create " anything, so that the attempt to create " new
worlds," instead of accepting the order of Creation, can only
lead to vast, grotesque and sanguinary scenes in future history.
With a genuine love of Russia, and a long personal devotion
to Alexander I, which was only too ready to overlook the well-
known weaknesses of this sovereign, and his tendency to strange
" illuminist " mysticism, de Maistre was perhaps the first
man to foretell prophetically the dangers which might one day
threaten Europe from this remote Empire of the North and the
East. His correspondence with Russian friends, and his
Quatre chapitres inédits sur la Russie show that he was full of these
anxieties. It was not the simple political anxiety, inspired in
Horace Walpole, in Joseph II and Kaunitz, by the size and
resources of Russia, her expansive ambition and the dynastic
instabilities which had often brought unscrupulous men and
women to posts of command in St Petersburg; neither was it
the anxiety which filled Metternich at the Vienna Congress,
and again during the Greek War of Independence and during
the various Polish crises, to combat which he tried, in the
months preceding the *Cent Jours*, and often afterwards, to make
Austria as much an ally of the West as of Russia, in order to be
able to play the mediating—or the decisive—part one day in
a conflict between East and West. Joseph de Maistre recognised in the penetration of Western ideas to Russia, and in the
uncritical spirit in which Russia was ready to accept ideas from
the West, a perspective which was frightening for discerning eyes:

*Tout me porte à croire que la Russie n'est pas susceptible d'un
gouvernement organisé comme les nôtres; et . . . si la nation, venant*

*à comprendre nos perfides nouveautés, si le peuple était ébranlé et
commençait, au lieu d'expéditions asiatiques, une révolution à l'européenne, je n'ai point expression à dire ce qu'on pourrait craindre:*

Bella, horrida bella!

Et multo Nevam spumantem sanguine cerno.[1]

Within less than ten years after de Maistre's departure from
Russia,[2] and only four years after his death, the " December
conspiracy " disclosed to an astonished world the widespread
presence in Russia of " our perfidious novelties "; young
noblemen and Imperial officers who had won their promotion
during the campaigns in Germany and France, in the last phase
of the Napoleonic Wars, had dreamed in their secret societies
of a future United States of all the Slavs, had taken the Pan-
Slav oath[3] and sworn on their daggers, to the glory of the
" Goddess of Reason," to build ports from Dalmatia to the
Arctic Sea, and to unite and " liberate " all Slav peoples in
Bohemia, Hungary and Transylvania, Moldavia, Wallachia
and Servia! Metternich's nightmare, that German philosophy
and Western modernism should prevail in Russia, rather than
the conservative and Christian concept of Monarchy, which
Russia held in common with Europe, was based on close knowledge of tendencies of this kind which were inherent in Russia's
political system and in the whole trend of the Czarist tradition
established by Peter the Great.[4]

One of the claims of Joseph de Maistre to the admiration of
posterity is this: he was the first European who, more than
half a century before Dostoievsky, visualised the prospect of a
Godless Russia, and urged on the schismatic Empire the alternative which may yet come in the future—integration into the
spiritual unity and authority of Christendom, instead of the
degradation and catastrophe of Godlessness.

[1] Op. cit. (*Quatre chapitres*, etc.), p. 218.

[2] He left Russia in 1816, and after meeting Vicomte de Bonald for the first time
in his life in Paris, returned to a post of no great importance, although it was of
Cabinet rank, in Turin. His last years in St Petersburg were embittered by the
conflict between Alexander I and the Holy See over the Church in Poland and
the Jesuit province in the Russian Empire. This cooled his relations with the
Czar. See Georges Goyau, *op. cit.*

[3] *La conspiration de Russie. Rapport de la Commission d'Enquête de St Pétersbourg à
S. M. Nicholas I, Empereur de Russie*, Paris, 1826, p. 70. The general conclusion
(p. 10) was that German ideas and German secret student societies had acted ever
since 1813 on the minds of young Russian officers.

[4] In addition to the many references in Metternich's posthumous *Mémoires et
Documents* (1880), see *Correspondance de Lebzeltern* (Austrian Ambassador in St
Petersburg under Alexander I) published by the Imperial Russian Academy, St
Petersburg, 1913.

5. THE PRIMACY OF POLITICS: FROM MONTESQUIEU TO BONALD

THE second most important thinker in the eighteenth century was, without any doubt, Montesquieu. The quintessence of Voltaire lay in the independence of morals from belief; Montesquieu's message was the primacy of politics over religious concerns. The author of *L'Esprit des Lois* was infinitely less hostile to Christianity than was Voltaire, he was even perhaps the most positive Christian amongst the outstanding writers of his century. He stated several times, in all sincerity, we feel, and not out of mere opportunism, that he preferred his own Catholic religion and that of his King to all others; he went so far as to engage in lengthy polemics with Pierre Beyle, the ex-Huguenot leader of a "natural" religion, which claimed that a perfect Christianity was incompatible with civic virtues and the interest of the State. In contrast to the witticisms of Voltaire, Montesquieu's humour and wit was never malicious, or inspired by hatred or bitterness; his aphoristic style is kindly and full of polish; the irony of the *Lettres Persanes* was not directed against sacred feelings.

Yet perhaps by reason of his greater moral seriousness and his more unselfish literary purpose—he was more concerned with objective truth than Voltaire ever was—the harm Montesquieu did was perhaps even greater than the harm Voltaire intended to do, and in fact accomplished.

Montesquieu saw the co-existence of various forms of religion in history. Some of them were more suitable in a Monarchy, others in a Republic. Social forms were largely a question of natural surroundings and climate. Even the desert could have a religion which was politically and socially suitable—for example, Islam. Political truth is relative; so, implicitly, is religious. The best form Liberty can take is one in which the three powers of the State, the executive, the judicial and the legislative, enjoy the greatest independence one from the other. Here again, more implicitly than explicitly, Montesquieu denied the unity of purpose in a governing power, the essential unity in diversity of social forms, the central significance of any revealed law or Scripture, the primacy of any Order over Liberty. The eighteenth century, still so near to Bossuet, interpreted the thesis of *L'Esprit des Lois* as a negation of that of the *Discours sur l'histoire universelle*.

L'Esprit des Lois was, of course, the great book of 1789 and of

almost the whole Liberal school of the nineteenth century. The
separation and the balance of the three powers within the
State has been the profession of Faith of all moderate revolutionaries, from Madame de Staël and Benjamin Constant, via
Guizot and Thiers, down to the recent constitution-makers of
the Fourth Republic in France. Precisely because Montesquieu
was sincere, and expressed in moderate terms his preference for
Christian Monarchy, his theory was taken up even by the post-
revolutionary and post-Napoleonic movements of Catholic
revival—Lord Acton in England and Montalembert in France
were both influenced by the ideal of a political and social
" equilibrium." We can recognise fragments of Montesquieu's
thought in the liberal-democratic half-truths of recent decades.
In the name of a political theory of equilibrium, some people
characterised Nazism as an " anti-progressive " reaction and
Bolshevism as " dictatorship "—terms as politically adequate
as would be the medical description of cancer as " indigestion,"
and tuberculosis as a " spring-cold "—and they postulated
compromise between parties as the supreme political ideal. This
supreme ideal of an " equilibrium " is, they say, only possible in
a " Democracy," a vague term for a form of government which
does not even claim to be right by any absolute standards, but
only to be " tolerant " out of consideration for the counterbalance of an opposition party, possessing likewise a half-truth.
     One may easily argue of course that Montesquieu was
superior to the many belated and sometimes only half-conscious
imitators of his thought. Texts to this effect could certainly be
found in abundance, but this is not our concern here, and in
any case such a defence of Montesquieu would not differ from
any defence put forward by disciples of Machiavelli or Hegel,
for example, in justification of the original thought of their
master, which was in most cases superior to any latter-day
interpretation of it. It is enough if we sum up Montesquieu
as the thinker who taught the primacy of political expediency
over absolute religious truth on society, who for the first time
envisaged religious truth as subordinate to the pragmatic moral
aims of government and society, and who judged governments
and social systems according to an outward criterion of the
formal legitimacy, intactness and inviolability of the respective
sphere of each power.[1] Only much later, when Equality

[1] The best recent study of the intellectual and political atmosphere of
Montesquieu's time and doctrine is *La crise de la conscience européenne au XVIIIe
siècle* by Paul Hazard, professeur au Collège de France. Paris, 1930.

became a new idol, one which was unforeseen by Montesquieu
—to whom aristocratic, senatorial and parliamentarian governments were more familiar than real democracies—was this
" inviolability of the spheres of power " combined with the
" people's will " as the criterion of formal legitimacy; this
caused no little surprise and considerable embarrassment to
those followers of Montesquieu who belonged mostly to the
privileged political and social classes, and who were unaware
that there was anything in the traditions of their master's
thought which justified such doctrines.

In the great debate concerning Authority and Liberty which
we have followed throughout the ages, until it reached its most
acute stage in the eighteenth and nineteenth centuries,
Vicomte de Bonald[1] was the counterpart of Montesquieu.

Bonald had more of a systematic, and even scholastic, mind
than Joseph de Maistre. Writing in a style which was not less
elegant than the latter's, he resisted all temptation to take his
opponent by surprise and deal the last stroke with some brilliant
paradox, which, final as it might be, would be questioned on
second thoughts by the defeated enemy. The author of the
Soirées de St Pétersbourg preferred the liveliness of the Platonic
form, being a master of dialogue. The author of the *Théorie du
pouvoir*[2] was more of a pure Aristotelian. De Maistre gave the
impression that he greatly enjoyed scoring over an opponent.
Bonald hits out almost accidentally, although he did it
frequently enough, at the anglophile school of Benjamin
Constant and Mme. de Staël, at Voltaire, Rousseau and
Montesquieu, at Locke and Kant, *si tristement célèbre*. Writing
in exile at Heidelberg, or in his provincial retreat during the
time of Napoleon (who would have much preferred to see this
Doctor of Authority serve him, " the restorer of Order and
Religion," instead of persevering in a discreet but indomitable
opposition), his starting point was naturally enough the

---

[1] We use his name thus, as he expressly disapproved, in *Considérations sur la
noblesse* and in *La théorie du pouvoir*, of the habit of putting Christian names instead
of titles before the family names of French noblemen, and because Joseph de
Maistre, himself less of a purist, in deference to his friend's insistence on this point,
requested a correspondent of his to write " Vicomte de Bonald," " M. de Bonald,"
or simply " Bonald," but never " de Bonald." The usual reference to the author
of the *Soirées de St Pétersbourg* as " Joseph de Maistre " and not " Comte de
Maistre " is to be explained by the fact that the title belonged also to his brother
Xavier de Maistre, who was hardly less known in the literature of his time.

[2] Practically speaking, he wrote one book only. The *Essai analytique sur les lois
naturelles* ; the *Intérêt général de l'Europe*, *Du divorce au XIXe siècle* and his countless
shorter essays, maxims, aphorisms and fragments are mere extensions and applica-
tions of, or additions to, his *Théorie du pouvoir*.

contemporary French and European scene. Yet, going far beyond the historical context of his time and country, he aimed at stating absolute truth in theology and philosophy, at making definitions which would hold good for all time.

Bonald gave a complete and full reply to almost every proposition which was part of the intellectual currency of the eighteenth century. The sensualist psychology of Condillac, the " natural man " of Rousseau, Locke's and Diderot's theory of knowledge which comes through the experience of the senses, were all answered by his monumental theory concerning language. He said that human language is unable to express, and is not meant to express, anything that is not either an image or an idea. The first proof of religious truth is the existence of the idea, that is of the word " God " in every human language. History is the evolution from the image to the idea, a transition of mankind from childhood to maturity:

Un enfant a des images avant d'avoir des idées; ainsi un peuple cultive son imagination avant de développer sa raison. Ainsi dans l'univers même, la société des images ou des figures, le judaisme, a précédé la société des idées, ou le christianisme, qui adore l'Etre suprême en esprit et en vérité.[1]

Instead of Montesquieu's theory of equilibrium through the separation of powers, Bonald propounded the unity of power, the unity of purpose seen in nature, because *one* mind has created nature and established its laws, which are gradually and progressively revealed to Man. We see a constantly recurring motive in all the political theorising of Bonald, a three-fold division, as in Montesquieu, but formulated differently and re-stated in order to establish a different conclusion. According to him, there is a singleness of purpose in society: Power is given for the preservation of religion and morals and of the natural law, i.e. for the preservation of identity to which every species in Nature tends. Judicial and executive power provide the means for this preservation, and fight the internal and the external enemy, which are obstacles to preservation. Thus, kings rule with the help of two classes, both of which are symbolised by the Sword—the Sword of Justice and the Sword of defence—although usually they are referred to as the *noblesse de robe* and the *noblesse d'épée*. In the spiritual society, the Church, power is transmitted to a spiritual successor. In the natural society, the State, power is transmitted in natural succession from father to son. The social unit is the family, not

---

[1] *Essai analytique sur les lois naturelles*, p. 221 in the first edition of 1800.

D

the individual. The liberties people really care about are not such things as the liberty of the Press, or the liberty of a jury, for few people publish anything, and few ever have to appear before a jury; but the liberty to preserve, in the form of safe property, the fruit of a family achievement, the liberty of a family to rise to a higher status, and the liberty to preserve this status for future generations.

It is fairly usual to identify Revolution with optimism, and post-revolutionary tendencies—the romantic period—as the reaction of pessimism, although they still professed a " religious attachment to Liberty."[1] The Italian historian Guglielmo Ferrero did much to spread this judgement in his numerous essays on the post-revolutionary era; he later revised it in his book *Bonaparte in Italy*, in which he classified the European parties into " groups of violence " and " groups of fear."

Reading Bonald's *Essai analytique*, we see that progressive optimism was not in the least absent from the anti-revolutionary party. He greets the new century with great hope, as one in which as much progress in the knowledge of the laws governing society will be made as the eighteenth century made in the knowledge of the laws governing nature. The law of society, he declares, is still in its infancy, just as religion was in the early centuries which saw the conversion of the Barbarian. The appeal for the unity of Europe is made by the anti-revolutionary party, not only in the writings of Bonald and Joseph de Maistre (in his *Essai sur le principe générateur des institutions humaines*, 1814) but also in the whole of the literature which prepared the way for, or commented upon, the Vienna Congress—Friedrich von Gentz, Adam Müller, Johannes von Müller, Friedrich von Schlegel, Novalis—all of whom, in their respective countries, looked for some principle to replace Spinoza's and Montesquieu's theories concerning the " balance " and the " equilibrium " of power; a principle which it was impossible to maintain in Schlegel's view[2] on account of the British possessions in Asia, and the extent of the Russian Empire the very vastness of which precludes any possibility of balance.

But we have to note a more radical change in European political thought, which was due mainly to Bonald—the revaluation of history as the science of social law and as the principal weapon in apologetics and religious controversy.

---

[1] Benedetto Croce: *Storia de l'Europa nel decimonono secolo*, Bari, 1932. See especially the introductory chapter.
[2] See his *Lectures on the Philosophy of History*, which we have already mentioned.

The immense change in the European outlook and in the modern historical sense, which pervades the artistic imagination with Chateaubriand, Walter Scott, the young Victor Hugo, Schiller, the German romantics, and Manzoni in Italy, is connected with the religious thought of the post-revolutionary era as exemplified in Bonald. Others had defended the religion of man: he would defend the religion of society; they had proved religion by religion, but he intends to prove it by history. Metaphysics is a science of *realities*; *et si certains écrivains qui ont traité de l'être sont vagues et obscurs . . . c'est qu'ils ont voulu expliquer l'être pensant par l'être pensant, au lieu de l'expliquer par l'être parlant, qui est son expression et son image.*

Bonald was the reply to Montesquieu as was de Maistre to Voltaire. As we have already pointed out, Montesquieu was the man whose intellectual influence was the least intentionally hostile to the Church in the eighteenth century. We find both religious and spiritual truth in him, disguised as irony, or even cynicism. When Montesquieu permitted himself such jokes as a defence of monogamy on sensual grounds, saying that the recollection of the by-gone youthful charm of women always acted as an attraction for husbands, he was still defending—in a curious manner—religious and social truth in the institution of marriage. When he justified slavery on the ground that the Africans are so stupid as to prefer shining glass to shining diamonds, *puis, ils ont le nez tellement écrasé qu'il est presque impossible de les plaindre*, he was stating the truth which Pascal never tired of demonstrating by all possible means: the truth concerning the extreme relativity and unreliability of every merely human judgement, one which Pascal himself had to wrap up in some cynical disguise. Bonald has much of Montesquieu's manner; we cannot help thinking of Montesquieu when we read Bonald's explanation of the English habit of eating raw meat, and the English legal institution of divorce, as the two signs of the raw and barbaric origin of this island people. But how much more deeply he goes into any subject proposed by Montesquieu for meditation, and how sternly he refuses to stop at any half-truth! Yet it was only a part of Bonald's achievement to reply to Montesquieu; of greater importance in his century was his discovery of a new field of historical and social theology. This historical argument in theology received its full elaboration in the work of Cardinal Newman, and still dominates a new Catholic spirituality, with Chesterton, Hilaire Belloc and Christopher Dawson in England, Theodor Haecker in Germany, Jacques Maritain and Étienne Gilson and Jean Guitton in France.[1]

Bonald stands for the transition from the *individualist* thought of the eighteenth century to the *social* thought of the nineteenth. It is sufficient to recall our last textual quotation from his *Théorie du pouvoir* to show how conscious he was of a *transition* period in human thought, the transition from individual to social religion, from rational to historical theology. We may also recall Metternich's frequent characterisation of his time as a " transition " period, Metternich who was almost the only statesman who understood Bonald's philosophy (and almost the only statesman of his time worthy of the name, in the opinion of Bonald's enthusiastic pupil, Honoré de Balzac). Metternich stood consciously at the close of an epoch, and was heroically determined to face the end of his world. In his view, the Primacy of Order was going to prevail[2] after the chaos which would separate the Old Europe from the New, and he wished he could have been born round about 1900 or later, so that he could have helped the new Europe come into being, instead of burying the old one.

Just as the Roman Emperor Marcus Aurelius, who wrote Greek in the same city of Vienna, was the last word of Classic Hellenism, the Imperial Chancellor of Austria, who wrote mostly in French, was the last great word of baroque, French-speaking, monarchical Europe. But as the ancient Greek wisdom expressed itself in melancholy, as befitted wise men, and was conquered by Christian hope, the last great word of monarchical Europe, Bonald or Metternich, gave a message not of melancholy, but of a transition towards an ultimate hope. We enter this period of transition from a rational to a historical and social theology, as we said, in the nineteenth century. Prophets in the Old Testament were men who announced a

---

[1] We allude here more particularly to Theodor Haecker's epilogue to a German translation of Cardinal Newman's *The Grammar of Assent*, written in 1921, to the *Rédemption du Temps* of Jacques Maritain and to Jean Guitton's comments on Newman's historical theology in *La justification du temps*.

[2] In his political testament (*Mémoires et Documents*, Vol. VII, p. 640) he writes —in French, which we prefer to keep, because it is Metternich's grand style—*Le mot de liberté n'a pas pour moi la valeur d'un point de départ, mais celle d'un point d'arrivée réel. C'est le mot d'ordre qui désigne le point de départ. Ce n'est que sur l'idée d'ordre que peut reposer l'idée de liberté* (sic!). *Sans la base de l'ordre, l'aspiration à la liberté n'est que l'effort d'un parti quelconque dans le but qu'il poursuit.*

Dans l'application à la vie positive, cette aspiration se traduira inévitablement par la tyrannie. À toutes les époques, dans toutes les situations, j'ai été un homme d'ordre, et j'ai toujours visé à l'établissement de la liberté véritable et non d'une liberté mensongère. La tyrannie, quelle qu'elle soit, a toujours été pour moi synonyme de la folie pure.

transition in time; transition always moves towards a new aspect of man's knowledge of God.

What was Bonald's concept of " Society " ? What does his repeated emphasis on the " social " and " historical " truth really mean ? He most certainly does not mean by " social law " the primacy of material concerns, as our time understands the term, led astray by a century of " material " Socialism, which even some emotional Catholic, or at any rate, Christian thought is ready to endorse and accept, confusing it with the primacy of charity. Neither does he mean by his notion of " historical situation " the distorted materialist sophistry of a variable relativity, determined by the temporary context of " economic conditions." He means the primacy of Order, such as we have tried to define it in these pages; the framework of real Liberty, that stability of consecrated Order, which for him was the only safeguard against the tyranny which the rule of individual judgement inevitably entails, for individual judgement is the *least* safe of foundations, and can only maintain its rule by violent means.

Society in Bonald's thought means first and foremost the family, " domestic society," of which God Himself was the legislator. The nations are extended domestic societies, i.e. they are " public societies." The international and European order is, or should be, a Society of Nations. The fundamental principle of association in all these phases is the social law, the law of God for the family, for the Church and for the nation.

History for Bonald is the science of the varying forms of an unalterable essence. His study of History is a prophetic one, a study of the transition from one stage of our knowledge of God to the next one, this new stage always being in his view a higher stage. There is a Progress. The word belongs to our vocabulary, therefore only Christians can understand the true meaning of the word. Only Christian society has known progress; non-Christian empires, at any rate before their contact with Christendom, only knew stability, so that the Muslim East presents a picture of arrested progress to all European observers.

With this summary of Bonald's thought, our earlier analysis of Joseph de Maistre, and the above—to our mind almost inevitable—comment on progress, we hope we have made it clear that such common-place descriptions as " reaction," " traditionalism," etc., are quite out of place in any characterisation of Bonald and Joseph de Maistre, who was fully aware of the truth that *si la Providence efface, c'est pour écrire*. Even a truly great mystic mind such as Léon Bloy could be so mistaken as to see " mere " traditionalism, unaware of God's plan to change the face of the world,[1] in the *Soirées de St Pétersbourg*, and in both de Maistre and Bonald to hear only *l'oraison funèbre de l'Europe civilisée*.[2]

Events inside the Church, however, were responsible for this widespread misunderstanding of the two foremost thinkers of the era of the French Revolution, which only a very close study of both Bonald and Joseph de Maistre can dispel. When on the death of Pope Gregory XVI in 1846, Cardinal Mastai Ferretti succeeded to the Papal throne under the style of Pope Pius IX, it seemed that the Catholic-Liberal school of thought would come into the forefront of Catholic action all over Europe.[3] These Catholic Liberals in France were, roughly speaking, the new variation of Gallicanism, as is shown by the support given them by members of the hierarchy known to have Gallican leanings—Mgr. Sibour, for instance, and Mgr. Dupanloup. Gallicanism had its counterpart in Germany under Joseph II, and derived new strength in the Napoleonic period under the régime of the Confederation of the Rhine and its Chancellor, Archbishop Dalberg. It also had its counterpart in England in the circle of Lord Acton—a nephew of Mgr. Dalberg, which is a biographical detail worth noting.

Did Pope Pius IX disapprove of the intransigent views expressed in Joseph de Maistre's *Du Pape*? Did he ever disapprove of the same author's sharp criticisms (and Bonald's also) of individual judgement as the basis of modern political institutions? There is not the slightest hint to this effect in any of his pronouncements. What he tried to achieve by the " Liberal " initiatives of his early years was the greater independence of the Papal See from European Powers, and what he achieved in his later period by the Bull of Infallibility (opposed by the same groups in 1869 who had hailed the new policy in 1846—by Montalembert and his friends) was a

[1] Léon Bloy: *Le Désespéré*. Ch. XLV.

[2] Léon Bloy: *Les dernières colonnes de l'Eglise* (essays, or rather polemics, against K. J. Huysmans, F. Brunetière, Paul Bourget, etc.).

[3] It had previously been discredited by the apostasy of Lamennais, though it was later strengthened by the prestige of the Dominican Fr. Lacordaire (a priest of holy zeal and ascetic spirituality, but at the same time a surprisingly conciliatory defender of the Faith), by the attractive oratory of Montalembert, and by the appearance in his circle of such a pure and zealous lay apostle as Frédéric Ozanam, the Catholic scholar and philosopher of the Romantic movement.

strengthening of the central power of the Papacy over the Universal Church. A monarch whose means of government were essentially spiritual, Pius IX was satisfied by the definition of this central power, and showed wise restraint and moderation in the exercise of it, as his successors have done ever since.

A whole generation after Napoleon's fall believed in the imminent conflict between the two victorious powers, both of whom were partly extra-European: Russia and Britain. Metternich's personal prestige in St Petersburg was one of the few obstacles to Russia's westward drive; Prussia's and Austria's reluctance to help Russia in any conflict (except in simple police operations against revolutionary upheavals, where the monarchical principle was at stake) was pointed out by Frederick von Gentz[1] as the chief factor delaying a conflict between East and West. Such a conflict Fichte had already foretold in 1814,[2] and its possibility was largely responsible for the desire of Emperor Francis I and Metternich to strengthen the Kingdom of Hungary by modernising reforms. With Metternich an old man, and the romantic-theocratic atmosphere which prevailed in Berlin since the accession in 1840 of Frederick-William IV (whom Europe believed to be a simple satellite of his brother-in-law Nicholas I of Russia), the conflict between East and West was more in the air than ever. Not wishing to be involved by Austrian protection of Italy on the side of schismatic and Muscovite concept of Imperial theocracy, not wishing either to rely on the protection of Protestant England and its Liberal and Radical admirers in Italy, the Papacy took the lead in the action to achieve Italian unity and independence. Two contemporary authors explain the full European background to this Papal policy, both of them Spaniards, Jaime Balmes and Donoso Cortés. Both were more inclined towards a pro-French, than to the pro-British tendency which prevailed over their country; for ever since the help given to Spain by Wellington against Napoleon, various British Foreign Ministers, and especially Lord Palmerston, had tried to bring that nation into the British orbit, through the influence of the *Exaltados* of the constitutional party. Both Balmes and Donoso believed in the concept of a great continental system of alliance to counterbalance the might both

---

[1] *Aus dem Nachlasse von F. v. Gentz.* Edited by General Count Prokesch-Osten. Wien, Leipzig, 1867. Vol. I, p. 206 seq.
[2] In his *Vermichtniss.*

of Britain and Russia,[1] and young as they were, they already had some experience of the minor revolutions which the *Exaltados'* admiration for British institutions and the British party-system had brought to Spain ever since the Cadiz constitution of 1812.[2]

With Balmes and Donoso, the leadership of Catholic thought might have passed from France to Spain, the country which had once led the way, before the *grand siècle*. A sign of the times, the stronger and the more original though not the more systematic of the two thinkers of the early years of Pius IX's reign was not the priest and theologian Balmes, but the secular historian and political philosopher, Donoso Cortés; this was the century of secular thinkers and of the secular concerns of the Church.

This promising new Spanish period of European Catholic thought had no time to mature. Balmes died at the early age of thirty-eight during the first phase of the European Revolution of 1848; Donoso lived only to his forty-fourth year, the last five years of his life being spent watching the European Revolution and its consequences from his diplomatic posts in Berlin and Paris. He lived to see that Revolution which was French no longer, but European in extent, and which we can now see was the first step towards the World Revolution which began with the 1914-1918 war, and in which we live today. He lived to regret much of his own earlier writing, and to hear Louis Veuillot refer to him as the future head of a new European party, as the new leader of secular spirituality. He also lived to suffer from the attacks of the neo-Gallican, Liberal-Catholic tendencies represented by Mgr. Dupanloup and a few members of the French hierarchy, but not long enough to see Rome set her final approval to his thought, or to hear Barbey d'Aurevilly call him " the third lay father of the Church "—Joseph de Maistre and Bonald being the first and second. Donoso's speeches and his thought provided melancholy consolation for Metternich after his fall.[3]

---

[1] A concept that was much discussed, and which owed its influence (in the opinion of many observers) to the personal rapprochement between Metternich and the French Prime Minister Guizot. Marx and Engels commented on it in the *Communist Manifesto* as the New Holy Alliance between the Pope, Metternich and Guizot against Communism, the mutual enemy.

[2] That ideological banner of Spanish military revolts, and even of the revolutionary movement in Italy, which began in Naples in 1820, where Spanish influence was still uppermost.

[3] See the present writer's *Metternich and Donoso Cortés—Christian and Conservative Thought in the European Revolution, Dublin Review*, No. 444, 1948, and *A Prophet of Europe's Disasters—Juan Donoso Cortés, The Month*, May 1947.

A deeper mystical, more passionate and dramatic version of Joseph de Maistre's and Bonald's thought began in France with Donoso Cortés, on the morrow of the European Revolution. Donoso sensed what Bonald and de Maistre had not yet sensed: the profound and universal cultural crisis of Europe—the great theme which Burckhardt and Nietzsche took up a little later—that deepening crisis which was promoted (so to say) by natural progress, the natural progress of mass movements of religious aberration. This, in Donoso's vision, could ultimately be arrested only by the triumph of supernatural over natural force; for the essence of history, according to him, is not the natural triumph of evil over good, but the supernatural triumph of good over evil.

6. THE PRIMACY OF IMAGINATION: FROM DIDEROT TO BARBEY D'AUREVILLY — THE PRIMACY OF EMOTION: FROM ROUSSEAU TO BLOY AND PÉGUY

FRANCE was still the foremost theatre of the European Revolution in the sense that here the social conflict predominated, whereas in other countries the principal element of the Revolution seemed to lie in the various national aspirations. The primacy of politics and of moral liberties, both of which were proposed by Montesquieu and Voltaire, seemed to come to an end. The dominating problem was henceforth to be the individual and society. Bonald and de Maistre saw a world which reasoned ill, erring in matters of religion, and removing itself from truth and law. Veuillot now saw a world which was ugly and decrepit in its self-sufficiency, and its vanity; his biting, satirical pages in *Les Odeurs de Paris* make Flaubert's aching sensitiveness, offended by bourgeois taste, and Baudelaire's despair at the decomposition of every beauty in modern life, appear as almost tame reactions to the social reality.

Bonald and Joseph de Maistre defended the Papacy and the Monarchy against the " party of the philosophers," and against the new institutions which Catholic Liberals tried to baptise from inside, but at the risk of some compromise with their non-Catholic theoretical and philosophical foundations. Barbey d'Aurevilly saw the Revolution when it had advanced a stage further; his main concern—and the concern of Bloy and Péguy after him—was the defence, not of old and consecrated institutions against new and man-made ones, lacking any authority for their basis or support, but the defence of spiritual truth and spiritual beauty against the materialistic ugliness of the masses, which was promoted by intellectual conceit and intellectual demagogy. Not that either Veuillot or Barbey d'Aurevilly, any more than Bloy or Péguy after them, would ever have been hostile to the " masses," or insensitive to the suffering of the poor. There are plenty of signs to the contrary. Nobody in the nineteenth century exalted the ideal of simplicity, or the virtue of humble work, higher than did Louis Veuillot in *Les Libres-Penseurs*; nobody imposed on himself the duty of active service in the cause of the poor more rigorously than Veuillot's master, Donoso Cortés.

Not in the sharpest polemical prose of Barbey d'Aurevilly was charity ever absent, even towards opponents; and with this went humanity and compassion for the multitude. Léon Bloy had no aristocratic contempt for the weak and the poor; on the contrary, his contempt was reserved wholly for the rich, and he never tired of prophesying the victory of the poor, although there was all the difference in the world in his eyes between the victory of the poor and the " suppression of poverty," which is the Socialist ideal—this debasement of man to an artificial, inhuman and impersonal life. If Léon Bloy disliked the Republic, it was because the republics of antiquity were founded by slave-owners, while the " Kingdom " was the promise given to the poor; because the poor delighted in Christ the King, who stood above mankind and did not govern a republic of equals. Finally, more than any other French or even European poet, Péguy has the child-like simplicity and sincerity of the hard-working and patient people.

There is a world of difference between the people and the " masses," and souls devoted to the people are all united, however much they differ in other things, in their disgust at the " masses," an ugly word for an uglier thing. The people are composed of men and women who have souls, of children who have hearts, the masses are a dead weight driven on by traffickers in murdered souls:

Ils ont voulu bannir Dieu et ressusciter César. C'est à quoi ils travaillent et ils sont en train de réussir. Déjà ils ne disent plus: Gloire à Dieu, et déjà il n'y a plus de paix. Ils ont diminué le nombre des hommes de bonne volonté, la bonne volonté a diminué avec l'intelligence de la vérité parmi ceux qui ont encore la vérité, et il n'y a plus de gloire ni de paix pour personne. Par un enchaînement formidable de bassesse et d'erreur, les peuples méprisent, haïssent et obéissent, formant mille désirs sauvages de briser le joug et de se venger. Ils se vengeront, mais ils ne briseront pas le joug, et plus ils le secoueront, plus il sera ignoble et dur.[1]

Louis Veuillot commented in these terms on the third revolution he had seen, that of the Paris Commune of 1871; this picture largely summarises the attitude of the great Catholic polemical writers who bring the last century to an end and usher in the present one.

We have seen the reply which Catholic thought gave to Voltaire's paradoxical moralism in Joseph de Maistre. We have seen also the full Catholic social and political theory which Bonald stated in reply to Montesquieu. Now we come to the third part of the dialogue between the eighteenth and the nineteenth centuries, that dialogue between Authority and Liberty which ever since the Middle Ages has been present in the Western conscience. This third and final part extends from the European Revolution to the First World War, which in turn began the World Revolution. The subject of the debate is now the individual and the world. Diderot gave his opinion on this subject as a neo-stoic, and worked out his argument in particular in a memorable discussion with a neo-cynic, *Le neveu de Rameau*, Goethe's favourite French masterpiece. It is exactly the same topic on which the stoics and the cynics of antiquity argued. The world, they said, makes all true sensibilities suffer. Diderot advised that moral principles should be elevated to a level higher than the world, he wanted us to give a fine example of principles, of a higher taste, of a sterner criticism of the profane world, and in this way he inaugurated a criticism of art and literature which was in itself literature, an art which was sometimes higher and more inventive than imaginative art—an art of which there have been many masters since Diderot, Sainte-Beuve being the foremost. In other words, Diderot postulated the stoic ideal of what we might call intellectual aristocracy, an ideal which greatly appealed to Goethe and attached him to Diderot more than to any of the other French authors of his youth. The " three Musketeers " were, as we know, four, and so were the three " masters of the European mind " in the eighteenth century. Diderot has a shadowy existence compared with the trio Voltaire, Montesquieu and Rousseau, and on account of his haughty artistic and

[1] Louis Veuillot: *Paris pendant les deux sièges en 1870-1871.* Vol. II, ch. xcviii, p. 23.

scientific pedantry, was less popular in his sensual age than Voltaire with his superficial brilliance, Montesquieu with his irony and Rousseau with his sentimental emotion.

In reply to Diderot, and his aesthetic descendants—Sainte-Beuve, Flaubert, the brothers Goncourt and others—Barbey d'Aurevilly made havoc of the aesthetic ideals of pedants. He showed that Judgement in the name of eternal law, rather than an endless comparison of relativities, is the key to true art; that true art, like true History above all, was a social responsibility. It is not an individual fantasy, or a pastime for the bored, or an emotional consolation for the over-sensitive. It is a task for the manly and the brave, and for them alone. It is a defence of Order for the sake of true Liberty. True art is Justice, which despite the frequent verbal violences and the unrestrained personal aversions, was the essence of Barbey d'Aurevilly's immense critical work, collected in over thirty volumes, *Les oeuvres et les hommes*. True art and true history mean judgement in the light of Eternity, and only one light has ever been cast on Eternity which was visible to human eyes. Barbey d'Aurevilly called himself the *sagittaire* of his century, and still near the preceding one in time, he replied to the eighteenth century by shooting his arrows at it:

Ce temps d'anarchie si universelle que le désordre passait dans la physiologie, faisant de Gustave III de Suède homme-femme et de Catherine femme-homme.[1]

Style is judgement, art is justice, history is a manifestation of public conscience. This theme of Barbey d'Aurevilly was to be elaborated and summed up in a very concise version in Ernest Hello's truly monumental study on *Le Style*.

While Barbey d'Aurevilly demolished affectation and pedantry, Louis Veuillot in the same generation was making havoc of the solemn pose of " stoic virtue," of the rhetorics of the politicians (" moderate," " understanding," " modern-minded," Catholics not excepted!), and of the learned commonplaces of all parties. Less of an artist than either Barbey d'Aurevilly or Léon Bloy, he was not less vigorous as a fighter. Vain are all the virtues, he showed, in which humility plays no part, and vain is all the learning that has any other motive than the charitable desire to teach those who have no knowledge. Between them, Barbey d'Aurevilly and Veuillot defeated presumption and pedantry.

But the virtuous neo-cynicism of emotional romance was to

---

[1] *Les oeuvres et les hommes. De l'histoire*, p. 333 of the first edition (1875).

be defeated by the poets, and by them alone. The isolation, the suffering which the hardness of this world inflicts upon the sensitive man, the suffering which comes from the violence of the senses, the hell-on-earth of poverty and loneliness—all these things Rousseau showed in a self-indulgent and a self-pitying way, to prove that man is intrinsically better than the society which surrounds him. At first hearing, nothing seems to be wrong with the proposition. Man has a soul, society has not. The incorruptible, divine substance of the soul was given to Man, the image of God, and not to society, to which only the Law was given. A whole life, noted down day by day, with humility, with humour, with outbursts of savage indignation and then again with overwhelming love—Léon Bloy's life—was needed to show not the abstract and the rational, but the vital and existential proof of the falsity of a proposition which had at first sounded plausible and seductive, and which has in fact seduced the world.

The immortal soul belongs to Man alone. But Man has a Creator, who gave him liberty within His order, and within His order alone. He suffers because God, in His moment of human Liberty, chose to suffer on the Cross, and because—and this is a thought so difficult to understand that it has separated the Muslim world from Christendom, probably until the end of History—He participates fully in human suffering. Léon Bloy interpreted his sufferings as a call from God to him to " conquer the world," to defeat worldliness. His Catholic spirituality was of the militant sort. This volunteer of 1870 never ceased to have a warrior's soul. Nothing is further removed from him than a Catholic spirituality of submission to an unpleasant world, as taught by Claudel or Mauriac, and while his polemics were direct and personal (and often coarse, absurd or unjust, the very opposite of what Barbey d'Aurevilly always strove to be) he was in the last resort infinitely more charitable in his indignations than writers who are satisfied with the mild observation of meanness and egotism, and the bestowing of Catholic consolation on weak souls. In spiritual as in physical suffering, the knife is often better than doubtful pills, coated with chocolate. Perhaps Léon Bloy dismissed too summarily the psychological approach to full and ultimate spiritual truth seen in Henri Bergson; perhaps, after helping Jacques Maritain towards conversion,[1] he was too impatient to

[1] See Madame Raissa Maritain's *Les Grandes amitiés*, 1946; Jacques Maritain: *Léon Bloy*, 1927; and the full and detailed biographical notes of M. Joseph Bollery in the first analytical edition of Léon Bloy's *Oeuvres complètes*, 1948-49.

see all " Bergsonians " travel along the same road—and as we now know, he did not guess what the final great gesture of Bergson's thought and life was to be. He ought perhaps to have shown more patience and humility towards a noble and generous Christian like Albert de Mun, who with the Austrians Vogelsang and Prince Aloys Liechtenstein began the Christian Social movement in the 1890's. He should have made a better attempt to understand the thought of Pope Leo XIII and *Rerum Novarum*, and he should perhaps have foreseen the high spirituality of Don Luigi Sturzo, Canon Cardijn and so many others, out of which would grow, like a new triumph of Christ, the social apostolate of the Church in an industrial society; perhaps he should have done all this instead of persevering in his endless mourning for the Salic Monarchy, destroyed, as he never ceased to reiterate, by God's wrath at the sins of kings. It may be that this hagiographer of the highest grace dwelt too long on the literary vanities of a world of mediocrity, and wasted time which he might otherwise have spent saying things that only he could say, on the saints of his own time in France—St Jean-Baptiste Vianney, the Curé d'Ars, on Chaminade and the *Société de Marie*, on Blessed Joseph Liebermann and his apostolate of the Holy Ghost in Africa, on the life of Père Foucauld and the White Fathers of the Desert.

The gravest and most frequent of his errors might have been that he altogether misunderstood the essence of religious peace in the secular order (as it is best defined by Friedrich von Schlegel) and this arch-enemy of modern Democracy completely failed to see how much nearer religious peace—counting mankind as spiritual units rather than as isolated individuals— was to perfect social wisdom, than was the individualistic, soulless and numerical " representation," which, as we have since seen in Germany and elsewhere, can only promote the domination of those units which are numerically and materially the strongest. Differing from Joseph de Maistre and Bonald, Balzac and Barbey d'Aurevilly, who were concerned to save society, since the individual was condemned by fallen human nature, he perhaps abandoned hope for society altogether, and was concerned only for the salvation of the individual soul, a path which once misled many into Protestantism or Jansenism.

Still, if we feel bound to register all these possible exceptions, without examining them in detail, we are happy to record the fact that chosen souls and hearts in our own days begin to understand Léon Bloy; they quite rightly prefer to be overwhelmed and over-awed by him, rather than to approach him by critical analysis, adequate enough for the spiritual artistry of Mauriac or Claudel, and perhaps the right approach to the passionate emotionalism of Georges Bernanos, but not the means of grasping the essence of Léon Bloy. The *Thankless Beggar* never wrote to please, to convince, or even to act. He wrote in tears, to move others to tears, and he still moves us.

We may dismiss the absurdities of his imagination, when they occurred in the wrong place; we may miss the humble sense of justice which we find in Barbey d'Aurevilly, or the immaculate elegance and the clear intelligence which reached out to the supernatural in Joseph de Maistre, Bonald and Donoso Cortés; yet it is in Léon Bloy that we find the prophetic thunder of Judgement Day. Living in a conceited and prosperous world, he saw this world on the eve of the Apocalypse. In a world of psychological curiosities, he could find the answer only in eschatology. With the great geologist Pierre Termier, he saw the full discovery of the physics and geography of the earth as the approaching fullness of time, with its urgent alternative of Grace or Doom, unknown to the ages of indifference. The Dreyfus affair was all that was needed to make him predict the devastating hatred and persecution which would be the lot of those Gentiles who were united in soul to the celestial Jerusalem, following upon the hatred and persecution which had fallen upon the Jews, the seed of Abraham. Of all those who, during a hundred years of " emancipated " Jewry, spoke and wrote on this question, Léon Bloy (and young Charles Péguy, as he then was at the time of the Dreyfus case) knew full well what was at stake in this controversy. For seven generations the sins of the fathers will be visited upon the heads of the sons, and for a thousand generations true love of God will be rewarded, as we know from Genesis. The spectacle of the material prosperity and the success of an apostate Jewry is hateful enough to God. But infinitely more hateful to Him is the envy of that success felt by Christians who desecrate the name they bear, and in their hatred for Abraham's seed deny the spirit transmitted through the seed of Abraham. The rest is clamour: the clamour of Lenin and Trotsky in 1917, the clamour of Hitler in 1933. A deafening, horrid, poisonous, unspeakable clamour, from which our generation seeks refuge in the spirituality of Max Picard's *Welt des Schweigens*. The clamour of horrid strident voices and desecrated words, which still rages despite the silence which follows upon massacres and exhausting famines.

The prophetic word on the eve of all this horror was said by Léon Bloy, Charles Péguy, and by at least two Germans who probably never knew either and were certainly unknown to them: Theodor Haecker and the Austrian Karl Kraus. Sovereign emotion, this poetic religion set up by the late eighteenth and early nineteenth century, came to its plenitude with these two Frenchmen and the two Germans, with a recall to God, the Word that was in the beginning. All that followers of the old sovereign emotion could describe after the First World War was a confession of failure, movingly told by André Gide, and differently by Paul Claudel—by him in avowed submission and with the right conclusion, although still with a remnant of vanity, and regret for out-moded forms.

Bloy, Péguy, Haecker, Kraus—these names mean the effort to create new forms in the two principal peoples of the Continent. It is the effort of a language unalterably personal, radically untranslatable and not for one moment utilitarian, once it is spoken in the personally-felt presence of God. The association of thought and word leads to such a complete expression of the thought, that nothing is left unsaid and nothing is left unexplored. They thirst for the spirit in its entirety. Total are the means of possessing the earth, total the means of destruction, and only the total Spirit can save the world and even the human person. It is from this perspective of the total dangers and the total hopes of consolation, that we survey the great debate between Authority and Liberty, between the individual and society, which is as old as the world.

To put the truth concerning this great debate into writing, God gave the written Law on Mount Sinai, and His prophets showed the writing on the wall. To demonstrate it fully, God gave His only Son. The long and laborious effort of the men of the West to understand it received its Crown, the Crown of the Christian Monarchy of Order and Liberty placed on the head of Charlemagne. Century followed century, until the immense temple of the West was built up, with stone laid correctly on stone, until the great age was reached when, with a perfect economy of words, passion spoke in the right place with Corneille, emotion with Racine, reason with Molière, divine truth and glory with Bossuet in the pulpit, while the congregation answered de profundis with the words of Pascal.

Then came the time of weakness and of collapse. This or

that stone of the Temple was removed, and faithless men transformed passion and emotion, reason and humour, into thrones
from which to preside as lawgivers. The temple was slowly
reduced to fragments and ruins—and around it we heard the
lament and the tears of the prophets, of the children of the
desolate city. But the sacred stones of Charlemagne reached
far away lands of the earth. Even now the construction of a
greater temple has probably begun, and the foundation has
been laid by invisible workers, who have nothing but scorn
and laughter for those who try to build the Tower of Babylon
once more, instead of their own new Temple of the World
Jerusalem. The scorn from above answers the tumult of Babel,
a tumult which will die down as others did before it. On high
no struggle rages between diversity and unity, between quality
and equality. The voice of prayer alone is heard there from the
altar of the Temple:

*Et in personis proprietas, et in essentia unitas, et in maiestate
adoretur aequalitas.*

E

I. JOSEPH DE MAISTRE

1753 - 1821

BORN in Chambéry, Haute Savoie, a hundred and six years before this province became part of France, Joseph de Maistre was a subject of the King of Piedmont and Sardinia. He belonged to a family of magistrates who had been honoured with the title of Count and he made his own legal studies in Turin. Appointed to the Court of Justice of Savoy in 1774 as Deputy Public Prosecutor, he became a member of the Senate in 1788 (in his country a judicial and not a legislative body). When the French Revolutionary armies invaded Savoy in 1793, Joseph de Maistre fled to Lausanne, where he took part in the activities of his fellow exiles who were loyal to the King of Piedmont, and was also in contact with the French Royalists. It was in Lausanne that the extraordinary circumstances of the political situation and the necessities of political action made him a writer. Although from early youth a man of all-round curiosity and wide studies outside his profession and his public service, his first book, *Considérations sur la France*, was not published until 1796, when he was forty-three years old.

The *Considérations* were hardly intended to be more than a pamphlet on the topical issues of the time, similar to many others that were published in the same year in Switzerland, mostly by authors belonging to the circle of Madame de Staël and Benjamin Constant. Intellectually, this group was the most active amongst those émigrés who, after the fall of Robespierre and the end of the Terror, believed that their hour had come, in the form of a moderate parliamentary and constitutional régime under the leadership of the educated and literary class—whom Napoleon contemptuously defined as the *idéologues*—perhaps as a consolidated Republic, or as a new constitutional—or rather merely " symbolic "—monarchy.

Joseph de Maistre was somewhat surprised to see himself put at the head of a new school of thought, an echo of which was heard in young Chateaubriand, and in the prodigious Vicomte de Bonald, who in his solitude in another part of Switzerland thought out independently much of Joseph de Maistre's philosophy long before he entered into a personal correspondence with him and almost twenty years before he actually met him after the fall of Napoleon, in Paris.

Joseph de Maistre raised the controversy on French political events to a clearly religious and metaphysical plane. Expounding

Burke's central theme, that constitutions are the slow, invisible work of history and are never made by individuals assembled in parliaments and conventions, which, at their very best, can only make administrative regulations, and approve or disapprove the way public money is spent, de Maistre goes a step further than Burke and asks the questions: Whose will is the Law? and Who moves History? Burke was certainly no agnostic; he was probably the first Anglican who, when discussing French events, dared to defend the Catholic Church, without fearing to be denounced by his fellow-countrymen as a " papist." But de Maistre openly calls for a return to the great tradition of the theologians, who see the problem of human government as one entirely subordinated to the will of God, politics as a branch of theology, and Providence as the only acceptable explanation of history.

In 1799 Joseph de Maistre was sent to St Petersburg as the plenipotentiary Minister of his King, who soon afterwards lost his kingdom of Piedmont and was confined to the island of Sardinia. Even before the accession of General Bonaparte to power, the unfortunate King Victor Amadeus had felt compelled to adapt himself to a policy of submission to French interests. Joseph de Maistre was in these circumstances unwelcome at home, as a letter captured by the French Republican army in Italy revealed that the Comte de Provence—later King Louis XVIII—showed a great personal interest in the author of the *Considérations*.

In the years that followed, Joseph de Maistre exerted a considerable personal influence in St Petersburg, somewhat out of keeping with his modest position as the Minister of a practically powerless King. Czar Alexander I was interested in his thought, which was considered not without misgivings and suspicion by Orthodox and Pravoslav circles, who had little or no objection to the spread of " free " thought from the Protestant Universities of Germany, propagated by the numerous German professors employed in Russia, but who did their best to prevent the penetration of " Jesuitism."

The sixteen years which Joseph de Maistre spent in St Petersburg bore considerable fruit. Here he wrote his various fragments on Russia, Orthodoxy and Protestantism, his comments on the philosophy of Bacon, his *Essai sur le principe générateur des institutions humaines* and, finally, the *Soirées de St Pétersbourg*, his greatest book, publication of which he never lived to see. De Maistre left St Petersburg after the fall of Napoleon, not without some bitter disappointment over the anti-Jesuit decrees of Alexander I, which temporarily put an end to the Society's activities in Russia; but he had the joy of seeing some excellent converts from Orthodoxy, amongst whom was Prince Dmitri Galitzin, S.J.

The main subject of the *Soirées* is the working of Providence in human institutions and in history. It is perhaps the best philosophy written in dialogue form since Plato; the persons taking part in the conversations are a Russian, a member of the Imperial Senate, a young French Royalist *émigré* and the " Comte," i.e. de Maistre himself. Almost every subject is touched upon in these dialogues: justice, human and divine, war and peace, social order and personal liberty, but first and foremost—for de Maistre was a true philosopher, though academic pedants deny him this title and treat him as a " mere writer," on account of the brilliant wit of his style—the ultimate sense and meaning of all words, which relate to the one " Word Incarnate." To quote Léon Bloy:

" Joseph de Maistre said, almost a century ago, that man is too wicked to deserve to be free.

" This seer was a contemporary of the Revolution; he meditated like a prophet on the grandiose horror it inspired, and confronted it face to face.

" He died, appalled at what he saw and full of contempt, pronouncing the funeral oration over civilised Europe."

1. HUMAN AND DIVINE NOMENCLATURE[1]

ONE of the great errors of a century which professed all possible errors, was to think that a political constitution could be written down and created *à priori*, when both reason and experience affirm that a constitution is a divine creation, and that precisely what is most fundamental and most essentially constitutional in the laws of a nation cannot be written down.

. . . The essence of a fundamental law is that nobody has the right to suppress it: now how can it be above *everybody*, if *somebody* made it ? The consent of the people is an impossible foundation for it; and even if it were otherwise, agreement by consent in no way constitutes a law, and constrains nobody, unless it is safeguarded by a higher authority. Locke attempted to define the nature of law as an expression of united wills; a fortunate man, who can thus discover the nature of law in something which, on the contrary, excludes the very idea of *law*. Indeed, united wills make a *ruling*, not a *law*, which latter necessarily and manifestly pre-supposes the existence of a higher will, strong enough to command obedience. " According to Hobbes's system "—the same one which has had so great a success in our century in the works of Locke—" the validity of

[1] Extract from *Essai sur le Principe Générateur des Constitutions Politiques.* H. Goemacre. Brussels. 1852.

the civil laws depends only on the consent of the people; but if no natural law exists which ordains the promulgation of the laws that have been made, of what use are they? Promises, contracts, oaths, are only vain words: it is as easy to break this frivolous link as it is to form it. Without the dogma of God the Lawgiver, all moral obligations are merely an illusion. Strength on the one hand and weakness on the other, that is all that binds human societies together."[1]

The words of this wise and profound theologian on the subject of moral obligation can be applied with equal truth to a political or civic obligation. Law is only really *law*, possessing a real sanction, when it is presumed to emanate from a higher will; with the result that its essential characteristic is *that it is not the expression of the general will*. Otherwise laws are *mere rulings*, as we have just said, and as the author whom we have quoted above goes on to say: " those who have been able freely to enter into these agreements, did not debar themselves from the right to revoke them; and their descendants, who took no part in them, are even less bound to honour them."[2] From whence it follows that primeval good sense, happily in existence before the birth of sophistry, sought on all sides a sanction for laws in an authority superior to man, whether such an authority acknowledged that sovereignty comes from God, or whether it venerated certain unwritten laws, as coming from Him.

The men who drafted the Roman laws discreetly interposed a very remarkable piece of Greek jurisprudence in the first chapter of their collection. " Amongst the laws which govern us," says this passage, " some are written down, others are not." Nothing could be simpler and yet more profound. Does anyone know of a Turkish law which expressly allows the sovereign to send a man to his death, without a court of law having first pronounced sentence? Does anyone know of any *written* law, even a religious one, which forbids the Christian sovereigns of Europe to do the same thing?[3] Yet the Turk is no more surprised at seeing his master order the immediate death of a man, than he is at seeing him go to the mosque. With the whole of

---

[1] Bergier: *Historical and Dogmatic Treatise on Religion.* Vol. III, ch. iv, para. 12, pp. 330, 331. (Following Tertullian, *Apologia*, 45.)

[2] Ibid.

[3] " The Church forbids her children, even more formally than the civil laws, to take justice into their own hands; and it is in this spirit that Christian kings abstain from doing so, even in crimes of high treason, and hand over the criminals to judges, so that they can be punished according to the laws and within the framework of justice." (Pascal, *Provincial Letters*, XIV.)

This passage is very important, and ought to be better known.

Asia, and indeed with the whole of antiquity, he believes that it is a legitimate prerogative of the sovereign to exercise an immediate power over life and death. But our princes trembled at the very idea of condemning a man to death; for according to our way of seeing things, this condemnation would be an atrocious murder; yet I doubt if it would be possible to forbid them to do it on the strength of a fundamental written law, without causing far greater evils than those it was intended to prevent.

Look at Roman history to see precisely in what the power of the Senate consisted; it throws no light on the matter, at least as regards the precise limits of this authority. It is generally speaking true that the authority of the people and that of the Senate counter-balanced each other, and were consistently hostile one to the other. It is easy to see that these dangerous struggles were always brought to an end either by patriotism or by lassitude, by weakness or by violence, but *we* know no more than that.[1] When we contemplate these great events of history, we are sometimes tempted to think that events would have turned out much better if there had been precise laws to circumscribe authority. This however would be a great error: such laws, perpetually compromised by unexpected happenings and by out of the way exceptions to the rule, would not have lasted six months, or they would have meant the overthrow of the republic.

The English constitution provides an example nearer home, and is therefore a more striking one to take. When we examine it carefully, we see *that it only works because it is unworkable* (if I may be allowed this play on words). It derives its stability from the exceptions to the rule, rather than from the rule itself. The *habeas corpus*, for example, has been suspended so often and for such long periods, that one wondered if the exception had not become the rule. Supposing for a moment that the authors of this famous Act had had the presumption to state cases in which it could be suspended, they would thereby have destroyed it.

The theory of names is a very important question. Names

---

[1] I have often meditated on this passage of Cicero (*De Leg.* II, 6): *Leges Liviae praesertim uno versiculo senatus puncto temporis sublatae sunt.* By what right did the Senate assume this liberty? And how did the people allow them to do so? It is certainly not an easy question to answer, but why need we be astonished at this, since after all that has been written on Roman history and Roman remains, men still have to write theses to show how the members of the Senate were recruited?

are in no wise arbitrary affairs, as so many men have affirmed *who had lost their names.* God says of Himself: *I am*; and all creatures say of themselves: *My name is This or That.* The name of a spiritual being relates necessarily to the action he performs, which is his distinctive quality; whence it follows that among the ancients, the greatest honour possible to a divinity was *polyonymy,* or *plurality of names,* which proclaimed the number of his functions or the extent of his power. Ancient mythology shows us Diana, when still a child, asking Jupiter to grant her this honour; and in the verses attributed to Orpheus, compliments are addressed to her under the title of *polyonymous spirit* (or spirit bearing many names). Which means, after all, that God alone has the right to give a *name.* Indeed, He has *named* everything, since He created everything.

It is the same with nations as with individuals: some there are *who have no name.* Herodotus observes that the Thracians would be the most powerful people in the world if they were united. " *But,*" he adds, " *this union is impossible, for they all have a different name.*" This is an excellent remark. There are also modern peoples *who have no name,* and there are others who have several; but *polyonymy* is as disastrous for nations as it has been thought honourable for spirits.

Since names have nothing arbitrary about them, and since, like all things, they derive their origin more or less directly from God, we must not think that a man has the unrestricted right to name even those beings of whose existence he has some right to consider himself the author, and to impose on them names according to his own ideas. God has reserved for Himself in this matter a sort of immediate jurisdiction, which it is impossible not to recognise. " *Oh, my dear Hermogenus! the imposition of names is a very important matter and one which cannot be the prerogative of a bad or even of a vulgar man. . . . This right only belongs to a creator of names (onomaturgos); that is, apparently, only to the legislator; but of all human creatures, the rarest is a legislator.*"

Man however likes nothing better than to give names to things. He does this, for example, when he applies significant epithets to words; a talent which is a distinctive mark of a great writer and especially of a great poet. The felicitous choice of an epithet enhances a noun, which becomes distinguished under this new sign. Examples can be found in every language; but to confine ourselves to the language of the nation which itself bears so great a name, since it gave its name to *frankness,* or else *frankness* received its name from the nation: what cultured man is not familiar with *miserly* Acheron, *careful* steeds, *shameless* bed, *timid* supplications, *silvery* rustling, *rapid* destroyer, *pale* sycophants, etc.? Never will man forget his primitive rights; we can even say in a certain sense, that he will always exercise them, but how curtailed have they become because of his degradation! Here is a true law, such as God made it: *Man is forbidden to give grand names to things of his own making, and which he thinks important; but if he has acted in a legitimate fashion, the commonplace name of the object will be ennobled by the object itself, and will achieve greatness.*

What is the real origin of this word *Tuileries*, which is so famous?[1] Nothing is more commonplace; but the ashes of dead heroes, mingling with the soil, had consecrated it and the soil consecrated the name. It is somewhat curious that at such a great distance in time and space, this same word TUILERIES, famous in olden days as the name of a tomb, should acquire new lustre as the name of a palace. The authority which came to dwell in the *Tuileries* did not think of giving it a more imposing name, which might have been more fitting. If it had committed this mistake, there would have been no reason why, on the following day, the place should not have been inhabited by pickpockets and street girls.

. . . There are therefore two infallible rules by which we may judge all human creations of whatever kind: their *basis* and their *name*, and these two rules of course are free from any pejorative interpretation. If the basis is purely human, the construction cannot last; and the more men there are who have been concerned in it, the more deliberation, science and *especially writing*, in a word, the more human the means of every kind that have been employed, the more fragile the institution will be. It is chiefly by applying this rule that we must judge all the enterprises of sovereigns or of assemblies of men in the cause of civilisation, and in the establishment or the regeneration of peoples.

. . . The second rule concerning names is, I think, neither less clear nor less decisive than the first. If the name has been imposed by an assembly; if it has been established by discussion before the object itself was created, so that the name precedes the object; if the name is pompous,[2] if it has a grammatical

---

[1] Tuileries, broadly interpreted, retains some connection with pottery.

[2] Thus, for example, if a man other than a sovereign confers upon himself the title of legislator, it is a sure sign that he is not one at all; and if an assembly has the temerity to call itself " legislative," not only is it a sure sign that it is nothing of the sort, but a sign that it has gone mad and will soon be the laughing stock of the whole world.

relation to the object it represents; finally, if it has been taken from a foreign language, especially from a dead language, all the characteristics of nonentity are there, and we can be sure that the name and the object will disappear in no time. The contrary assumptions proclaim the principle of legitimacy, consequently that the institution will last. We must take care not to pass over this subject lightly. A true philosopher ought never to lose sight of the language as a real barometer, the variations in which are an infallible guide to *good and bad weather*. To confine myself to the subject in hand, it is certain that the disproportionate introduction of foreign words, applied in particular to national institutions of every kind, are one of the most infallible signs of the decadence of a people.

If the formation of every empire, the march of civilisation and the unanimous verdict of all history and all tradition were not enough to convince us, the destruction of empires would complete the demonstration begun by their origin. Just as the religious principle created everything, so the absence of this same principle has destroyed everything. The sect of Epicurus, which might be called the scepticism of antiquity, first degraded, then destroyed every government which had the misfortune to give it protection. Everywhere, Lucretius proclaimed the coming of Caesar.

2. WAR, PEACE, AND SOCIAL ORDER[1]

THE fearful sight of carnage does not harden the true soldier's heart. Amidst the blood he sheds, he remains as human as a wife is chaste in the ecstasy of love. Once he has sheathed his sword, sacred humanity comes into its own again, and it is probably true to say that the most exalted and the most generous sentiments of all are felt by the soldier. Cast your mind back, Sir, to the *grand siècle* in France. The harmony which existed in that century between religion, military courage and science, is responsible for the noble character which all nations have hailed with universal acclamation as the pattern of the European man. Take the first element away from it, and the unity, or in other words, the whole beauty of it, disappears. Men do not realise how necessary this element

[1] Extract from the 7th Dialogue of the *Soirées de St Pétersbourg*. H. Goemaere. Brussels. 1852.

is in all things, nor the part it plays in matters in which it might seem irrelevant to superficial observers. The divine spirit, which has singled out Europe as its dwelling-place, even mitigated the scourges of eternal justice and the *type* of war waged in Europe will always be outstanding in the annals of the universe. Men killed each other of course, burned and ravaged and committed thousands of useless crimes, I admit, yet they began their war in May and stopped in December; they slept under canvas; the fighting was confined to soldiers. Never were nations as such at war with each other, and weakness was held to be sacred in the lamentable series of devastations which this scourge brought in its train.

It was moreover a magnificent sight to see all the sovereigns of Europe, restrained by a mysterious and irrepressible urge towards moderation, refuse ever to demand the utmost, even in moments of great peril, that their people could give them; they used men gently, and all of them, guided by an invisible inspiration, avoided dealing any of those blows to the sovereignty of the enemy *which could rebound on them*: glory, honour and eternal praise to the law of love which was unceasingly proclaimed at the heart of Europe! No one nation triumphed over the other; the wars of antiquity were forgotten, except in books, or amongst people *seated in the shadow of death*; fierce wars were brought to an end when a province, or a town or even in many cases a few villages, changed hands. Mutual consideration and the most delicate courtesy could be found amidst the clash of arms. Bombs were never directed at the palaces of kings; balls and displays on more than one occasion interrupted the course of battle. The enemy officer, who was invited to these celebrations, would come in order to joke about the battle to be fought on the morrow; amidst all the horror of the most sanguinary engagement, the dying man could still hear the voice of compassion and words of courtesy. The first shots were no sooner exchanged, than huge hospitals sprang up everywhere: doctors, surgeons, chemists flocked to offer their skill; from their ranks would arise the presiding genius of St John of God, or of St Vincent de Paul, greater and stronger than ordinary men, constant as faith itself, as active as hope, and as skilful as love. Every victim of the battle who still breathed was picked up, received treatment and was given consolation: every wound was touched by the hand of science and of charity!

Gentlemen, the functions of a soldier are terrible, but they surely derive from a major law of the spiritual world, and we must not be surprised that all nations agree in seeing something more particularly divine in this scourge than in the others. Believe me, it is for a great and fundamental reason that the title *GOD OF HOSTS* illumines every page of Scripture. . . .

War is divine then of its very nature, because it is a law of the world.

War is divine in its consequences, both general and particular, which are of a supernatural order; consequences which are little known because few people care for them, but which are none the less beyond all question. Who could doubt that death on the battlefield entails great privileges ? Who could think that the victims of this fearful judgement shed their blood in vain ? Yet the time is not propitious for insisting on these subjects; our century is not prepared yet to think about them. Let us leave natural philosophy to this world and keep our own eyes ever fixed on the invisible world, which will give us the answer to everything.

War is divine in the protection granted to the great leaders, even to the most daring, who seldom fall in battle, and then only when their fame can reach no further heights and their mission is fulfilled.

War is divine in the manner in which it is declared. I have no desire to exonerate any man inopportunely, but how obvious it is, that those men whom we consider to be the immediate authors of wars are themselves swept along by circumstances! At the exact moment prepared by men and prescribed by justice, God intervenes to avenge the iniquity which the inhabitants of the earth have committed against Him. . . .

War is divine in its results, over which human reason speculates in vain: for they can be totally different in two nations, although both were equally affected by the war. Some wars debase nations and debase them for centuries; others exalt them, perfect them in every way, and within a short space of time, even repair momentary losses with a visible increase in population, which is very extraordinary. History often presents us with the picture of a population which remains rich and goes on increasing while the most desperate battles are being fought. But some wars are vicious and accursed, which our conscience, rather than our reason, recognises to be so: nations receive their death-blow in these wars, both as regards their power and their character. Thus even the conqueror seems degraded and impoverished, and although he is crowned with laurels, he is left sad and lamenting, while in the vanquished country there is soon not a workshop or a plough which is not working to capacity.

3. ON SOPHISTRY AND TYRANNY[1]

THINK of him, if you will, as possessing a fine talent; it is none the less true that when we praise Voltaire, we ought to do so with certain reservations, I nearly said with reluctance. The unbridled admiration lavished on him by too many people is an infallible sign of a corrupted soul. Let us be under no illusion: if a man runs his eye over his book-shelves and feels attracted to the *Works of Ferney*, God does not love him. People have often laughed at ecclesiastical authority for condemning books *in odium auctoris*; in reality, nothing was more just; *Refuse honours due to genius to the man who abuses his gifts*. If this law were severely applied, we should soon see poisonous books disappear; but since we are not responsible for promulgating it, at least let us beware of going to the extreme (far more reprehensible than we think) of praising guilty writers to the skies. Voltaire above all. He pronounced a terrible judgement against himself without realising it, for it was he who said, " A corrupt mind never reached sublime heights."

Nothing is more true, and that is why Voltaire, for all his hundred books, is never more than *attractive*. I make an exception of his tragedies, in which the nature of the medium obliged him to express noble sentiments which were alien to his character; yet even in his dramatic work, in which he triumphed, he does not deceive the experienced eye. In his best plays he resembles his two great rivals as the most cunning hypocrite resembles a saint. I do not intend in any case to question his merits as a dramatist, but maintain what I said in the beginning: that as soon as Voltaire speaks in his own name, he is nothing more than *attractive*; nothing can arouse his enthusiasm, not even the battle of Fontenoy. *He is charming*, people say; I agree, but I use the word in criticism of him. Moreover, I cannot endure the exaggeration which makes him

---

[1] Extract from the 4th Dialogue of *Soirées de St Pétersbourg*.

universal. To tell the truth, I see certain exceptions to this universality. He is a complete failure in the ode: and no wonder. His deliberate impiety had killed the divine flame of enthusiasm in him. He is also a complete failure, even a ridiculous failure, in lyrical drama, his ear being as completely deaf to the beauties of harmony, as his eye was blind to the beauties of art. In the genres which best suited his talent, he is dull: he is mediocre, cold and often (who would credit it ?) heavy and coarse in comedy; for the evil man is never comic. For the same reason, he was unable to coin an epigram, the smallest outpouring of his venom needing at least a hundred lines. If he tries his hand at satire, he borders on scurrility; he is unbearable when he writes history, despite his art and the elegance and grace of his style; no quality in him can replace those he lacks, namely a feeling for the life of history, a serious purpose, good faith and dignity. As for his *epic* poem, I am not qualified to speak on it: for we have to read a book before we judge it, and we must be wide awake before we can read it.

A monotonous torpor hangs over most of his writings, which consist of two subjects only, the Bible and his enemies: he is either blasphemous or insulting. His jokes, which receive so much praise, are however far from being beyond reproach: the laughter they arouse is not real laughter; it is a grimace. Have you ever noticed that the divine anathema was written large on his face ? After the lapse of so many years, there is still time to prove it for yourself. Go and gaze at his face in the *Hermitage* Palace; never do I look at it without congratulating myself that it has not been handed down to us by some sculptor, who took his inspiration from the Greeks, and who would perhaps have idealised it. Everything is as nature made it in this portrait. There is as much truth in this head as there would be if a death mask had been taken of him. Observe the abject brow, which never blushed for shame, the eyes like two extinct craters, in which lust and hatred still seem to be seething. That mouth—perhaps I should not say so, but I cannot help myself—that frightful *grin* stretching from ear to ear, like a spring ready to open and release a blasphemy or a piece of sarcasm, when his cruel malice demands it.

Do not talk to me of this man, I cannot endure the thought of him. Oh, what harm he has done us! Like the insect which is the scourge of our gardens, because it attacks the roots of our most precious plants, Voltaire unceasingly pricks with his *goad* at the two roots of society, women and young men; they imbibe his poisons, which he is thus able to transmit from generation to generation. It is in vain that, in order to cover up his unspeakable outrages, his stupid admirers deafen us by quoting the sonorous tirades in which he spoke of the most venerated objects in a masterly fashion. These people, who are wilfully blind, do not see that they are putting the final touch to the condemnation of this guilty writer. If Fénelon had written *The Prince* in the same style in which he painted the joys of Elysium, he would be a thousand times more vile and more guilty than Machiavelli. Voltaire's great crime is the abuse of a talent, and the deliberate prostitution of a mind created to sing the praises of God and of virtue. He cannot allege in excuse, as so many other men can, his youth, thoughtlessness, the allurements of passion, or, finally, the melancholy weakness of our nature. Nothing can absolve him: his corruption is in a class by itself; it takes root in the deepest fibres of his heart, and is fortified by all the powers of his understanding. Always closely linked with sacrilege, it defies God by leading men astray. With a fury which is unequalled in this world, this insolent blasphemer goes to the length of declaring himself the personal enemy of the Saviour of mankind; from the depths of his nothingness, he dares to give Him a ridiculous name, and the adorable law which the God-Man brought on earth he calls INFAMOUS. Abandoned by God, who punishes by withdrawing Himself, he throws off all restraint. Other cynics have startled virtue, Voltaire startles vice. He plunges into the mud, rolls himself in it, slakes his thirst with it; he delivers his imagination up to the enthusiasm of Hell, which lends him all its strength to drag him to the extreme limits of evil. He invents wonders, monsters which make us grow pale. Paris crowned him, but Sodom would have banished him. Shameless desecrator of the universal language, and of her greatest names, the very last of men, after those who love him! How can I express the feelings he arouses in me? When I see what he was capable of doing, and what he in fact did, his inimitable talents inspire nothing less in me than a kind of sacred rage, which has no name. Divided between admiration and horror, I sometimes feel I would like to have a statue erected to him . . . by the hand of the common hangman.

. . . There is moreover a certain *rational anger* which goes very well with wisdom; the Holy Ghost Himself has expressly stated that it is free from sin.

4. RUSSIA AND THE CHRISTIAN WEST[1]

" HUMAN nature was created for the benefit of the few."

This maxim, expressed in natural terms, shocks us no doubt by its Machiavellian turn of phrase, but from another point of view it is well said. Everywhere the mass of the people is led by the few; for without a reasonably strong aristocracy, the public authority is weak.

There were far fewer free men in antiquity than there were slaves. Athens had forty thousand slaves and twenty thousand citizens. Rome, towards the end of the Republic, had about twelve hundred thousand inhabitants, of whom barely two thousand were landowners; which by itself proves the enormous number of slaves that there were. One man sometimes had several thousands of slaves in his service. Once four hundred slaves were executed in a single house, by virtue of the terrible law which pronounced that all the slaves who lived under the same roof should perish when a Roman citizen was killed in his own home.

. . . Then the divine law appeared on earth. It immediately took possession of the hearts of men and changed them in a way which arouses the eternal admiration of any sincere observer. Above all, religion began to work unremittingly for the abolition of slavery, a project which no other religion, no other legislator or philosopher had ever dared to undertake, let alone conceive. . . .

Generally speaking, human nature is only fit to receive civic liberty in proportion as it is penetrated and led by Christian principles.

Wherever any religion other than Christianity is practised, slavery exists as of right, and wherever religion grows weak, the political power becomes proportionately more dominant and the nation is less fit to enjoy general liberty.

This paramount truth has just been demonstrated before our very eyes in the most illuminating and terrible way. For an entire century, Christianity suffered continuous attack by an abominable sect. Those princes who were perverted by their doctrine allowed them to pursue their work, and on more than one deplorable occasion even helped on their ill-intentioned endeavours, undermining, with the very hands that were created to preserve, the pillars of the temple that later crashed around them. What was the result? There was finally too

---

[1] Extract from *Quatre Chapitres inédits sur la Russie*, ch. i. Paris. Aug. Vaton. 1859.

much liberty in the world. The depraved will of men, having cast off all restraint, gave itself up completely to pride and corruption. The mass of emancipated men attacked the first institution in the land that had the greatest influence over all the others. In less than twenty years, the European edifice crumbled, and the principle of sovereignty still struggles to survive amidst the ruins, compromised perhaps for ever.

In our day, the two anchors of society, religion and slavery, have been lost, so that the vessel of State has been cast adrift and shattered by the storm.

These truths are so obvious that it is impossible to question them. It is now an easy matter to apply our conclusions to Russia.

If we ask why serfdom is still the common lot of the Russian masses today, the answer is self-evident. *Serfdom is present in Russia because it is a necessity and the Emperor cannot rule without it.*

The primordial antipathy between Rome and Constantinople; the crimes and the orgies of the Byzantine Empire; the extraordinary paroxysm which overwhelmed the West round about the tenth century; the ill-chosen and consequently the vicious Popes who were created at the time by petty, semi-barbaric princes and even by base women who had seized power; the Tartar invasion; the previous invasion by a power of another kind, which had entered Russia as a liquid flows into an empty vessel; finally the disastrous dividing wall which had been deliberately erected during the eleventh and twelfth centuries; all these causes, I repeat, removed Russia perforce from the general stream of civilisation and emancipation which came from Rome.

. . . In the West, the civil authority did not abandon slaves to their own devices when it freed them; they lived under the protection of the priests, and in any case, life at that time was very simple. Science had not yet kindled the pride which, like a devouring flame, has already destroyed a part of the world and will destroy the whole of it, if it is allowed to continue.

Circumstances in Russia are very different. Every lord, or rather every noble, is a real magistrate, a kind of civil governor who is responsible for the policing of his estate, and who is endowed with the necessary authority to repress, at least to a large extent, the reckless impulses of individual wills.

If this magistrature should ever be suppressed, what authority could the sovereign put in its place to maintain order? The laws, you will say; but the laws are precisely the weakest

F

part of this great empire. The tribunals all have more duties to perform than authority to wield; they complain of public opinion, which in turn is dissatisfied with the tribunals; these grievances are one of the things that strike foreigners especially the most forcibly. As a crowning danger, Russia, alone amongst nations, ancient or modern, refuses to exercise the death penalty in the public interest; a circumstance which must be borne in mind.

. . . Now the great conservative and preservative force of loyalty to the throne does not exist in Russia. Religion has a certain influence on the human mind, but none at all on the heart, the seat of all desires and all crimes. A peasant would probably rather risk his life than eat meat on one of the forbidden days; but if the problem is to prevent an outburst of passion, the outcome is uncertain. Christianity does not consist of words only, it is a concrete thing; if it no longer possesses its strength, its penetrating influence, its primeval simplicity and a powerful priesthood, it is not *itself* any more, it is no longer what it was when it made a general liberation of slaves possible. Let the Russian Government beware: its clergy do not even possess a voice in the State, they dare not speak and are only consulted when it cannot be avoided; a foreigner by no means says: *It is unfortunate*; he simply says: *It is a fact*.

. . . The danger of rebellion, following upon an emancipation of the serfs, would be indescribably great on account of the peculiar character of this nation, which is the most excitable, impetuous and enterprising in the whole world. The writer has sometimes said (and I hope the joke is not entirely without foundation) " that if the longing in a Russian heart could be imprisoned in a citadel, it would blow it to pieces." No man *longs* for something as ardently as the Russian does.

Watch how he spends his money, and how he pursues all his pleasures as the fancy takes him; you will see how he wants things. Watch him as he engages in trade, even amongst the poorer classes, and see how intelligent and alive he is to his own interests; watch him as he fulfils his most hazardous enterprises, watch him finally on the battlefield, and you will see the full extent of his daring.

If we imagine liberty being given to thirty-six millions of men, more or less of this calibre—never can it be repeated too often—we should immediately see the outbreak of a conflagration which would destroy Russia.

. . . Russia does not possess any powerful reinforcements to authority (such as Turkey possesses in the Koran, or China in the maxims and laws of Confucius); consequently she ought to beware of giving full reign to too many individual wills. Moreover, her legislators ought never to lose sight of a fact of the greatest importance: Russian civilisation coincided with the period of the greatest corruption the mind of man has ever known; and that a series of circumstances which we cannot examine here put the Russian nature into contact with, and amalgamated it, so to speak, with the nation which has been at one and the same time the most terrible instrument and the most pitiable victim of this corruption.

Such a thing has never been seen before. Priests and oracles have always presided over the infancy of nations; here we have the opposite. The germs of Russian civilisation were fermented and developed in the corruption of the Regency period in France. The dreadful literature of the eighteenth century arrived in Russia suddenly and without any preparation; the first French lessons which this people received consisted of blasphemies.

This fatal disadvantage which Russia possesses over other nations ought to make her rulers take special precautions when it comes to the point of giving liberty to the immense mass of the nation which still does not enjoy it. As these serfs receive their liberty, they will find that they are placed between teachers who are more than suspect, and priests who are weak and enjoy no special consideration. Exposed in this unprepared fashion, they will infallibly and abruptly pass from superstition to atheism and from passive obedience to unbridled activity. Liberty will have the same effect on these temperaments as a heady wine on a man who is not used to it. The mere sight of liberty given to others will intoxicate those who still do not share it. With men's minds prepared in this way, any University Pugatscheff[1] has only to appear (they can be manufactured easily enough, as all the factories are open) and if we add indifference, incapacity, the ambition of a few nobles, foreign bad faith, the intrigues of a detestable sect which never rests, etc., etc., the State, according to all the rules of probability, will literally *burst asunder*, like an over-long beam which only holds firm at the two extremities. *Elsewhere there is only one danger to fear; here there are two.*

If an emancipation of the serfs is to take place in Russia, it

---

[1] Pugatscheff: Leader of a peasant revolt in the reign of Catherine II, whom his followers proclaimed to be the murdered Czar, Peter III. Executed 1775.

will come about in the course of nature. Quite unforeseen circumstances will make it generally desirable. The whole process will take place quietly and will be carried through without a hitch (like all great enterprises). If the sovereign gives his blessing to this national movement, it will be his right and his duty to do so; but God forbid that he should ever stimulate it of his own accord!

II. VICOMTE DE BONALD

1754 - 1840

LOUIS-GABRIEL-AMBROISE, Vicomte de Bonald, came from an ancient noble family of Provence, was educated at the Oratorian College at Juilly, and after serving with the Artillery he held a post in the local administration of his native province. Elected to the States General of 1789 as a deputy for Aveyron, he strongly opposed the new legislation on the civil status of the clergy and emigrated in 1791, as many Royalists did, to Germany, when Louis XVI, a virtual prisoner of the Revolution, lost all control over the situation. After serving for a few years in the Royalist army of Prince Condé, Bonald retired to Heidelberg when the Condé army was disbanded. In 1797 he published his *Théorie du pouvoir politique et religieux dans la société civile démontrée par le raisonnement et l'histoire* in Constance, which was banned by the *Directoire* in France. Although he returned to France later, Bonald remained faithful to the Bourbon dynasty and declined every offer of public service under Napoleon. With his *Essai analytique sur les lois naturelles* (1800), *Du Divorce* (1801), *La Législation primitive* (1802), *Recherches philosophiques sur les premier objets des connaissances morales* (1818) and with the hundreds of shorter essays and newspaper articles on topical subjects which he wrote, Bonald became for a generation the leading theorist of Legitimism. He was also an active exponent of this principle in the Peerage, in the French Academy, in the Royal Council of the Universities, to which Louis XVIII appointed him, and at the head of the Ministry of Education under this same King. In 1830 Bonald retired from politics and adopted an attitude of passive opposition towards King Louis Philippe and the Orleanist monarchy.

Bonald is a foremost apologist of Catholic political and social doctrine, combating the various schools of romantic political thought and of English utilitarianism. His importance lies in the fact that he was a most penetrating critic of the ethics of Kant, of Rousseau's notion of the " general will " and of Montesquieu's " division of powers." To Kant's individual judgement Bonald opposes dogma and authority; against Rousseau he establishes the primacy of thought over will in his analysis of primitive legislation and of the origin of human language; in place of Montesquieu's " division of powers," he demonstrates his brilliant historical and theological theory of the " unity of power," given by God for a

unique and undivided purpose. According to Bonald, the safeguard
against the misuse of power does not lie in institutions to curb
power, as the Liberal school thought, but in the ethical limitations
of power set by the religious conscience.

Bonald distinguishes between the " social " and the " political "
sphere, the first comprising all legitimate private concerns and
activities, and the second providing force in the service of justice.
The foundation of the Christian State is in Bonald's view justice.
The sword against the internal and the external enemy—the sword
of justice and the sword of defence—are one and the same and are
carried by the same monarch, in whose service there are two kinds
of nobility, the *noblesse de robe* and the *noblesse d'épée*. The foundation
of both society and State is the family, marriage being " eventual
society," which becomes " actual " with the birth of children. The
sacred character of family life safeguards it against interference by
the State in the social sphere. All ethical principles governing State
and society are derived from the family and thus Bonald wishes to
see at the head of the State, not a " first citizen," but a " first
family," and the political and public services assured, not by
individuals, but by such families who are ready to renounce otherwise legitimate and lucrative private activities for political honours
and distinctions.

Bonald preached the essential unity of Europe as a society of
Christian public law, and he may be quoted as the classic opponent
of modern tendencies of nationalism, which he showed are of
revolutionary origin.

Among the great Catholic writers of the post-Revolutionary era,
Bonald occupies a first and unique place. Less of an elegant paradoxical wit than Joseph de Maistre, with whose apologetic thought
he concurred in many essential points, he is a more systematic
thinker, whose achievement shows a rare consistency and unity in
thought, an unusual purity of style and an unmatched conformity
of life to the principles he constantly defended.

The light and the truth of the Christian heritage, reached by men
like Donoso Cortés, Louis Veuillot or Barbey d'Aurevilly after hard
struggles against the intellectual trends of their time, Bonald
inherited safely; he was never misled by the aberrations of his
century and transmitted it safely to future generations. In the
history of French philosophy, he will be mainly remembered for
his theory of the origin of human language. Bonald concluded from
the fact that the name of God exists in every language, that it
expresses a correct and *plausible* idea, and sees in this the proof of
God's existence: man, in his view, is only capable of imagining
what exists in reality. While Descartes, and the whole school of
thought which followed his method, took individual thought and
reasoning as their point of departure, the existence of society is for
Bonald the first and foremost problem. Society exists, in his view,

for a Thought conceived, human association being the means employed to achieve this end. The expression of this Thought is the *Word* and the Word became incarnate in Christ.

Thus Bonald's reasoning leads to a perfect harmony and perfect faith, and he is perhaps the first modern philosopher to rejoin the great medieval tradition of Christian philosophy.

The first part of the following extracts was written by Bonald in 1799, the second in 1819. The two essays from which they are taken both relate to the same subject, the pacification of Europe after the wars of the Revolution. In the *Analytical Essay on the Law of Nature* we follow Bonald's thought during the period of consolidation after the fall of Robespierre, and which soon afterwards took a more definite shape in the Consulate of Bonaparte, proclaimed on the 18th Brumaire of the Year VIII (November 9th, 1799). The *Essay on the General Interest of Europe* (1814) was meant as a piece of advice to the Congress of Vienna, and as a comment on the basic principle of this Congress, which Metternich proclaimed to be the restoration of " the public law of Europe, as it can be seen in facts incontestably established by history." Bonald takes the principle formulated in Vienna as his point of departure and also as a method of approach. He underlines very emphatically the central importance of the Church in the making of Europe, and at the same time he directs his polemics by implication against the political theories of non-Catholic philosophical schools: Spinoza's theory of the geometrical equilibrium in the division of powers, and Kant's theoretically Republican " Eternal Peace," which neglect to define, or relegate to the second plane the first principle of Power (a human part of the divine attribute of the Almighty) and the principle of facts and rights clearly established by history.

1. THE UNITY OF EUROPE

I

THERE has arisen in our time, in the midst of Christian Europe and at the very heart of civilisation, an independent State which has made atheism its religion and anarchy its system of government. Although it was at war with society, this monstrous State has yet shown all the marks of a society; its sovereign was a stupendous spirit of error and of lies; its basic law, a hatred of all order; its subjects were men tormented by the passions of covetousness and greed; its instruments of authority and its ministers were men who were either thoroughly corrupt, or had been wretchedly seduced from their duty, men who, bearing titles and names which will remain for ever celebrated, united by the same oaths, united more closely still by the same crimes, led this terrible *action* with all the devices of genius and carried it out with the blind devotion of fanatics.

Scarcely had this sinister society been formed and so to say constituted, than the *inevitable* and metaphysical distinction between truth and error, and good and evil, which began with man himself and will last as long as he lives, became a physical reality. Then France, where this infernal State materialised for a time, intoxicated with *the wine of prostitution*, and as if carried away by a superhuman frenzy, despatched her principles, her soldiers and the memory of her famous men to extinguish all truth, to overthrow every semblance of order, and threatened the whole world with a return to savagery.

Anarchy has been dethroned and the armies of atheism are defeated; but the precedent lives on after these successes and the principles survive the precedent. A generation has grown up which hates authority and is ignorant of its duties, and which will transmit to succeeding generations the fatal tradition of so many accepted errors and the noxious memory of so many crimes which remain unpunished. The causes of disorder, which always subsist at the heart of society, will sooner or later reproduce their terrible effects, unless the authority vested in the different societies substitutes its unlimited powers of preservation for this thorough system of destruction; unless our rulers return to the natural constitution of societies, in order to make their social action completely effective; unless finally they bring the whole might of public institutions into play, to fight and call a halt to the deadly consequences of occult institutions.

In France especially, it is both possible and necessary to relate the question of authority, and those who administer it, back to their natural origin; that is to say, to form a society. France has always served as a model to other nations, in good things as well as in bad; and alone perhaps in Europe, she is in just the requisite position to establish a society in a final and complete form, because she is, I think, the only nation which has reached the limits set to her territory by nature. A nation which has reached this stage ought not, and even cannot, have any other ambition than to maintain her position, to arm herself only against the enemy from without, and still more against the enemy from within: that spirit of pride and revolt which, curbed but never destroyed, and ever present in society because it is always alive in man, will wage an internecine and stubborn war until the end, in the bosom of society as well as in the heart of man. For let us make no mistake: society itself is a real state of warfare, in which virtue combats error, and good combats evil, while nature, which desires that all men should combine in a society, wars against man, who tends to isolate himself from society, or rather to create a society all by himself; the name of the *Lord of Hosts*, which is assumed by the creator and preserver of human nature, means first and foremost the God of societies.

We are approaching a great phase in the social development of the world. The Revolution, which, like all revolutions, was both religious and political, was the result of the general laws governing the preservation of societies, and is to be compared to a terrible and salutary crisis, by means of which nature roots out from the social body those vicious principles which the weakness of authority had allowed to creep in, and restores to it its health and pristine vigour.

Hence the Revolution will restore to the principle of authority in France the requisite strength which will enable it to preserve society, that same strength which it had lost in proportion as it repudiated the real bases of authority and in some cases over-estimated its scope. " Upheavals have always strengthened the hand of authority," says Montesquieu, who observes the fact without referring back to the principle. Hence the Revolution will restore religious and political *unity* to Europe, that natural constitution based on the authority of religion and the authority of the State, from which she was separated by the Treaty of Westphalia. It was, as a matter of fact, in this treaty, famous for all time, that the *atheistic* dogma of the religious and political sovereignty of man was first propounded and in a sense consecrated, that principle of every revolution and the germ of all the evils which afflict society, the *abomination of desolation in high places*, in other words, in a society which is subject to the sovereignty of God. Then it was that the leaders of the nations, united in the most solemn act that has been performed since the foundation of Christian society, recognised the public and social existence of political democracy, in the illusory independence of Switzerland and the United Provinces, and of religious democracy, in the public establishment of the reformed religion and the evangelical body of German princes, thus legalising in Europe usurpations of religious and political authority, which had hitherto only received a provisional and precarious recognition in imperfect States.

The treaties which sooner or later will bring the present war to an end will be based on contradictory principles, irrespective of the period in which they are signed. They will propose the abolition of all government by the mob, the organisation of Europe into great States, and perhaps even the overthrow of that dividing wall which, thanks to a policy torn by party hatreds, has separated certain peoples from the ancient faith of Christian Europe. Already we see the opposition to religious unity weakening in England, as, on account of the accession of Ireland and other events which are perhaps already in preparation, she becomes more firmly attached to the principle of monarchy. Russia, weary of the despotism which, as Montesquieu says, " is more burdensome to her than to her peoples themselves," is progressing towards a *unified* and natural organisation of political authority, through the law of succession which she has recently promulgated; at the same time, we can discern unequivocal signs in her government that she is trying to return to religious unity and that she will perhaps be able to bring the Orient back into that unity. Finally, in France herself, pseudo-authority is refraining from persecuting pseudo-religion, until such time as authority can lend religion its support. Every event of this ever-memorable era brings nearer to us the universal revelation of this fundamental truth of the science of society: that *outside religious and political unity, man can find no truth and society no salvation.*

The greatest genius the world has perhaps ever seen, Leibnitz,[1] who lived at the beginning of this century, and who, placed historically as he was between the reverses which afflicted the old age of Louis XIV and the upheavals which were inevitable during the minority of his successor, dared, at the time of France's greatest weakness, to foretell her future greatness, and to write these remarkable words to his friend Ludolphus: " Would you like me to tell you my fears more explicitly ? It is that France, bringing the whole of the Rhine under her domination, will, with a stroke of the pen, reduce the College of Electors by one half, so that the foundations of the Empire being already destroyed, the structure itself will fall

---

[1] See Note 3, p. 94.

into ruin." Leibnitz wrote in his *Further Essays on Human Under-standing* lines which are no less prophetic: " Those who imagine that they have broken free from the inconvenient fear of a watchful Providence and a threatening future, give their brute passions full rein and apply their minds towards seducing and corrupting others. If they are ambitious and *somewhat hard men*, they are capable of *setting the four corners of the earth ablaze* for their own pleasure or advancement, and some I have known of this metal. . . . I have even come to the conclusion that similar opinions, which gradually insinuate themselves into the minds of those great men who control other men and are respon-sible for government, and which slip into fashionable books, prepare the way for *the general revolution which threatens Europe*. . . . If we still have the strength to cure ourselves of the spiritual infection, the bad effects of which now begin to be visible, the evils can perhaps be averted; *but if it spreads, Providence will punish the faults of men by that very revolution to which it will give birth:* for whatever happens, *everything will in general and in the long run happen for the best. . . .*" In other words, all things will tend towards the improvement of mankind or of society, an opinion which is in conformity with this great man's system, a religious and philosophical optimism which was misunderstood and ridiculed by Voltaire,[1] and to which so many other men have subscribed, without fully understanding it.

Therein, and therein only, lies that *social perfectibility* which is promised us by men who do not understand the term, and whose opinions, at least in their consequences, drag down society to a state of ignorance and barbarity. Writers who attempt to hasten the progress of society reject it without examination, when they defend the principles of morality, reason and good taste against the encroachment of barbarians; a remarkable contradiction in terms, which proves that truth and error are often but the same things, seen from two different angles. Indeed, the opponents of *perfectibility* can be excused for failing to recognise it, when it is offered to them by men who, in morality, politics and literature, mistake the unnatural and the *extraordinary* for a novelty, who think that they are progres-sive, when they are only caught in a circle of errors and follies taken over from the Greeks in a new form, and when they see happiness for the peoples of the world only in riches, and pro-gress for society only in the arts.

[1] See Note 4, p. 95.

II

Until the sixteenth century the life of Europe had been based on the two principles of monarchy and the Christian religion. Peace had been disturbed from time to time by wars between neighbours. Yet these wars, in which hatred was unknown, these passing disputes between peoples who were united in political and religious doctrine, merely provided a means of testing the strength of States, without there being any danger to their power or their independence; furthermore, they had often yielded to the intervention of the head of the Church, the common father of all Christian peoples and the universal link between members of the great family.

A great schism in religion occurred in the sixteenth century and a great cleavage in politics was the inevitable result.

A new system of religion, which was soon extended to politics, the presbyterian and popular system, hostile to the idea of monarchy, was born in Europe. Principles so diametrically opposed to each other were bound to come into conflict. So the struggle began in Europe, and will never perhaps be concluded.

The two great parties had resort to pen and arms alike; controversy divided intellects and war disturbed States. Each party endeavoured to retain power, or if it was not in power to seize it; and when they were exhausted by this bitter struggle, they drew breath under cover of treaties which were broken as soon as they were signed, so that for a while they were evenly matched. Then it was that Europe had its first glimpse of the idea of political equilibrium, which the publicists of the Northern countries[1] adopted enthusiastically, hoping thereby to tilt the balance in their own favour.

It might be interesting to examine this notion of political equilibrium, at a time when it appeared to be as *weighted* and steady as was possible. " After the peace of Aix-la-Chapelle," says Voltaire, " Christian Europe was divided into two great parties, who treated each other with consideration, maintaining in their own fashion the balance of power, *this pretext for so many wars*, which was supposed to guarantee eternal peace. One of these great factions consisted of the States of the Queen-Empress of Hungary,[2] a part of Germany, Russia, England, Holland and Sardinia; the other comprised France, Spain, the

[1] See Note 1, p. 93.   [2] See Note 2, p. 93.

Two Sicilies, Prussia and Sweden. Each power remained *under arms*. It was hoped that a lasting truce would result from the fear that each half of Europe inspired in the other. They flattered themselves for a long time that no aggressor could arise, because each State was armed in self-defence. Vain hope. A trifling quarrel between France and England over some native territory in Canada led all the sovereigns of Europe to formulate a new policy." Such was, and always will be, the strength and the extent of this system of the balance of power, *in which each power remains under arms*. It is an exact parallel to the principle of mechanical equilibrium, which only consists of a pause of a second between the two swings of the pendulum.

In vain can weights be changed, or the two halves which should counter-balance each other be combined in different ways: only war will result. The reason is that according to this system *each power remains under arms*, and it is only by putting their swords into the balance that they can achieve a moment's equilibrium: a situation more dangerous than ever today, when third-rate powers produce, or hold in reserve, a military strength which is quite disproportionate to the size of the population. Moreover, when we balance interests, or even military strength, is it possible for us also to put into the balance the moral strength of nations and the passions and talents of those who govern them ?

It was on less unsure foundations than this, that one of the greatest kings of modern times, and one of the greatest minds of all time, endeavoured to build order and peace in Europe. Both of them set at the head of Christendom, as arbiter and moderating influence, the common father of Christians. Although this plan for a Christian republic would have been difficult, not to say impossible, to realise, and although today we could not persuade that part of Europe which has rejected his spiritual supremacy to appreciate the political pre-eminence of the head of the Church, we must be careful not to reject contemptuously a plan which seemed practicable to Henry IV and Leibnitz.[1]

These two excellent minds understood to the full that Christendom is a great family, composed of young and old, a society in which there are strong and weak, great powers and small ones. The whole of Christendom was subject to the law common to families and States alike, which are not governed by a system of balances, but by various authorities.

[1] See Note 3, p. 94.

Dare we hope that in the facts we are about to present, and the opinion we are going to give, reason and experience will triumph over national prejudices ?

Since the time of Charlemagne, there has always been an authority in Europe which was respected, even by its rivals, and recognised, even by its enemies: the preponderance of France. It was not a preponderance based on force, for French politics have always been more successful than her arms, but it was based on the dignity, respect, influence and good counsel which her age and her memories brought her. There was also such consistency in the counsel she gave, her progress was so felicitous, in spite of mistakes in administration and military reverses, that a great Pope was moved to say that " France was a kingdom governed by Providence." France was the eldest of all these European societies. While the peoples of Great Britain and the Germanic lands were still living in their forests and marshes, Gaul, cultured through her study of Greek and Latin literature, strong in the Roman discipline, educated in the school of these masters of the World, refined by their arts and their urbanity, which had even in the end been driven into exile from Rome and had taken refuge within the confines of the Empire; Gaul, like a well-prepared soil, received all the advantages of Christian civilisation. Soon she became a monarchy; the antiquity of the noble line of her kings, itself older than any other royal line, the excellence of her constitution, the virtues and the intelligence of her clergy, the dignity of her magistrature, the fame of her chivalry, the learning of her Universities, the wisdom of her laws, her gracious way of living, the character of her inhabitants, rather than the strength of her arms, which were always evenly matched and often unfortunate—above all, the genius of Charlemagne, had raised her to a position in Europe which none contested. No great political act was ever performed without France; she was the trustee of every tradition of the great family, and the repository of all the *State secrets* of Christendom. I dare to say that no great act will ever be performed without her, and what assures her of this pre-eminence for all time, and in a measure sets the final seal on it, is the universality of her language, which has been adopted by Cabinets and Courts, and is consequently the language of politics: the mildest and at the same time the strongest domination which one people can exercise over another, since by imposing its language on others, a people bestows at the same time a measure of its character, its spirit and its thought, which is faithfully reflected in its language.

Hence France has always exercised a sort of authority over Christendom. She was always destined to teach Europe, sometimes by the example of her virtues, sometimes by the lesson to be drawn from her misfortunes. If we can trace great motives which led to great events, every nation is guilty and every nation has been punished; and France, the guiltiest nation of all, because she had received the most, has found a frightful retribution in the terrible revenge which made her its instrument.

The most striking tribute however to the importance of France in the social field, and to the political *need* for her existence, comes from the prodigious events we have just witnessed. I dare to say that no other society could excite the same interest, or call forth the same effort. The peoples of the North and East have had to join forces in order to restore to France that legitimate authority over herself which she had lost, when all they thought they were engaging in, and all they perhaps had desired to do, was to escape from her tyranny. All the noble scions of Christendom have had to bring back the first-born of this illustrious family with their own hands, to the house of his fathers. The elements themselves collaborated with mankind in this great undertaking; and when the head of the family crossed the threshold of France, this superhuman authority, the most formidable that the world has ever seen, and *before whom the earth was silent*, vanished like a dream, with all its fortresses, its treasure and its armies. This mighty storm grew calm in an instant and the last roar of gunfire seemed to be the signal for the piping days of peace.

Let nobody place on France the entire responsibility for the madness into which she fell, and for the unparalleled misfortunes she brought on Europe; the foreign doctrines brought into France over a period of years, and propagated by our writers with such lamentable success, have had only too great an effect on our destinies. It was easy to see through the foreign intrigues, even in the very early days of our troubles. The inconceivable tyranny beneath which in the end the whole of Europe groaned was connived at and supported by people outside France; she can say with a clear conscience to other governments: Let him who is without sin amongst you cast the first stone.

It would be a big mistake at the present time, and a great danger for the future, if political action, which is responsible for the wellbeing of Europe, were consciously to be motivated by memories of the past, instead of by a vision of the future.

This line of policy has been in the position of misleading Europe for a long time. With her eyes turned towards the past, she does not take the future sufficiently into account; in her desire to be forearmed against any imaginary peril, she exposes herself in her defenceless position to real dangers.

Because the House of Austria united for one historical moment the most splendid parts of the Old and the New World under her domination, France, who had no real reason to fear her, always imagined that Austria was anxious to swallow her up; their mutual hostility, under Charles V and Francis I, brought about the ruin of Europe, since it gave Lutheranism the opportunity to spread its influence. Richelieu reduced the nobles to the status of courtiers and paid officials, because he still feared the shadow of the great landed aristocracy which had long since been broken. Coming to our own days, France was only able to win such sweeping victories because the great powers of the North could not forget that they were age-old enemies and spent their strength in jealous rivalry.

There is no doubt that France has shown extraordinary might and caused Europe infinite misfortunes; yet it was the might that fever brings in its train, nay, a real frenzy. The revolution, like some supernatural engine which had been applied to a powerful nation, transformed her suddenly, and by means of terror, into a blind and dumb instrument whose only action was destruction and whose only movement was a flight towards ruin. This incredible combination of events, inconceivable until our own day, cannot happen again. To take precautions against such an unlikely event at the expense of France would be like conjuring up phantoms merely for the pleasure of fighting them. It is not the revolutionary armies of France which other States have to fear now, but rather the principles of licence and insubordination which she has sown in Europe, and which probably have more supporters outside France than in France herself.

We must not therefore reproach each other with our mistakes and errors, but must guard against the only danger which peoples who have reached a high level of civilisation and knowledge need fear, the danger of false doctrines which imperceptibly undermine laws, morals and institutions. When Europe emerges from this violent crisis, she cannot perish except by wasting away. The day when the atheistic dogma of the sovereignty of the people replaces in politics the sacred dogma of the sovereignty of God; the day when Europe ceases to be Christian and monarchical, she will perish, and the sceptre of the world will pass to other hands.

*   *   *

As we have said before, Bonald defines the unity of Christendom as a " Society of States," the State as a " public society " and the family as a " domestic society." The family is therefore, in his view, the first social unit, and the principle of the family is the basis of every other larger association. In his *Theory of Power*, Bonald expounds the idea that in the analysis of any phenomenon, three problems have to be faced and defined by every philosophy worthy of the name: the Cause, the Effect and the Means employed to achieve the Effect. In the social order, this means power (or authority, or will), ministry (or the service of power), and in the religious society spiritual wellbeing, or in the political society the security and the liberty of the subject. In the religious society, the Power (or Authority, or Will) is God; the ministry is the clergy; the effect aimed at is the salvation of the community. In the State, the Power is represented by the principle of Sovereignty; in its service, " ministry " is exercised by all those who administer the law and defend the territory (i.e. all those who " combat the obstacles to integral sovereignty," " the internal and the external enemy "); the effect to be desired is the security and the liberty of the subject to fulfil the natural purpose of Man, which is the procreation and preservation of the divine substance through the medium of the family. Within the family, the Power belongs to the man, whose " ministry " is exercised by the woman, and the effect desired is the child, i.e. the preservation of the divine and human substance in a new generation.

It follows from these fundamental notions of Bonald's system of philosophy, that in the political controversies of his time he considered the defence of marriage to be a foremost task. The following extract is taken from *Divorce in the Nineteenth Century*, a pamphlet published in 1802 and intended as a piece of advice to the Committee presided over by the First Consul Bonaparte, which was to codify the civil and penal laws of France. This was one of the rare writings of Bonald which achieved an immediate and practical result: Bonaparte read it, and under the influence of Bonald's arguments, he took the initiative of withdrawing the original draft authorising divorce.

2. ON DOMESTIC SOCIETY

THE authors of the draft Bill on the statute book, after having informed us " that until today, the nature of marriage has been misunderstood, and that it is only in recent times that people

G

have had clear ideas on marriage . . . are convinced that marriage, which existed before the establishment of Christianity, which preceded all positive law, and which derives from the very composition of our being, is neither a civil nor a religious act, but a natural one, which attracted the attention of legislators and which has been sanctified by religion." (Introduction, on the draft Bill of the statute book.)

It is well worth while to discuss the principles set forth in the passage which we have just quoted, since they form the basis of all the draft bills on the possibility of divorce, from the first bill in which it was proposed to grant divorce, to the final one which received the sanction of the legislature.

How has it been possible to maintain in France, after fifteen centuries of the public profession of Christianity, that is, of everything that was most perfect in public morality and in the principles underlying the laws, according to all men in the most enlightened nations who are versed in the knowledge of civil and religious legislation, " that until today people have mis-understood the nature of marriage," this element which is present in all societies, this *contract* which really is *social*, the act by which a family is founded, the laws governing which are at the basis of all political legislation ? How has it been possible to suggest " that it is only in recent times that people have had clear ideas on marriage " ? And to which period do " *recent times* " refer ? Are they referring to the time of Luther, who allowed the dissolution of marriage, or to the period of modern philosophy, which, not content with allowing the greatest possible facility in the dissolution of the conjugal tie, has justi-fied concubinage and extended its indulgence as far as adul-tery ? And are they not already biased in favour of the useful-ness of divorce, when they state in the preamble of the Bill which authorises it, " *that only in recent times has marriage been understood* " ?

" Marriage, which existed before the establishment of Christianity, which preceded all positive law, and which derives from the very composition of our being, is neither a civil nor a religious act, but a natural one, which attracted the attention of the legislator and was sanctified by religion." *Marriage existed before Christianity and preceded all positive laws;* but did it precede the natural relationships between men in society, the most per-fect evolution of which is seen in the Christian religion, and to which all religions and civil laws give expression and bear wit-ness ?

The sentence we have just quoted deceives the mind, and the differing meanings which it seems to suggest will not bear examination.

Marriage is a civil affair from the point of view of the interests at stake; it is religious, spiritually speaking; it is *animal* and physical from the point of view of the body; and as the family has never at any time been able to subsist without the social proprieties, and as man has always embarked on marriage in possession of all his moral and physical faculties, it is true to say that the nature of marriage has always fundamentally been a simultaneous civil, religious and physical act. It was not a civil affair in the earliest times, in the sense that the interests of the family were protected by public authority and regulated according to public laws, which comprise what we call our civil status. But they were protected by domestic authority, which is an element of the public authority, and regulated by domestic customs and laws, which are themselves the germs of the public laws, just as the domestic society, or the family, is itself the element and the germ of public society. Marriage was not religious in the sense that it was divine, and that the Creator had said of the woman: " She shall leave her father and her mother and cleave unto her husband," and of husband and wife: " They shall be two in one flesh." It is because marriage was, in the earliest times, and before the establishment of public, political and religious societies, a divine and at the same time a human act (I mean by human: moral and physical), just as it has been a civil and religious act since the foundation of public societies; I say it is because it derives from the very composition of our being and of our nature, that it is a *natural* act. For the real nature of man, and the true composition of his being, consist in a natural relationship with the author of his being, and in his natural as well as his moral and physical relationship with his fellow-men. It is entirely because marriage was a divine and a human institution, in the sense in which I understand it, that it *attracted the attention* of civil legislators, and that it was sanctified by religion. For if the orator, whose reasoning I question, because he makes a distinction between the *natural* and the civil or religious state, as if what is civil and religious is not also natural, understands by nature the animal instincts of man, he is falling into the same error as the senator who submitted the government draft of this Bill, when he says: " Philosophers are only concerned with the physical side of marriage." They are certainly curious philosophers, be it said in passing; apparently only anatomists are allowed to consider the union of man and woman in this light.

Natural marriage, which is neither *civil* nor *religious*, gives birth to the *natural* man of J. J. Rousseau, who is likewise neither *civil* nor *religious*; and to say that marriage *is neither a civil nor a religious act, but a natural act,* is to suggest that the civil and religious state is not within the nature of man. It is to descend to the level of the doctrine of the writer whom we have just quoted, when he says " that society is not natural to mankind," and elsewhere that " everything that is not contained in nature has certain disadvantages, civil society having more than all the rest put together."

Let us say then that marriage is simultaneously a social, domestic, civil and religious act; the act by which domestic society is founded, the interests of which are bound to be safeguarded by the civil authority as it comes to the aid of domestic harmony, and in which religious authority introduces the divine element in an external and sensible manner, in order to consecrate the union of two hearts and purify the union of two bodies.

No problem could be clearer in its principles, or more fruitful in its consequences, than the question of divorce, since by its nature it brings into play all those problems of *authority* and our *duties*, which are fundamental to society. I do not hesitate to affirm, and I hope even to prove, that on the dissolution or the indissolubility of the conjugal tie depends the fate of the family, of religion and of the State, in France and in the whole world.

Divorce was made legal in 1792, to the surprise of nobody, since it was the inevitable *consequence*, long foreseen, of that system of destruction which was pursued with such enthusiasm at that time. But today, when we want to reconstruct, divorce appears to be almost a *principle* at the base of the social edifice, and those who are destined to inhabit it ought to tremble.

I will go further. Divorce was in harmony with that brand of democracy which has held sway for too long in France, under different names and in different forms. We have seen domestic and public authority delivered up on all sides to the passions of *subjects*; it brought about disorder in the family and disorder in the State: there was an analogy between the disorganisation in both of them. There is indeed, if one may say so, even some semblance of order, when everything is confused in the same style, and for the same reason. Furthermore, divorce is in direct contradiction with the spirit and the principles of hereditary or indissoluble monarchy. We have, then, order in the State and disorder in the family, indissolubility of the one and dissolution of the other, with a subsequent lack of harmony, so that the situation is such that the family will finally disorganise the State or the State will have to govern the family. Nay, more. In a democracy, the people have the privilege of making the laws, or abolishing them, according to their fancy. Since the magistrates they elect only hold office for a short time, it rarely happens that individual men are powerful enough to make the laws serve their passions, whereas in a monarchy, where men hold eminent positions, which can be hereditary, or else are conferred for life, and derive from them a great reputation and a great fortune, it can happen that laws are not made by influential men, but are interpreted in their favour. What judgements could be solicited with greater passion than those concerning divorce, and what laws lend themselves to arbitrary interpretation to a greater degree than those which limit or extend facilities for divorce ? Now where great men have trod, the crowd treads in its turn. What was once difficult becomes easy; what was once rare becomes a frequent occurrence; what was forbidden is now permitted; the exception acquires all the force of law; the law is soon nothing but the exception and the time comes when there is no other alternative to disorder than extreme disorder or revolution.

*   *   *

Note 1: " publicists of the Northern countries."

Bonald mainly refers to the seventeenth-century Swedish statesman of German birth, Puffendorff, whose *States of Europe* was for a century or more considered to be the classic handbook of diplomacy. He may, however, equally have in mind Spinoza's *Tractatus theologico-politicus*, another classic (and more metaphysical) summary of the theory of the balance of power, the perfect balance being the result of politics conceived *more geometrico*, like an architectural construction.

This idea of Spinoza was very popular among English Whig publicists of the early eighteenth century. Dean Swift however thought that the diplomatic balance of the European house might become so perfect that any sparrow which settled down on the roof would upset it!

Note 2: " Queen-Empress of Hungary."

Maria-Theresa, Archduchess of Austria, daughter of Emperor Charles VI, b. 1717, d. 1780. By the Act of Pragmatic Sanction of

her father, promulgated at the Hungarian Diet in 1723, she succeeded to the Crown of Hungary in 1740. As this Act was also
endorsed by the Imperial Diet, the hereditary " Kingdoms and
Provinces " of the House of Habsburg (Bohemia, Moravia, Silesia,
Upper and Lower Austria, Tyrol, Vorarlberg, etc.) belonging to the
Holy Roman Empire were to remain " undivided and inseparable "
under her rule, although on account of her sex she could not succeed
to the Empire, which fell in 1740 to the Prince-Elector of Bavaria,
who ruled as Charles VII until 1747, and to which Prince Francis
of Lorraine, Grand Duke of Tuscany, Maria-Theresa's husband,
was afterwards elected (d. 1765 and succeeded by his son Joseph II,
who, on his mother's death in 1780, also became King of Hungary
and ruler of the hereditary States). Thus, in the diplomacy of her
time, Maria-Theresa, ruling Queen in Hungary and Empress-
Consort, later Empress-Mother, was referred to as " Queen of
Hungary," or more ceremoniously as " Her Apostolic Majesty," a
title which referred exclusively to the Papal privileges of St. Stephen
of Hungary, and not to her other dominions.

The European situation here described by Voltaire underwent
changes, by reason of the fact that Britain and France could never
be on the same side during the great eighteenth-century rivalry.
During the War of the Austrian Succession, which ended with the
Peace of Aix-la-Chapelle in 1748, Britain supported Maria-Theresa
against France and Prussia. Subsequently the Austrian Chancellor,
Prince Kaunitz, conceived the plan of a great continental alliance
between France, Austria and Russia, mainly in order to moderate
growing Russian aims in the East by having greater security on the
Western flank of the Austrian power. As a reply, Walpole and the
Whig party sided with Prussia, against both France and Austria.
The European situation which Voltaire summarises here and
Bonald quotes, prevailed between the end of the War of the
Austrian Succession (1748) and the Seven Years' War (1756-1763).

Note 3: " Leibnitz."

Gottfried Wilhelm Leibnitz, 1646-1716, a German philosopher
writing mostly in Latin and French, a mathematician and scientist,
also an author on politics and international law, one of the most
versatile intellects of modern Europe. The fundamental notion of
his philosophical system is the " pre-established " or " pre-existing "
harmony between spiritual and material reality. Each species
(" Monadology ") follows its own intrinsic law and naturally tends
towards its reproduction for the sake of the perfect preservation of
its internal value.

Bonald's *Theory of Power* which considers " preservation " as the
aim of the power established in religious and political societies,
and " perfectibility " (i.e. the capacity to realise the " best possible "
order), the principle of which is the " pre-established harmony of

Creation," is very largely an application of the methods and principles of Leibnitz in politics and society.

Leibnitz was the first Protestant thinker to advocate the reunion of the Protestant communities with the Church: a leading idea in his correspondence with Bossuet, Bishop of Meaux, which extends over a period of years.

Note 4: " ridiculed by Voltaire."

Bonald alludes here to Voltaire's *Candide*, the grotesque and fantastic story of an unfortunate young man educated in Leibnitz's doctrine that the world lives under " the best possible order." The aversion of Voltaire and of many other writers of the eighteenth century to Leibnitz is to be explained by the fact that (unlike other thinkers of the great European philosophical movement which followed the religious wars and which relegated the theological issue to a secondary plane), Leibnitz aimed at a definition of the metaphysical world order, and not only at a method of individual reasoning (like Descartes), at experimental science (like Bacon or Locke), or an analysis of the critical mind (like Kant). In other words, Leibnitz was the philosophical opposite, for the eighteenth century, of rationalistic and ethical individualism.

At the same time, Leibnitz is still nearer to the Realism of St Thomas than either Descartes or Bacon and he emphatically recognises the primacy of belief and the conformity of rational knowledge with the truth of Revelation.

III. FRANÇOIS RENÉ DE CHATEAUBRIAND

1768 - 1848

CHATEAUBRIAND'S place in a chronological survey of Catholic thought since the French Revolution comes immediately after Joseph de Maistre and Vicomte de Bonald. The *Considérations sur la France* of the first writer, the *Théorie du Pouvoir* of the second and Chateaubriand's *Essai sur les Révolutions* were the three great commentaries published on the events of 1789-93. All three were written abroad and were influenced by, and to a great extent inspired by an English book, Burke's *Reflections on the French Revolution*.

Bonald's book was the final expression and the systematic summary of the thought of an author in his forties; everything else he wrote in his life was but an addition or glossary to it. Joseph de Maistre, about the same age as Bonald, wrote his principal book—the *Soirées de Saint Pétersbourg*—a quarter of a century later; his *Considérations sur la France* and even *Du Pape* were but prefaces to his final thought. In Chateaubriand's case, however, his comment on the Revolution was not so much as a preface even to the ultimate summary of his thought and it merely marked one step towards the final pinnacle of his style. The subject, however, was of immense importance in his life. Like Joseph de Maistre and Bonald, Chateaubriand, half a generation younger than they, became a writer because of the French Revolution; a principal feature in his work is the new historical and political approach to theology, which resulted from the context of the Revolution. Yet, he is, above all, one of the masters, perhaps the foremost one, of a new concept of literature. He is a master among the new post-Revolutionary secular religious writers. He is the first of those modern poets who are not craftsmen of rhyme and stage technique—there were many such during the eighteenth century—and he it was who gave to the word " poet " that larger, more universal meaning which it still keeps in German. According to this new concept, the poet is a writer, often a prose-writer (Chateaubriand himself wrote almost entirely in prose, for his attempts at verse and at poetic tragedy were a failure), who must be judged above all by standards of personal feeling and temperament. In other words, Chateaubriand was the father of Romanticism. In aesthetics he saved that part of Rousseau's message which was valid truth, and the rest of which was otherwise so disastrous in politics.

A recapitulation of Chateaubriand's life and work is hardly necessary here; he is a writer whom few read today, but who is nevertheless known to all. This has happened because, as Oscar Wilde said of himself, he gave to his books his talent only, while he gave to his life his genius. Chateaubriand created at least one work of genius, which was the story of his life, the *Mémoires d'outre-tombe*. The conclusion of these Memoirs tell what was the central inspiration of his life and his work.

This inspiration was already clear in *Le Génie du Christianisme* and in *Les Martyrs*. In his early sensualist outlook he was still a son of the eighteenth century, of Condillac and especially of Rousseau. His return to the old religious foundations of France was only partly political and social in origin; it was to a large extent visual and aesthetic. He rediscovered Gothic architecture at a moment when medieval art found no defenders and when the Greek colonnade, with its more geometrical form, was the fashionable ideal of the day. He introduced into the art of epic prose imaginative detail, colourful landscape, historical atmosphere and spectacular costume—all visual elements—and so he became the master of Sir Walter Scott and the historical novel. Chateaubriand revolutionised European taste and European art almost more than any other writer contemporary with the Revolution. He discovered the East and the Holy Land for many of his contemporaries; he was perhaps the first French author fully to understand Shakespeare; the first modern writer who interpreted the saints, the Fathers and the early teachers of the Church as thinkers and mystical poets, rather than as theologians and authorities on the liturgy—a new approach at the end of the eighteenth century and an unusual and a new angle for scholarship and letters, which before Chateaubriand had kept secular humanism and theology apart.

There are, of course, as we have already pointed out in the Introduction, obvious limitations and shortcomings in this artistic and aesthetic religiosity. They were already present in Chateaubriand's work; they led to worse aberrations in his followers and imitators: to a superficial pose of melancholy over a lost tradition and to the *culte du moi* of Maurice Barrès, for example. Chateaubriand had neither the grave objectivity of Bonald, nor the penetrating, critical wit of Joseph de Maistre, so that ultimately little survives which is of any objective value in his religious, political and philosophical thought.

As to his career as a statesman, he was Plenipotentiary Minister of the First Consul Bonaparte to the Vatican, Ambassador in London and Berlin and once more at the Vatican, and Minister of Foreign Affairs for a short while under the Restoration; he was the author of pamphlets such as *De Buonaparte*[1] *et des Bourbons* (1814)

---

[1] By insisting on the Italian spelling of the name which the family abandoned when they left Corsica for France during the Revolution, Chateaubriand wished to emphasise the fact that he considered Napoleon to be a usurper.

and *La Monarchie selon la Charte* (1816), great political events at the
time. Yet he left behind him only the memory of a temperamental
opposition, first to Napoleon, then even to the Bourbons, whose
cause he had promoted, and finally a long voluntary exile from the
political scene in Paris, at the memorable salon of Madame
Récamier, during which he foresaw the future triumph of Democracy over Louis Philippe's imitation-Monarchy and over the
bourgeoisie, the "*monarchie de la boutique*," and during which he
once more espoused the lost cause of the elder branch of the
Bourbons.

He ended his long career with this melancholy love for a cause
he believed to be lost, dying at the age of eighty on July 4th, 1848.
Mental decay preceding his physical end, during the last year of his
life he was hardly conscious of the new Revolution and of the
fighting at the barricades in June 1848, which absorbed the general
attention, while Chateaubriand, the great personal link between
the eighteenth and the nineteenth centuries in France, was on his
deathbed.

His life exhausted all the possibilities of an age. He saw America
during the life-time of Washington, Europe under Napoleon; he
knew the destitution and solitude of an exile in London during the
Revolution; he enjoyed the adventures of a soldier in the Royalist
cause and the flamboyant but hollow splendours of the victorious
diplomacy of the era of the Congresses. And to this life he gave an
imperishable monument, the great story of an indefatigable sensibility, of the emotions of a long and varied life, of a personality
which was too exuberant to create a consistent system of thought.
Chateaubriand's greatness lies in his imagination, his sensibility and
emotion.

Any account of Chateaubriand's life is bound to centre round the
problem of " pose," so that both his critics and admirers must devote
a fundamental study to the question of sincerity and ostentation.
Chateaubriand, no doubt, liked ostentation. Yet there is hardly a
more insincere book in existence that Sainte-Beuve's attack on
Chateaubriand's sincerity. Sainte-Beuve, the least sincere of the
Romantic generation, the least loyal character among men of
talent, if anything a Jansenist in religion (not on account of a misguided religious passion, but out of spite for the spiritual gifts of
others and out of spite for the Church), Sainte-Beuve was a bad
judge of Chateaubriand's sincerity in religion, and was not even
the best qualified judge of his genius. Sainte-Beuve's talent grew
in the service of those greater than he; Chateaubriand, even at his
worst, was a sovereign temperament. The proud ostentation of
honour is to be preferred to that of informed pedantry; the pose of
a hopeless love for lost causes is preferable to the critical pose of a
bitter and pedantic talent, who, after all, placed himself voluntarily in Chateaubriand's shadow for over twenty years before he

discovered any blot on his sun. As the deliberate distortions and, we may say, the bad faith of Sainte-Beuve's *Chateaubriand et son groupe littéraire* has been exposed by two Catholic literary scholars of incontestable probity, this debate may be considered closed.[1]

There is ostentation in Chateaubriand, but no morbid self-seeking, no indecent and effeminate exhibitionism, nothing approaching decadence. His place in the history of secular spirituality is best defined by himself in the conclusion to *Mémoires d'outre-tombe* which follows here.

PROGRESS[2]

DURING the eight centuries of our monarchy, France was the centre of the intelligence, the continuity and the peace of Europe; no sooner had that monarchy been lost than Europe tended in the direction of democracy. The human race, for good or for ill, is now its own master; princes once had the keeping of it; having attained their majority, the nations now claim that they have no further need of tutelage. From the time of David down to modern days, kings have always been called; now the vocation of the peoples begins. Apart from the short-lived and minor exceptions of the Greek, the Carthaginian and the Roman republics, with their slaves, the monarchical form of government was normal throughout the entire world. Modern society in its entirety has forsaken the monarchy since the flag of the kings of France no longer flies. In order to hasten the degradation of royal power, God has in various countries delivered up the sceptre to usurper kings, to young girls who are either still in the nursery, or are just of marriageable age; it is lions such as these, without any jaws, lionesses without any claws and baby girls suckling at the breasts, or giving their hand in marriage, whom the men born of this believing age must follow.

The wildest principles are proclaimed under the very noses of monarchs who imagine that they are safeguarding themselves behind the triple hedge of a doubtful protection. Democracy is overtaking them; stage by stage, they are retreating from the ground floor of their palaces to the topmost part, so

---

[1] L'Abbé G. Bertrin: *La sincérité religieuse de Chateaubriand.* 1893. Edmond Biré: *Chateaubriand, Victor Hugo, Balzac.* 1897.

[2] Taken from the epilogue to *Mémoires d'outre-tombe.* Written in November 1841, this epilogue was first published in *La Presse*, edited by Emile de Girardin, in October 1850.

that finally they will cast themselves upon the waters from the attic windows.

Furthermore, consider a phenomenal contradiction: material conditions are improving and education is spreading, yet instead of this being a boon to the nations their stature is diminishing—from whence comes this contradiction ?

The explanation lies in this: that we have deteriorated in the moral order. Crimes have always been committed, but they were not committed in cold blood, as they are today, because we have lost all feeling for religion. They no longer fill us with revulsion today, they seem only to be a consequence of the march of time; if they were judged differently in former times, it was because, as they dare to assert, our knowledge of human nature was not advanced enough. Nowadays crimes are analysed; they are passed through a crucible in order that we may discover any useful lesson accruing from them, as chemistry discovers constituents in garbage. Corruption of the mind, far more destructive than corruption of the senses, is accepted as a necessary result; it is not only to be found now in a few perverted individuals; it has become universal.

Men of this type would feel humiliated if it were proved to them that they had a soul and that after this life they will discover the existence of another one; they would think themselves devoid of all steadfastness, strength and intelligence if they did not rise above the pusillanimity of our fathers; they accept nothingness, or if you prefer it, doubt, as an unpleasant fact perhaps, but nevertheless as an incontestable truth. How admirable is our fatuous pride!

The decay of society then and the increasing importance of the individual can be accounted for in this manner. If the moral sense developed logically from the increase in intelligence, we should have a counterweight and humanity would increase in stature without any danger, but the exact opposite happens; our apprehension of good and evil grows dim as our intelligence becomes more enlightened; our conscience contracts as our ideas broaden. Yes, society will certainly perish; liberty, which might have saved the world, will not work, because it has cut itself off from religion; order, which could have ensured continuity, cannot be firmly established because the present anarchy of ideas prevents it. The purple, which once denoted power, will henceforth serve only to cradle disaster; no man will be saved unless he was born, like Christ, on straw. When the monarchs were disinterred at St. Denis, as the revolutionary tocsin rang out; when, dragged from their crumbling tombs, they were awaiting plebeian burial, rag merchants came upon this scene of the last judgement of the centuries; holding high their lanterns, they gazed into the eternal night; they rummaged amongst the remains which had escaped the original pillage. The kings were no longer there, but royalty was still there; they tore it out of the entrails of time and cast it on the rubbish heap.

So much for ancient Europe: it will never live again. Does the young Europe offer us any higher hopes ? The world of today, lacking any consecrated authority, seems faced with two impossibilities: it is impossible to return to the past or to go forward into the future. Do not run away with the idea, as some people do, that if we are in a bad pass today, good will be reborn out of evil; human nature, when it is out of order at its very source, does not function so smoothly. The excesses of liberty, for example, lead to despotism, but the excesses of tyranny lead only to tyranny; tyranny, by degrading us, makes us incapable of independence; Tiberius did not have the effect of making Rome return to the republican form of government, he merely left Caligula behind to succeed him.

Not desiring to find the true explanation of our present situation, men are content to say that a political constitution which we cannot as yet discern may possibly be hidden in the bosom of time. Did the whole of antiquity, including the most splendid of its geniuses, understand that a society could exist without slaves ? Yet we know that it can. People say—I have said it myself—that mankind will increase in stature in this new civilisation which is to come: yet is it not to be feared that the individual man will decrease in stature ? We can well be busy bees, engaged in making our own honey together. In the *material* world, men group themselves together for the purpose of work, because many people working together find what they want quicker and by devious means; individuals working in the mass can build pyramids; these individuals, studying each in his own way, can make scientific discoveries and explore all the corners of the physical creation. But do things work out in this wise in the *moral* order ? A thousand brains can collaborate in vain: they can never compose the masterpiece which comes out of the head of a Homer.

It has been said that a city, all the inhabitants of which have an equal share of wealth and education, will be a more pleasing sight in the eyes of Divinity than was the city of our fathers.

The folly of the age is to achieve the unity of the peoples, while turning the whole species into a single unit—granted; but while we are acquiring these general faculties, is not a whole chain of private feelings in danger of perishing ? Farewell to the sweetness of home; farewell to the delights of family life; amongst all these white men, yellow men and black men, reputedly your brothers, you will not find one whom you can embrace as a brother. Was there nothing then in your former life, nothing in that restricted piece of space which you could see from your ivy-mantled window ? Beyond your immediate horizon, you conjectured the existence of unknown countries from the presence of the birds of passage, the only travellers that you saw in the autumn days. Happiness lay in knowing that the surrounding hills would always be there; that they would be the scene of your friendships and your loves; that the sighing of the night wind around your retreat would be the only sound to lull you to sleep; that the peace of your soul would never be disturbed and that the familiar thoughts would always be waiting for you to commune with them. You knew where you had been born, you knew where your tomb would lie; as you penetrated deeper into the forest you could say:

> *Beautiful trees that saw my birth,*
> *Soon you will see me die.*

Man has no need to travel to become more powerful; he carries immensity within him. The impulses of your heart cannot be measured, they find an echo in thousands of other hearts; he who has nothing of this harmony in his innermost being will implore the universe to give it to him in vain. Sit on a fallen tree-trunk deep in the woods: if in these moments of complete self-forgetfulness, in your immobility and silence, you do not find the infinite, it is of no avail to wander along the banks of the Ganges.

What sort of a universal society would it be which possessed no individual country, which would be neither French nor English, nor German, nor Spanish, nor Portuguese, nor Italian, nor Russian, nor Tartar, nor Turkish, nor Persian, nor Indian, nor Chinese, nor American, or rather, what would all these societies be like if they were rolled into one ? What would the effect be on the way of life, on the sciences, the arts and the poetry of a universal society ? What expression could be given to passions felt at the same time by different peoples under different climates ? How would this medley of needs and images which the sun produces in divers lands, and which light up the youth, the maturity and the old age of men, enter into the language ? And what language would it be ? Will a universal idiom be born out of the fusion of societies, or will there be a business dialect for everyday purposes, whilst each nation retains its own language, or, on the other hand, will all the divers languages be understood by all ? Under what sort of rule and under what sort of universal law would this society live ? How should we find a place on an earth which has been extended by the power of ubiquity and shrunk by the small proportions of a globe which is everywhere dishonoured ? It only remains to ask science to show us how we can go and live on another planet.

Let us suppose that you have had enough of private property and that you propose to turn the government into a universal landlord, who is to distribute to the destitute community that share which each individual deserves. Who is to be the judge of individual merits ? Who will have the strength and the authority to carry out your decrees? Who is to be responsible for and assess the capital value of this human property ? What is to be the contribution of the weak, the sick and the stupid in a community burdened by their unfitness ?

There is another suggestion: instead of working for a salary, men could form limited companies, or limited partnerships between manufacturers and workers, between intelligence and matter, whereby some would contribute ideas and others their industry and their work; profits would be shared in common. It is an excellent thing thus to acknowledge complete perfection in mankind: excellent, if quarrels, avarice or envy are unknown: but once an associate registers a grievance, the whole edifice crumbles; dissension and lawsuits will henceforth be the order of the day. This method, which is slightly more plausible than the others in theory, is as impossible in practice.

Would you prefer to follow a moderate line and build a city in which each man has a roof, fuel, clothing and adequate food ? You will no sooner have presented each citizen with these things, than individual qualities and defects will either upset your system of distribution, or will make it unjust: one man needs much more food than the other; this man cannot work as hard as that one can; men who are frugal and work hard will become rich, those who are extravagant or idle will relapse into poverty; for you cannot bestow the same temperament on all: an innate inequality is bound to reappear in spite of all your efforts.

Do not be under any illusion that we are going to allow ourselves to be caught up in all the legal processes which have been invented for the protection of the family, for inherited rights, the guardianship of children, claims to property, etc.; marriage is notoriously an absurd oppression: we shall abolish all that. If a son kills his father, it is not the son, as we can very well prove, who is guilty of patricide, it is the father, who, by the very act of living, sacrifices the son's chances. Do not let us trouble our heads then with the labyrinths of an organisation which we intend to raze to the ground; it is a waste of time to linger over the obsolete nonsense of our grandfathers.

Notwithstanding this, some of our sectarian modernists, having an inkling of the impractibility of their doctrines, introduce certain phrases concerning morality and religion, in an attempt to make them more palatable; they imagine that all they can realise at the moment is to bring us into line with the American ideal of mediocrity, ignoring in their blindness the fact that the Americans are not only landowners, but very enthusiastic ones, which makes all the difference.

Others, who are of a kindlier disposition still, and who are not hostile to the polish which a civilisation can confer on men, would be satisfied if they could transform us into *constitutional* Chinamen, atheist to all practical purposes, enlightened and free old gentlemen, sitting for centuries amongst our flower-beds in our yellow robes, whiling away our days in a wellbeing which has spread to the masses, having invented all things and discovered all things, peacefully vegetating amidst all the progress which has been accomplished, carried in the train like a parcel merely to go from Canton to the Great Wall to discuss with another business man of the Celestial Empire a piece of marshland which has to be drained, or a canal which is to be cut. In either hypothesis, American or Chinese, I should be thankful to have departed this world before such felicity befell me.

There is one final suggestion: it could happen that, as a result of the total deterioration of the human character, the peoples of the world would be content to make do with what they have got: love of gold would take the place of a love of their independence, while kings would barter their love of power for love of the civil list. A compromise would thus be reached between monarchs and their subjects, who would be delighted to fawn upon them without let or hindrance in a bastard political order; all men would display their infirmities in front of each other, as they used to do in the old lazar houses, or as sick people do today, when they take mudbaths as a cure for their ailments; mankind would flounder in unmitigated mud after the fashion of a peaceable reptile.

It is, nevertheless, a mere waste of time at the present stage of our development to desire to replace intellectual pleasures by the delights of physical nature. These latter, as we can well imagine, filled the lives of the aristocratic peoples of antiquity; masters of the world, they possessed palaces and vast numbers of slaves; their estates comprised whole regions of Africa. But under which porticoes can you wander now, in your rare moments of leisure? In which huge and ornate baths can you find nowadays the perfumes and flowers, the flute-players and courtesans of Ionia? You cannot be Heliogabulus[1] for the asking. Where would you lay hands on the necessary treasure for these material delights? The spirit is frugal, but the body is extravagant.

And now, to be more serious, a few words on the question of absolute equality: such an equality would mean a return not only to bodily slavery, but to spiritual slavery; for it would mean nothing less than the destruction of the moral and physical inequality of the individual. Our wills, controlled and supervised by all, would witness the atrophy of our faculties. The infinite, for example, is part of our very nature; if you forbid our intelligence, or even our passions, to dream of unbounded prosperity, you reduce a man to the level of a snail and you metamorphose him into a machine. For make no mistake, if we cannot hope to penetrate the ultimate, if we do not believe in eternal life, there is annihilation everywhere; no man is free if he does not possess any property of his own; a man who has no property cannot be independent, he becomes a member of the proletariat or he works for a wage, whether he live within our present system of private property, or in a future one of communal property. Property held in common would mean that our society would be like one of those monasteries which used to distribute bread to the needy at the gates. Property which we hold inviolate from our fathers is our means of personal defence; property really means the same thing as

---

[1] Roman Emperor, b. 204 A.D. Reigned from 218-222. The prototype of dissolute and pleasure-loving youth.

H

liberty. *Absolute equality*, which presupposes *complete submission* to this *equality*, would make us revert to the most wretched servitude; it would make of individual man a beast of burden, submitting to his bonds and obliged to walk endlessly along the same path.

. . . Enlightened people cannot understand why a Catholic such as I should so obstinately take my stand in the shadow of what they think are ruins; according to them, it is bravado on my part, or prejudice. But for pity's sake, tell me where I could find a family or a God in the individualistic and philosophical society which you propose for my acceptance ? Tell me, and I will follow you; if you cannot, do not take it amiss if I lay myself down in the tomb of Christ, the only refuge you left me when you abandoned me.

No, it is not out of bravado: I am sincere; my conclusion is this: that out of all the plans and studies I have made, and after all my experiences, there only remains a complete disillusionment with all the preoccupations of this world. As my religious convictions developed, they absorbed all my other convictions; no man here on earth is a more faithful Christian, or more sceptical in the things of this world, than I. Far from being exhausted, the religion of the Liberator is just entering its third phase, the political phase of *liberty, equality* and *fraternity*. The Gospel—that verdict of acquittal—has not yet been proclaimed to all men; we have progressed no further than the maledictions pronounced by Christ: Woe to you who weigh men down with burdens too heavy to be borne, and who would not touch them with the tips of your fingers!

The Christian religion, stable in its dogmas, is yet mobile in its inspiration; as it develops, it transforms the whole world. When it has reached its highest point, darkness will finally be made light; liberty, crucified on Calvary with the Messiah, will descend from the Cross with Him; it will put back into the hands of the nations that New Testament which was written for their benefit, and the message of which has hitherto been fettered. Governments will pass, moral evil will pass and the renewal will announce the consummation of the centuries of death and oppression which started with the Fall.

When will this longed for day dawn ? When will society be reorganised according to the secret ways of the principle of generation ? No man can tell; the resistance which human passions will offer cannot be measured.

Death will more than once engulf the peoples in torpor and

will enshroud events in silence, as the snow fallen in the night deadens the noise of the wagon. Nations do not develop as rapidly as the individuals who comprise them, and do not disappear so quickly. How long it takes to find out the meaning of a certain event! The Byzantine Empire believed that its agony would be prolonged for ever; the Christian era, already so long drawn out, has still not seen the abolition of slavery. Such considerations do not, I am aware, suit the French temperament; we have never admitted the element of time in our revolutions: that is why we have always been dumbfounded at the results, which were the opposite of what we so impatiently desired. Young men hurl themselves into the fray, animated by generous courage; with their eyes on the ground, they climb towards the heights which they can dimly see and which they struggle to attain: nothing is more admirable; but they will waste their lives in these attempts and when they have reached the allotted span and piled error upon error, they will impose on succeeding generations by bestowing the burden of their disillusionment upon them, which they in turn will carry to neighbouring graves; and so on. The times of the desert have returned; Christianity starts afresh in the sterility of the Thebaid, amidst a formidable idolatry, the idolatry of man for himself.

History has two sequels, one which is both immediate and instantly recognised, the other which is more distant and not immediately perceived. They are often mutually contradictory, for one derives from our brief human wisdom and the other from the eternal wisdom. The providential event appears after the human event. God is seen to have worked through the actions of men. Deny as much as you please the supreme purpose, refuse to acknowledge its action, quarrel over words, name what the vulgar call Providence the force of circumstances, or reason—observe what the result of a certain course of action was and you will see that the opposite of what was intended invariably came to pass, if it was not primarily based on standards of morality and justice.

If Heaven has not pronounced its final decree; if a future is to come into being which will be both strong and free, this future is still very distant, far beyond our present horizon; we can only attain it with the help of that Christian hope whose wings extend ever wider, as all things appear to betray it, a hope which is more lasting than time itself and stronger than disaster.

IV. HONORÉ DE BALZAC

1799 - 1850

An account of Balzac's life and even a short appreciation of his immense achievement would be out of place here. Studies of the great novelist's art abound in every language, as do anecdotes on the great eccentric. He has even sometimes been introduced as a moralist and author of aphorisms.

None the less, Balzac is little known as a defender of the Faith. Despite the Preface to his *Human Comedy*, in which he describes himself as an author " definitely on the side of Bossuet and the Vicomte de Bonald," and in which he expressly states that he wrote on human society " in the light of the spiritual truth of the Church and the social truth of the Monarchy "; despite his declarations of faithful attachment to the elder branch of the Bourbons under Louis Philippe and the Second Republic, not a few critics have tried to prove that various contrary philosophies can just as well be derived from the *Human Comedy*—a utilitarian Liberalism, which encourages unlimited speculation for material gain, or a Socialism or a Communism, which unmasks the corruption and the inner rottenness of the rich ruling classes. Sometimes even Catholic critics—Ferdinand Brunetière, for example, whom some people considered to be the official Catholic voice in literary criticism round about 1900, and whom few care to read today—advanced the opinion that the often-quoted appraisal of " the two great truths, the Church and the Monarchy " is more vocal in the Preface to the *Human Comedy* than it is borne out in the novels, in which the reader may easily find a lesson of immorality.

Again, Balzac has often been claimed as a master and precursor by schools far removed from Catholic spirituality: by Flaubert and the Brothers Goncourt, as a master of minute observation and description; by the numerous commentators and critics of Sainte-Beuve's school, as the prophet of scepticism, and able exposer of " conventional values "; even by Zola and the " Naturalists," as the precursor of the " photographic " novel, which largely owes its success to the needless accumulation of unsuppressed filth. The most combative and fearless Catholic critics of Balzac's period and of French society as a whole did not altogether accept the author of the *Human Comedy* as one of their own. In his *Literary Confessions*, Louis Veuillot is not too favourable to Balzac. He places him above his imitators, but is hardly prepared to exonerate him from the suspicion of being a literary exploiter of the commercial possibilities of a well-described social corruption, and he praises him mainly for stopping short at mere discreet allusion, where Eugène Sue would have given a prolonged exhibition of bad taste and cynicism.

Still, the whole case of Balzac is perhaps wrongly placed on this plane of good taste and decency, to which a great part of contemporary criticism reduced it. Balzac is somewhat outside this central concern of aesthetics, just as the moral lesson of his world is outside the classic concern of ethics. This most strange and curious world of his imagination has few, perhaps no characters which are symbolic of moral virtues. Indeed, he would have been the last to defend his invented world on moral grounds, and the last to claim to be a teacher of good ways by inventing good examples, or by a consoling and redeeming and extenuated representation of historical and social reality. Balzac did not compose a world of essentially good men, accidentally corrupted by society, such as the fictitious Citizen of Jean-Jacques Rousseau. He did not plead the mysterious and unexplored laws of pathological heredity as an explanation of vice, and an excuse for it, like Zola. His most monumental convict, Vautrin, is not a half-innocent victim like Victor Hugo's Jean Valjean. He is a hardened criminal, capable of one virtue only, a frank and cynical appreciation of the ambition of others, and of one sacrifice, to support the ambition of those men whose minds and will he is prepared to recognise as superior to his own.

For it is this very harshness, this lack of any emotional element or sentimentality, that brought Balzac close to the Church. He had shown a world which was without hope—except for the Redemption. A society which was lost—except for the infinite wisdom of the first Principle ruling it. A contemporary society which was rotten, composed of men who were capable of doing anything—except to strive after the ultimate social truth, which an infinite and almighty wisdom had placed beyond their devilish and devastating power, by sending them, not apostles and priests, whom they would once more have scorned and in the end martyred, but bad priests, who, in the shape of the unholy trio, Talleyrand, Fouché and Siéyès, saved France from the French, their hidden theological intelligence giving them the gift of statesmanship, although their sinful hearts refused the milder gifts of Christ. (*Une Ténébreuse Affaire*.) The ambition of a Napoleon and the intelligence of the three bad priests saved France from the dissolution and anarchy which was produced by the complacent sentimentality of Rousseau's followers. Balzac was ultimately on the side of a God who saves men, not because of their merits, but because He is infinitely more wise and generous than men are. If Balzac sometimes failed to be touched by the compassion of the Son, he did not fail to pay trembling respect to the Father, nor to proclaim in humble admiration the wisdom and the firmness of the Holy Ghost as man's surest guide.

The redeeming feature in Balzac's mankind is its Secret, a word used with a capital letter in Balzac's sense. The uncommon man differs from the rabble because he has a Secret: the secret knowledge of the law governing the world. Balzac saw the Church as the depositary of wisdom. Wickedness is stupid, although he thought—and this may be a dangerous doctrine indeed—that wisdom itself has no choice but to fight wickedness by evil means. Christ never appeared to Balzac otherwise than as the Judge of the Last Day, of iron firmness, like the vigorous, bare-armed figure painted by Michelangelo on the wall of the Sistine Chapel. Perhaps because he saw the shrewdness of the serpent too clearly and praised it too often, Balzac was too inclined to forget the gentleness of the dove, which should always take precedence over the serpent for those who follow the evangelical precept. But if there are dangerous precepts which could be derived from the philosophy underlying Balzac's art, let us not have the slightest doubt on his firm and unmistakable adherence to the Catholic order of values and Catholic reasoning. He often described moral and even physical filth at great length, just like Zola and the naturalists who came after him. But he put it into its right sphere, into the sphere of the grotesque and the comic (*Les Contes drôlatiques*, or the description of the boarding-house in the Rue Neuve Ste. Geneviève in *Père Goriot*). He was not the father of Zola, but the son of Rabelais. Not the finest spiritual ancestry, to be sure, and no guarantee against grossness and even a streak of vulgarity.

We need not idealise either Balzac or Rabelais. Rabelais was a scandalous friar, who ran away from his monastery, which would have been wiser to chase him away in time, and what he wrote was of course not intended to be an auxiliary of the Daily Missal, or a companion-book for readers of the *Imitation*. An avowed spiritual descent from Rabelais does not put Balzac necessarily among the guides to good religion and good morals. Yet, may we not argue that a *healthy* faith is better than " good religion," for the very reason that it is a more definite and precise term? " Religion " may be vague, may stand in danger of being " a " religion, or even of degenerating into " some sort of religion," " the religious need of mankind," and like things that we hear from doubtful quarters today. Faith, however, does not tolerate misunderstanding. A man believes, and then he is ready to sacrifice intellect to belief, or the belief is missing, and the lack of it deprives a man of all the gifts of the intellect. Balzac believed in the primacy of the gifts conferred by Faith. Much as he thought intellect to be a supreme agent in history and in human action, his search was for the Absolute, not for " lost time," not for subtle observation and not for good social guidance, as did his decadent imitators of later generations. Faith stood in the same relation for him to the intellect, as Charity stood to Faith for St. Paul.

SOCIETY AND THE INDIVIDUAL

I[1]

Man is neither good nor bad. He is born with certain instincts and aptitudes. Society, far from corrupting him, as Rousseau says, perfects him. But self-interest brings out his evil propensities also, and Catholicism is the *only* complete system which represses the vicious tendencies in man. Hence it is the greatest element in social order.

Every thinking man must march under the banner of Christ! He alone consecrated the triumph of spirit over matter; He alone revealed in practical terms the intermediate world which separates us from God.

Christianity created the nations of the modern world; it will preserve them.

Nations can only achieve long life by husbanding their vitality. In this the life of society resembles the life of a man. Education, or rather up-bringing, by the religious bodies is therefore the great principle on which the existence of nations depends.

Crimes which are of a purely moral order and escape human justice are the vilest and the most hateful of all. . . . God often punishes them on earth. Herein lies the explanation of those dreadful misfortunes which seem incomprehensible to us.

Any moral regeneration which does not spring from a deep religious feeling, and which is not pursued within the bosom of the Church, rests on foundations of sand. All the practices prescribed in such detail by Catholicism, and which meet with so little comprehension, are so many breakwaters indispensable to withstand the storms of the Evil One.

---

[1] Extracts from Balzac's *Maximes et Pensées,* collected and edited by Barbey d'Aurevilly.

The cult of a religion lies in its form, and societies only exist by their form: the national colours and the Cross.

Have you noticed the deep sense of security in the true priest, when he has given himself to God, listens to His voice and strives to be a submissive instrument in the hands of Providence ? . . . There is neither vanity nor pride left in him, nor anything which, to those in the world, is a continual source of offence. His tranquillity is as complete as that of the fatalist and his resignation helps him to endure all things.

All the religious who were forced to leave their monasteries by the Revolution and who engaged in politics have proved, by the coolness of their demeanour and their reserve, the superiority which ecclesiastical discipline confers on all the children of the Church, even on those who desert her.

Patriotism only inspires transitory sentiments. Religion gives them a permanent character. Patriotism is a momentary forgetfulness of self-interest, whilst Christianity is a complete system of opposition to the corrupt tendencies in man.

Christianity is a perfect system which combats the corrupt tendencies in man and absolutism is a complete system which controls the divergent interests of society. Each one is necessary to the other. Without Catholicism the law has no sword to defend it, and we see the result of this today.

Protestants have done as much harm to art as they have done to the political body.

That man amongst us who makes the most fun of his religion in Paris would not abjure it in Constantinople.

The Virgin Mary (even if we only consider her as a symbol) eclipses in her greatness all Hindoo, Egyptian or Greek prototypes. Virginity, the mother of great things, *magna rerum parens*, holds the key to higher worlds in her fair white hands. In short, this grandiose and terrible exception deserves all the honours which the Catholic Church bestows upon her.

In the Protestant faith, there is nothing woman can do after her fault, whilst in the Catholic Church, the hope of forgiveness makes her sublime.

Suicide ought to be the final word of unbelieving societies.

When it beheaded Louis XVI, the Revolution beheaded in his person all fathers of families. The family no longer exists today; there are only individuals. When they wanted to become a nation, Frenchmen gave up the idea of being an empire. By proclaiming the equal division of the father's property, they killed the family spirit and created the tax-gatherer mentality! On the other hand they paved the way for the weakening of the better elements, and the blind impulses of the masses, the extinction of the arts, the reign of self-interest, and opened up the path to conquest.

The family! I repudiate the family in a society which, on the death of the father or mother, divides up the property and tells each member to go his own way. The family is a temporary and fortuitous association, which is dissolved immediately by death. Our laws have broken up our homes, our inheritance, and the perennial value of example and tradition. I see only ruins around us.

The march of civilisation and the wellbeing of the masses depends on three men: the priest, the doctor and the judge; these are the three authorities who can immediately make people conscious of the interplay of actions, interests and principles—the three great consequences brought about in a nation by events, property and ideas.

With the advent of Luther, the question at stake was not the reformation of the Church, but rather the undefined liberty of man, which means the death of all authority.

Authority can only come from above or from below. To attempt to find it half-way is to want to make nations walk on their belly, to lead them by the lowest interest of all, individualism.

There are no more than fifty or sixty dangerous men in a nation, whose minds are on a level with their ambition. The secret of government is to know who these men are, so that they can either be executed or bought.

A feudal aristocracy can be subdued by cutting off a few heads, but a hydra with a thousand heads cannot be subdued. No, unimportant people are not crushed; they are too flat under the feet!

When Europe is no more than a drifting herd of men, she will have no leaders and will be devoured by uncouth conquerors. Twenty times has the world presented us with this sight. Europe will repeat the process. Ideas eat up the centuries as men are eaten up by their passions. . . . When man is cured, humanity will be able to cure itself perhaps; but will man ever be cured ? . . .

The prophecy of the eagle plucked by diplomacy will be fulfilled before the eyes of a selfish generation, lacking in all religious sentiment, which is the principle of resistance, in patriotism, which has been destroyed by revolutions, and in fidelity to an oath, which is a peculiarly monarchical principle.

There are in the world countries which are no longer defended by their peoples: countries where individuals are no longer linked together and where *nationality* is replaced by *personality*. M. Lainé[1] has said: " Kings are disappearing." He might have added: Nations are advancing, but they advance from North to South. People who like to lie peacefully in their beds at night say: " Our industry is flourishing, our arms are equal to the enemy and nations do not easily let themselves be swallowed up." Does anybody think by chance that the invasions of the Goths, Franks and Saxons did not find flourishing industries and armed nations barring their way ? The interests of the fourth century were the same as those of the nineteenth. Only they took a different shape, and the barbarians found themselves faced by rival interests, just as we see today.

The day will come when people will say to each other: " Why not the Czar ? " as once they said: " Why not the Duke of Orleans ? " People do not care much about anything nowadays (1840). In fifty years time they will not care about anything at all.

If the Press did not exist, it would not be necessary to invent it.

[1] Vicomte de Lainé, Minister of the Interior under Louis XVIII, a leading Parliamentarian of the Constitutional Royalists and opponent of the " ultras."

We all know that newspapers outstrip kings in ingratitude, the shadiest business enterprise in speculation and cunning, and that they destroy our intelligence with the mental raw spirits which they sell us every morning; but all of us write in them, like those people who exploit a quicksilver mine, knowing that they will meet their death thereby.

There was once a journalist who confessed to having written the same article every day for twelve years. His now celebrated confession makes us smile, but ought on the contrary to make us shiver. Does not a mason always strike at the same spot with his pick-axe, in order to demolish a particularly fine building ?

II[1]

IN order to destroy the principle of authority, the new political doctrines (an absurd phrase, since authority can only take one of two forms: aristocracy or democracy) claim that systems are born and grow, that a total philosophy would be an absolute science and an impossibility. This assertion is made by people who talk nonsense about free-will and liberty. The doctrine of authority is complete and final.

There is no absolute authority in the universe. The only absolute authority which the imagination has been able to conceive, the authority of God, works according to rules which He has imposed upon Himself. He can destroy all His worlds and return to His rest, but while He allows them to exist, they continue to be governed by the laws which together create order.

Politically speaking, man is the basis of society. It would be a mistake not to understand by man, three people: a man, his wife and child. " Man " means " family."

When man existed in a primitive state, did he live alone ? This question is very important, for many philosophers, in fact all who have wanted to apply their theories on man to society, and their theories on society to religion, have first begun by examining man in his primitive state, to find out whether he was naturally good or bad, and whether society corrupted or perfected him.

Hobbes said: Man is born bad and society perfects him.

[1] Extracts from the unfinished *Catéchisme Social*.

J. J. Rousseau said: Man is born good and society corrupts him. Religion says: Man is born with the stain of original sin and religion helps him to curb all his passions, so that he may be made worthy of God, Who holds the secret of his destiny.

Imagine a fight between five Iroquis, a hundred leagues away from their own country, and five Mohicans. They have had nothing to eat for many days. The Iroquis kill a Mohican and remain masters of the field and of the enemy; they proceed to eat their prisoner.

It is an easy step to make a custom out of something which was done once out of necessity. Custom can engender abuse, just as it can in Society. The aim of religion is to curb bad desires and inculcate good ones. Religion comprises the whole of society. If it were not a divine institution, it would be a human necessity.

Men have always wanted to discover the laws which govern society in nature, but when we observe the laws of nature carefully, we find that they provide a complete justification for the social laws, such as every society has always imagined them to be, and which prove that Equality is the most terrible illusion.

The earth has no exact geometrical limits and cannot be separated from the surrounding atmosphere. It has been proved that none of her products, neither man, animal, nor plants, could survive without this girdle of air, which determines their food, their physical shape and their species.

Hence, nature has given all its earthly creations the *right* to live on this sphere, the *right* to draw from it the elementary substances which they need. Here we have a complete picture of social rights. Social rights, taken in the broadest sense, really mean the right to moral and physical life, in a given environment and in a given place, the whole regulated by a network of customs. The analogy is not only an exact one; it is perfect.

What do we see as the result of the natural and visible law which governs the creatures of the earth, and allows them to develop in these atmospheric conditions ? The most striking inequality, and a variety of species which is the signal beauty of the universe.

Man's free-will lies at the heart of any problem of his liberty. If man has no free-will, the question of his liberty does not arise. The problem is no longer whether he should be allowed to gratify every whim, but what society allows him to do. If

nature has set limits to man's action, instead of giving him unlimited powers, and confines this action within a ruthless circle,
society is not under a greater obligation to its citizens than man
is to nature.

Free-will means then in its truest sense the power a man
possesses to do what he likes, without any let or hindrance, and
without being influenced in his decision by any moral or
physical law.

Industry attracts workmen, and concentrates them in centres
where they are not able to produce any food. Industry, while
it doubles the population, does not increase agricultural
products two-fold; on the contrary, by forcing up the price of
labour, it forces up the price of food. A clash between industry
and agriculture is inevitable, for industry, which is up against
competition, wants food to be cheap, so that the cost of labour
may fall, while agriculture cannot afford to sell food at prices
below cost. This is a problem which modern politics finds
insoluble.

The poverty of a certain section of the population is not only
a reproach to a government, it is an indictment which will
bring about its fall. When the numbers of the oppressed pass a
certain limit, and they see how many rich people there are in
the world, revolution soon breaks out. All revolutions depend
on a leader, and on a contingency which suddenly precipitates
it; every contingency has a leader, since every leader knows
how to engineer the necessary contingency.

Religion is based on an innate sentiment in man, which is a
universal phenomenon; no uncivilised peoples, tribes, hordes
of savages, or men in a state of nature, have ever been discovered, who did not have a faith of some sort. This emotion,
inborn in man, is the mine which has been exploited by all the
philosophies of the world, and which has furnished them with
weapons against the so-called sensualist and materialist schools
of thought, etc. . . .

This sentiment, which is so strong in peoples who lived
nearest in time to the disaster known as the Flood, pre-supposes
a fall, a punishment, the result of a battle, a decline in the
knowledge of a superior being and an angry victor.

The scientific knowledge which we possess today, thanks to
progress and the indefatigable human brain, corroborates this
feeling in man. Mammoth creatures belonging to the early life

of the earth have now disappeared. Earth itself has perhaps fallen and become detached from a hierarchy of superior worlds. It has certainly undergone modification. Material science has vindicated the idea of religion, which is the common basis of all societies: in other words, divine revelation. The idea of reparation is almost universally accepted also.

These two general ideas, common to man, or this divine revelation, are at the root of Christianity. These findings, this conclusion of history, are beyond dispute. Whether God co-exists in the world, or is separated from His creation, whether He exists in Himself and for Himself, or is indissolubly linked to His creation or not, we can see that a part of that creation has been vitiated and punished, and while it has not been withdrawn from the whole, it has been condemned to undergo modification and purification, before it returns to the general stream.

Hence humanity can journey from worse to better (or from better to worse, if the globe has a life of its own, for it is going towards its death). Humanity has a future, and man likewise.

It is dangerous for man and for society to lose sight of these points. They contain the idea of obedience, which is fundamental to any society.

Catholicism is the most perfect religion of all, because it condemns the discussion of questions on which the Church has pronounced judgement, and because the Church admits those time-honoured practices of religious observance, which thereby bring us nearer to God. The fate which the various heresies have brought on Europe is an argument in favour of Catholicism. Revelation is always present within the bosom of the Church; it is restricted in the heretical sects.

When authority comes from the people it is vacillating; when it comes from God it is steadfast. It is either beyond all question, or it is no authority at all. Such is the lesson of history.

V. FRIEDRICH VON SCHLEGEL

1772 - 1829

FRIEDRICH VON SCHLEGEL, poet, historian and translator of Shakespeare, together with his brother August-Wilhelm, the poet and philosopher Friedrich von Hardenberg (better known under his pseudonym, Novalis), Clemens Brentano, and Count Friedrich Stolberg—these are the Germans of the period who, as the result of the French wars, the Napoleonic conquests and the fall of the last remnants of the Empire, moved towards the eternal and central light of European history and culture, and who gave a Christian and European meaning to a belated German Renaissance. Certainly none of them is a major teacher of the Church, fighting the aesthetic-pantheist heresy of the nineteenth century (which was mainly German) in the sense that St Augustine fought the Manichean heresy, or St Thomas the Albigensians. All the same, the German convert thinkers of the Napoleonic era, by the very fact of their conversion, took up the struggle against all the perils of agnostic deviation from a firm system of truth, against the trend in German philosophy which reached its fullest expression in Hegel's dialectics, against all the pitfalls of a " historicism " which confuses all standards by its pantheism.

It was a Protestant historian, the Swiss Johannes von Müller, who first showed, with great brilliance and learning, that the law of Europe governing the relations between the individual states was originally laid down by the Papacy, and that the European concept of personal liberty is inseparable from the law of Christian morality. It was a Protestant publicist, the Prussian Friedrich von Gentz (who later became an Austrian, for some decades the theoretical organ of Metternich's policy), who showed the dogmatic—ultimately the theological—character of the common law of Europe. But the last consequences of the principles laid down by German political thinkers in the struggle against Napoleon were drawn by such Germans who, in the critical years of Napoleon's rise to hegemony, placed their hopes in Catholic Austria. For some years, Vienna was the centre of German thought and the German awakening. Johannes von Müller (born in Switzerland) and Friedrich von Gentz (born in Prussia) spent the most important years of their lives in the Imperial city, the birth-place of the " Romantic " school of thought and of art.

The central figure of the Vienna circle was a priest and preacher who, less than a hundred years after his death in 1820, became a canonised saint of the Church, the Redemptorist Father Clemens Hofbauer, whose Congregation, for forty years, replaced the dissolved Society of Jesus. From all parts of the German-speaking world, converts came to Vienna, the philosophers of a re-Christianised Europe: Zacharias Werner, Adam Müller and many other outstanding scholars and writers, some of whom were not only received into the Church, but even followed the priestly vocation among the Redemptorists of Father Hofbauer.

The following pages of Friedrich von Schlegel were written in 1827. They form the epilogue to his *Lectures on the Philosophy of History*, given in Vienna some twenty years earlier. Between these lectures and the epilogue, important events occurred in Schlegel's life: his failure to persuade his brother August-Wilhelm to follow him into the Church; his disappointment over Goethe's hostility to the " romantic " tendency and to Catholicism. There were also the years he spent on Metternich's staff at the State Chancellery of Austria, and his journey to Rome in 1819 in the Chancellor's company in connection with important negotiations with Pope Pius VII and Cardinal Consalvi. The close links which existed between Metternich and Friedrich von Schlegel allow us to consider the pages that follow as the foremost document of the political theory of a whole era of German and European history.

THE REGENERATION OF CHRISTIAN STATES AND NATIONS[1]

THERE are, in the history of the eighteenth century, many phenomena which occurred so suddenly, so instantaneously, and were so contrary to all expectation, that although on deeper consideration we may discover their efficient causes in the past, in the natural state of things and in the general situation of the world, yet there are many circumstances which prove that there was a deliberate, although secret, preparation of events, as indeed has been actually demonstrated in many instances. I must now say a few words on this secret and mysterious branch of illuminism, and on the progress it made during the period of its influence, and show the influence of this principle, both in regard to the origin and general spirit of the revolution (which in its fanaticism believed itself to be a regeneration of the world) and in regard to the true restoration

[1] Friedrich von Schlegel: *Lectures on the Philosophy of History* (Lecture XVIII). Translated from the German by James Burton Robertson, London, Henry G. Bohn, 1846 (slightly revised).

of society founded on the basis of Christian justice. One circumstance, however, is peculiar to this historical enquiry, that
those who could best speak from their personal experience cannot always be considered the most reliable eye-witnesses; for
we never know, or can know, what their particular views and
interests may lead them to say, or conceal, or suppress. However,
it has so happened that, in the universal convulsion and overthrow of society, many things have come to light on this
mysterious and esoteric clue in modern history—things which,
when combined together, furnish us with a not incorrect and
reasonably complete idea of this mighty element of the Revolution, and of illuminism both true and false, which has exercised so evident and varied an influence on the world.

As to the origin of this esoteric influence, the impartial
enquirer cannot doubt that the order of Templars was the
channel by which this society in its ancient and long-preserved
form was introduced into the West. The religious *Masonic*
symbols may be explained by the traditions of Solomon connected with the very foundation of the order of Templars; and
indeed the existence of these symbols may be traced in other
passages of Holy Writ, and in other parts of sacred history, and
they may very well admit of a Christian interpretation. Traces
of these symbols may be found in the monuments of the old
German architecture of the Middle Ages. Any secret spiritual
association however, spread simultaneously amongst Christians
and Mahometans, cannot be of a very Christian nature, nor long
remain so. Indeed, the very idea of an esoteric society for the
propagation of any secret doctrines is not compatible with the
very principle of Christianity itself; for Christianity is a divine
mystery, which according to the intention of its divine Founder
lies open to all, and is daily exposed on every altar. For this
reason, in a Revelation imparted to all alike, there can be no
secrecy, as in the pagan mysteries, where, side by side with
popular mythology and the public religion of the State, certain
esoteric doctrines were inculcated amongst the initiated alone.
This would be to constitute a church within a church—a
measure to be as little tolerated or justified as an *imperium in
imperio*; and in an age where worldly interests and public or
secret views of policy carry far more weight than religious
opinions or sentiments, such a secret parasitical church would
unquestionably, as experience has already proved, be very soon
transformed into a secret directory for political changes and
revolutions. That in this society the unchristian principles of a

I

negative illuminism, disguised as they often were into sentiments of universal philanthropy, were reasonably modern in
date, all historical analogies would lead us to suppose. On the
other hand, the Christian opinions which survived in this order
(although in our day the adherents to Christian principles form
a minority in our society, agitated as it is by the quarrels of in-
numerable factions) assumed, in conformity with the historical
origin I have described, more of an oriental and Gnostic
character. The great, or at least not inconsiderable influence
which this society exercises in politics, we may discover in those
revolutions which, after having convulsed our part of the globe,
have rolled onwards to the New World, where the two principal
revolutionary factions in one of those South American states
whose troubles are not yet at an end, are called the Scots and the
Yorkists, from the two parties which divide the English Masonic
lodges. Who does not know, or who does not remember, that
the ruler of the world in the period we have just lived through
made use of this vehicle in all the countries he conquered, to
delude and deceive the nations with false hopes ? And on this
account he was styled by his followers the man of his age and,
in fact, he was a slave to the spirit of his age. A society from
whose bosom, as from the secret laboratory of Revolution, the
Illuminés, the Jacobins and the Carbonari have successively
proceeded, cannot possibly be termed, or in fact be, very beneficial to mankind, politically sound, or truly Christian in its
views and tendency. Still, I must observe here, that it has been
the fate of the oldest of all secret societies to have its venerable
forms, which are known to all the initiated, made a cloak for
every new conspiracy. In the next place, we must not forget
that this order itself appears to be split and divided into a multitude of different sects and factions; and on this account we
must not suppose that all those fearful aberrations and wild
excesses of impiety, all those openly destructive or secretly
undermining principles of revolution were universally approved
by this society. On the contrary, such a supposition would be
utterly false, or at least very exaggerated. A glance at all the
highly estimable characters, mistaken only on this one point—
most distinguished and illustrious personages in the eighteenth
century, who were members of this association—would be
sufficient to remove, or at least materially to modify, this
sweeping censure. From many indications, we may consider it
certain, or at least extremely probable, that in no country did
this esoteric society harmonise so well with the State and the

whole established order of things as in that country where all the conflicting elements of morals and society are combined in a sort of strange and artificial balance—I mean England. If now we turn our attention to the continent of Europe, and even to those countries which were the chief theatre of the Revolution, we shall see that there, among many other factions, a Christian party had sprung up in this society, a party which, although it formed a very small minority in point of numbers, possessed by its profounder doctrines and the interesting fragments of ancient tradition it had preserved, a great moral ascendancy; and this, many historical facts and many written documents which have since been published place beyond the shadow of a doubt. Instead of mentioning the names of some German writers less generally known, I prefer to quote in confirmation of what I have said the example of a French writer who is typical of the internal and more hidden character of the revolution. The Christian theosophist St Martin, who was a disciple of this school, stands quite apart in his age from the other organs of the then prevailing atheistic philosophy. He was, however, a most decided revolutionary (yet at the same time a disinterested fanatic whose conduct was entirely guided by high moral motives) because of his utter contempt and abhorrence for the whole moral and political system of Europe as it then stood—a contempt in which, if we cannot entirely agree with him, we cannot in many instances withhold from him at least a sort of negative approval; and secondly, he was a revolutionary by reason of his enthusiastic belief in a complete Christian regeneration of society, conceived it is true according to his own views, or the views of his party. Among the French writers of the Restoration, no one has so thoroughly understood this remarkable philosopher and so well understood how to appreciate him in all the depths of his errors, as well as in the many excellent things which his writings contain, as Count de Maistre.

This secret clue in the history of the revolution must not be overlooked, if we desire to form a due estimate of its character; for it greatly contributed to the illusion of a great many by no means ill-intentioned persons, who saw, or wished to see, in the revolution merely the inevitable and necessary, although in its origin harsh and severe, regeneration of Christian states and nations, which had then gone so far astray from their original course. This illusory notion of a false restoration of society was particularly prevalent during the imperial rule of that extraordinary man whose true biography—I mean the high moral law of his destiny, or the theological key to his life—still seems to exceed the critical powers of our age. Seven years were allotted to him for the growth of his power, for fourteen years the world was delivered up into his hands; and seven years were left him for solitary reflection, the first of which he misused by embroiling the world anew. On the use he made of the extraordinary power that had been granted him, of that formidable dominion which had fallen to his lot, history has long ago pronounced sentence. Never is it permitted to exercise such power, unless it is in a period of some awful reckoning to which it leads, for the purpose of a still more fearful probation of mankind. But if his restoration—that is to say, the restoration which his infatuated supporters attributed to him—was most certainly a false one, the question naturally occurs whether the restoration which his successors attempted to effect has been perfectly sound, or at least quite complete; and what are the defects in the new system and how can they be remedied ?

A mere treaty of territorial adjustments could not, and never can, constitute a great religious and international pacification of the whole of Europe. The re-establishment of subverted thrones, the restoration of exiled sovereigns and dynasties will not in themselves have any security or permanence, unless they are based on moral principles and maxims. After the severe and unexpected lesson which was again inflicted upon Europe, religion was at last made the basis of European policy; and we must not make it a matter of reproach that this principle still retained so indefinite a character; for this was necessary, at least in the beginning, in order to remove any misconception, or any possible suspicion of interested views. And not only does the stability and future existence of the whole Christian and civilised world depend on this bond of religious confederation —which we can only hope will be ever more and more firmly knit—but each individual great power is especially called upon to play its part. That the moral strength and stability of the Russian empire mainly depends on religion, that every departure from its sacred spirit must have the most fatal effects on its whole system, has already been stated by her late monarch, distinguished alike in adversity and in prosperity, and is an axiom of State policy, which can hardly ever be forgotten again. But in that country, where the elements of Protestantism (to use that word in its most comprehensive sense) obtained such weight at the outset of its literary refinement, and are incorporated to such a degree into the whole political system of the State, the toleration extended to every form of worship should not be withheld from that Church which is the mother-Church of the rest of Europe, including Poland; nor should the religious liberty of individuals be in that respect at all restricted.

It is equally evident that in that country of Europe where monarchy has been restored, the restoration of religion must go hand in hand with that of monarchy, and that the latter would lose all security if the former were removed. In the peace-loving monarchy of Austria, unchangeably attached as she is to her ancient principles, religion, rather than any other principle, has always been the recognised basis of her existence. As to the fifth Germanico-European monarchy of Prussia, recently created, the solid maintenance of religion is the only means of allaying the disquiet inevitably caused by such a State, and of securing its future existence. Any act of even indirect hostility towards the Catholic body—one half of the nation—any infringement of the liberty of individuals in that sacred concern —a liberty which must be guaranteed not only by the letter of the law, but by real, effective and practical measures—would not only be in complete opposition to those religious principles rapidly spreading as they are all over Europe and particularly in Germany but would violate and render insecure the great, fundamental and long-established principle of toleration, such as it has up to now been understood. It is only in England that Anglicanism has raised her doubts as to the utility of a religious fraternity among the Christian states and nations—doubts which are connected with the still exclusively character of the English constitution, and which on many occasions may lead England to a sort of schismatic rupture with the rest of Europe. On several occasions, we must regretfully note that mighty England, in the eighteenth century so brilliant and so powerful by the influence she exerted over the whole European mind, no longer seems to feel herself at home in the nineteenth century, and no longer knows where to find her place in the new order of things.

If we consider Europe as a whole, the maxims and principles of liberalism are but a partial return to the revolution—they can have no other tendency than to revolution. Liberalism will never obtain a majority among the well-thinking persons of any of the European states, except by some gross error, some singular degeneration in that party, which really does not

constitute a party and ought not to be called such—I mean the
men who in politics are attached to the monarchy, and in
religion to Christianity.

The mere principle of a mechanical balance of power, to
serve as a negative check on excessive power—a system which
emanated from England and was in the eighteenth century
universally accepted—has ceased to be applicable, or to be of
any service in the existing state of things in Europe; for all the
remedies which it can offer tend only to aggravate the evil,
when once it has occurred. In religion alone are to be found the
remedies, the safeguards, the emancipation and the consolidation of the whole civilised world, as well as of each individual
State. The most imminent danger for our age, and the possible
abuse of religion itself, are the excesses of the absolute. Great
is the danger when, in a vindictive spirit of reaction, a revolutionary conduct is adopted by the legitimist party; when
passion itself is consecrated into a maxim of reason, and held up
as the only valid and just way of proceeding; and when the
sacredness of religion itself is hawked about as if it were some
fashionable opinion; as if the world-redeeming power of faith
and truth consisted only of the dead letter and the recited formula. True life can only spring from the vivifying spirit of
eternal truth. In science, the absolute is the abyss which swal-
lows up the living truth, and leaves behind only the hollow idea
and the dead formula. In the political world, the absolute in
conduct and in speculation is that false spirit of time, opposed to
all good and to the fulness of divine truth, which in a great
measure rules the world, and may entirely rule it and lead it for
ever to its final ruin. As errors would not be dangerous or
deceptive, and would have little effect, unless they contained a
portion or an appearance of truth, this false spirit of time, which
successively assumes all forms of destruction, since it has abandoned the path of eternal truth, consists in this: it withdraws
particular facts from their historical context and holds them up
as the centre and term of a system, without any qualification
and without any regard for historical circumstances. The true
foundation and the right term of things, in the history of society
as in the lives of individuals, cannot be severed in this way from
their historical context and their place in the natural order of
events. In any speculation or enterprise conducted by this
passionate spirit of exaggeration, the living spirit must
evaporate, and only the dead and deadening formula survive.
What idols may successively be worshipped by the changing

spirit of the age, which easily jumps from one extreme to the other, cannot be determined beforehand. It is even possible that for a while eternal truth itself may be profaned and perverted to such an idol of the day—I mean the counterfeit form of truth; for the spirit of the age can never attain the inward essence and living energy of truth, even if it assumes the appearance of it. Whatever may be the alternative idol, and the reigning object of its worship, or of its passionate rhetoric, it still remains essentially the same—that is to say, the absolute, as deadening to the intellect as it is destructive to life. In science, the absolute is the idol of vain and empty systems, of dead and abstract reason.

The Christian faith has the living God and His revelation for its object, and is itself that revelation; hence, every doctrine taken from this source is something real and positive. The defence of truth against error will then only be attended by permanent success when the divine doctrine, in whatever department it may be, is represented with intellectual energy as a living principle, and at the same time is placed in its historical context, with a due regard for every other historical reality. This calm, historical judgement of things, this acute insight into subjects, whether they be real facts or intellectual phenomena, is the invariable concomitant of truth, and the indispensable condition to the full knowledge of truth. This is the more so, indeed, as religion, which forms the basis of all truth and of all knowledge, naturally follows with an attentive eye the mysterious clue of divine Providence and divine permission through the long labyrinth of human errors and human follies, both of a practical and of a speculative nature. Error, on the other hand, is always unhistorical; the spirit of the age is almost always passionate; and both, consequently, are untrue. The conflict against error cannot be brought to a prompter or more successful issue by separating, in every system of moral and speculative error, and according to the standard of divine truth, the absolute, which is the basis of such systems, into its two component parts of truth and falsehood. For when we acknowledge and point out the truth to be found in those systems there only remains error, the stupidity of which it requires little labour, little cost of time or talent, to expose and make evident to every eye. But in real life, the struggle of parties often ceases to be purely intellectual, their physical energy is displayed in violent upheavals and in proportion as all parties become absolute, so their struggle becomes one of violent and mutual destruction, a circumstance which most fatally impedes the great work of religious regeneration—the mighty problem of our age—which so far from being brought to a satisfactory conclusion is not yet even solved. In this respect, it is no doubt a critical fact, that in certain parts of Europe, nay, even in some entire countries, parties and governments should be more and more carried away by the spirit of absolutism. For this is not a question of names, and it is very evident that those parties which are called, or call themselves, absolute, are not the most so in reality; since now, as in all periods of violent party struggles, a whimsical mistake in names, a great disorder of ideas, and a Babel confusion of tongues, occur even in those languages otherwise distinguished for their clearness and precision.

. . . The dogmatic decision and definiteness of Catholic faith on the one hand, and the firmly rooted private convictions of Protestantism on the other, are very compatible with an historical judgement of historical events. Difficult as this may appear to the absolute spirit of our age, it is this very historical impartiality which must prepare the way for the complete triumph of truth and the consummate glory of Christianity. In the absolute spirit of our age and in the absolute character of its factions, there is a deep-rooted intellectual pride, which is not so much personal, or individual, as social, for it refers to the historical destiny of mankind, and of this age in particular. Actuated by this pride, a spirit exalted by moral energy or invested with external power fancies it can give a real existence to that which can only be the work of God, as from Him alone proceed all those mighty and real regenerations of the world, Christianity among them—a revolution in the high and divine sense of the word—occupying the first place; and in these plastic moments, everything is possible that man can wish or dare to hope, if, in what he adds for his own part, he does not mar in any considerable degree what the bounteous monarch of the universe pours out upon His earth from the overflow of His ineffable love. For the last three hundred years, this human pride has been at work, a pride that wishes to originate events, instead of humbly awaiting them, and of resting content with the place assigned to it among those events, and of making the best and most charitable use of those circumstances which Providence has decreed.

The idea of Illuminism is perfectly blameless, and it is unfair to pronounce on it an indiscriminate censure, and to treat it as an unqualified abuse. It was indeed a very small portion of this Illuminism of the eighteenth century that was really derived from the truths of Christianity and the pure light of Revelation. The rest was the mere work of man, consequently vain and empty, or at least defective, corrupt in parts and, on the whole, destitute of solid foundation, and therefore devoid of all permanent strength and duration.

But when once, after the complete victory of truth, the divine Reformation appears, then that human Reformation which has existed until now will sink to the ground and disappear from the world. Then, with the universal triumph of Christianity and the thorough religious regeneration of the age, the era of a true Christian *Illuminism* will dawn. This period is not perhaps so remote from our own as the natural indolence of the mind, which after every great occurrence loves to sink again into the death-sleep of ordinary life, is disposed to believe. Yet this exalted religious hope, this high historical expectation, must be coupled with great apprehension as to the full display of divine justice in the world. For how is such a religious regeneration possible, until every species, form and denomination of political idolatry is eradicated and finally extirpated from the earth?

Never was there a period that pointed so strongly, so clearly, so generally towards the future as our own. On this account, we should endeavour clearly and accurately to distinguish between what, on the one hand, man may by slow, progressive, but unwearied exertions, by the pacific adjustment of all disputed points, and by the cultivation of his intellectual qualities contribute towards the great work of the religious regeneration of government and science, and what, on the other hand, he should look for in silent awe from a higher Providence, from the new creative fiat of a last period of consummation, unable as he is to produce or call it into being. We are directed much more towards the future than the past; but in order to understand the problem of our age in all its magnitude, it is not enough to seek this social regeneration in the eighteenth century—an age in no way entitled to praise—or in the reign of Louis XIV and his times of false national glory. The birth of Christianity must be the great central point to which we must recur, not to bring back, or counterfeit the forms of past ages, which are no longer applicable to our own; but clearly to examine what has remained incomplete and what has not yet been attained. For, unquestionably, all that has been neglected in the earlier periods and stages of Christian civilisation must be made good in this true, consummate regeneration of society. If truth is to obtain a complete victory—if Christianity is really to triumph on the earth—then the State must become Christian and science must become Christian. But these two objects have never been generally or completely realised, although during the many ages in which mankind has been Christian it has struggled for the attainment of both, and though this political struggle and this intellectual aspiration form the purport of modern history. The Roman Empire, even after the true religion had become prominent, was too thoroughly and too radically corrupt to form a truly Christian State. The sound, unvitiated, natural energy of the Germanic nations seemed far better fitted for such a destiny, after they had received from Christianity a high religious consecration for this purpose. There was, if we may say so, in the interior of each State, as well as in the general system of Christendom, a most magnificent foundation laid for a truly Christian structure of government. But this groundwork remained unfinished, after the internal divisions in the State, then the divisions between Church and State, and lastly the divisions in the Church and in religion itself, had interrupted the successful beginnings of a most glorious work.

The ecclesiastical writers of the first ages furnish a solid foundation for all the future labours of Christian science; but their science does not comprehend all the branches of Christian knowledge. In the Middle Ages, undoubtedly, the foundation of a Christian science, laid down by the early Fathers, was slowly and in detail advanced; but on the whole, many hurtful influences of the time had reduced science and speculation to a very low ebb, when suddenly, in the fifteenth century, all the literary treasures of ancient Greece, and all the new discoveries in geography and in physics, were offered to philosophy. Scarcely had philosophy begun to examine these mighty stories of ancient and modern science, in order to give them a Christian form, and to appropriate them to the use of religion and modern society, when the world again broke out into disputes; and this noble beginning of a Christian philosophy was interrupted, and has since remained an unfinished fragment for a later and happier period. Such, then, is the two-fold problem of a real and complete regeneration which our age is called upon to solve; on the one hand, the further extension of Christian government and of Catholic principles of legislation, in opposition to the revolutionary spirit of the age and to the anti-Christian principle of government hitherto so exclusively prevalent; and on the other hand, the establishment of a Christian philosophy, or Catholic science. As I have already characterised the political spirit of the eighteenth century by the term Protestantism of State (taking that word in a purely philosophical sense, and not as a religious designation), a system which found its one main support in an old Catholic Empire—Austria; and as I characterised the intellectual spirit of the same age by the term Protestantism of science, a science which made the greatest progress and exerted the widest influence in another great Catholic country—France; systems in which nothing irreligious was originally intended, but which became so by their too exclusive or negative bearing: so I may here permit myself to say in like manner that the destiny of this age, the peculiar need of the nineteenth century, is the establishment of those Catholic principles of government and the general construction of a Catholic system of science. This expression is used in a purely scientific sense, and refers to all that is positively and completely religious in thought and feeling. In the certain conviction that this cannot be misunderstood in an exclusive or polemical sense, I will expressly add that this foundation of Catholic legislation for the future political existence of Europe may be laid by one, or more than one, non-Catholic power; and that I even cherish the hope that it is our own Germany, one half of which is Protestant, which more than any other country is destined to complete the fabric of Catholic science and of a true Christian philosophy in all the departments of human knowledge.

The religious hope of a true and complete regeneration of the age by a Christian system of government and a Christian system of science forms the conclusion to this Philosophy of History. The bond of a religious union between all the European states will be more closely knit and more comprehensive, in proportion as each nation advances in the work of its own religious regeneration, and carefully avoids any relapse into the old revolutionary spirit, any worship of the false idols of mistaken freedom and illusory glory, and rejects every other new form or species of political idolatry. For it is the very nature of political idolatry to lead to the mutual destruction of parties, and consequently it can never possess the elements of stability.

Philosophy, as it is the vivifying centre of all other sciences, must be the principal concern and the highest object of the labours of Christian science. Yet history, which is so closely and so variously connected with religion, must be by no means forgotten, nor must historical research be separated from philosophic speculation. On the contrary, it is the religious spirit and views already pervading the combined efforts of historical learning and philosophical speculation that chiefly distinguish this new era of a better intellectual culture, or as I should rather say, this first stage of a return to the great religious restoration. And I may venture to assert that this spirit, at least in the present century, has become ever more and more the prevailing characteristic of German science and on this science, in its relation to the moral needs and spiritual callings of the nineteenth century, I have now a few observations to make. Like an image reflected in a mirror, or like those symptoms which precede and announce a crisis in human events, the focal-point of all government, or the religious basis of legislation, is sure to be reflected in the whole mental culture, or in the most remarkable intellectual productions of a nation. In England, the equilibrium of a constitution that combines in itself so many conflicting elements is reflected in its philosophy. The revolutionary spirit was prevalent in French literature of the eighteenth century long before it broke out in real life, and the struggle is still very animated between the intellectual defenders and champions of the monarchical and religious Restoration and the newly-awakened liberal opposition. In like manner, as the German people were, and still are, half Catholic and half Protestant, it is religious peace which forms the basis of their modern intellectual culture in all literature, and particularly in philosophy. The mere aesthetic part of German letters, as regards art and poetry—that artist-like enthusiasm peculiar to our nation, the struggles which convulsed our literature in its infancy, the successive imitation and rejection of the French and English models, the very general diffusion of classical learning, the newly-enkindled love for our native speech and for the early history of our country and its older monuments of art—all these are subjects of minor interest in the European point of view which we take here, and form but the prelude and introduction to that higher German science and philosophy which is now more immediately the subject of our enquiries. Historical research should never be separated from any philosophy, still less from the German; as historical erudition is the most effective counterpoise to that absolute spirit, so prevalent in German science and speculation.

Art and poetry constitute that department of the intellect in which every nation should in general follow the impulse of its own spirit, its own feelings and its own turn of fancy; and we must regard it as an exception when the poetry of any particular nation (such, for instance, as that of the English at the present day) is felt and received by other nations as a European poetry. On the other hand, history is an intellectual field open to all European nations. The English, who in this department were extremely active and distinguished, have, in recent times, produced works on their own national history which really merit the name of classical monuments of the new religious regeneration. Science in general, and philosophy in particular, should never be exclusive or national, should never be called English or German, but should be general and European. And if this is not so entirely the case as in the nature of things it ought to be, we must ascribe it to the defects of particular forms. The example of the French language may convince us of this truth; for no one will deny the metaphysical profundity of Count de Maistre, or the dialectic perspicacity of the Viscount de Bonald. Although these absolute principles which appear to characterise the European nations at this time have much less influence on real life and on social relationships in Germany than in any other country, yet the false spirit of the absolute seems to be quite native to German science and philosophy, and for a long time has been the principal cause which has cramped the religious spirit and feelings so natural to the German character, or at least has given them a false direction.

That in this progress of mankind a divine Hand and guiding Providence are clearly discernible; that earthly and visible power has not alone co-operated in this progress and in the opposition which has impeded it, but that the struggle has been carried on in part under divine and against invisible might —this is a truth, I trust, which if not proved on mathematical evidence, has still been substantiated on firm and solid grounds. We may conclude with a retrospective view of society, considered in reference to that invisible world and higher region from which the operations of the visible world proceed, in which its great destinies have their root, and which is the ultimate and highest term of all its movements.

Christianity is the emancipation of the human race from the bondage of that inimical spirit who denies God, and, as far as in him lies, leads all created intelligence astray. Hence the Scriptures style him " the prince of this world," and so he was in fact, but in ancient history only, when among all the nations of the earth, and amid the pomp of military glory and the splendour of pagan life, he had established the throne of his domination. Since this divine era in the history of man, since the beginning of his emancipation in modern times, this spirit can no longer be called the prince of this world, but *the spirit of the age*, the spirit opposed to divine influence and to the Christian religion, which is apparent in all those who consider and estimate time and all things temporal, not by the law and feelings of eternity, but for temporal interests, or from temporal motives, change or undervalue and forget the thoughts and faith of eternity.

In the first ages of the Christian Church, the spirit of the age appeared as a beguiling sectarian spirit. This spirit attained its highest triumph in the new and false faith of a fanatical Unitarianism, utterly opposed to the religion of love, and which severed from Christianity so large a portion of the Eastern Church, and whole regions in Asia. In the Middle Ages, this spirit displayed itself, not so much in hostile sects, as in scholastic disputes, in divisions between Church and State, and in the internal disorders of both. At the beginning of the new era of the world, the spirit of the age claimed as an urgent need of mankind, full freedom of faith, the immediate consequence of which claim was only a bloody warfare and a fatal struggle of life and death, protracted for more than a century. When this struggle was brought to an end, or rather appeased, it was succeeded by an utter indifference for all religions, provided only their morality was good; and the spirit of the age proclaimed religious *indifferentism* as the order of the day. This apparent calm was followed by the revolutionary tempest; and now that this has passed away, the spirit of the age has in our days become absolute, that is to say, it has perverted reason to party-passion, or exalted passion to the place of reason: and this is the present form and last metamorphosis of the old, evil spirit of the age.

Turning now to that Divine aid which has supported mankind in its everlasting struggle against its own infirmities, against all the obstacles of nature and natural circumstances, and against the opposition of the evil spirit; I have endeavoured to show that in the first thousand years of primitive History, Divine Revelation, although only preserved in its native purity in the one original source, still flowed in copious streams through the religious traditions of the other great nations of that early era; and that troubled as the current might be by the admixture of many errors, yet it was easy, in the midst of this slime and pollution, to trace it to its pure and sacred source. Every religious view of universal history must begin with such a belief. We shall prize with deeper, more earnest, and more solid affection, the great and divine era of man's redemption and emancipation, the more accurately we discriminate between what is essentially divine and unchangeably eternal in this revelation of love, and the elements of destruction which man has opposed to it, or mingled with it. And it is only in the spirit of love that the history of Christian times can rightly be understood and accurately judged. In later ages, when the spirit of discord has triumphed over love, historical hope is our only remaining clue in the labyrinth of history. It is only with sentiments of grateful admiration, of amazement and awe, that we trace in the special dispensations of Providence for the advancement of Christianity and the progress of modern society, the wonderful concurrence of events towards the single object of divine love, or the unexpected exercise of divine justice long delayed.

VI. PRINCE CLEMENS METTERNICH

1773 - 1859

THE name Metternich signifies a European era. Without any exaggeration, we can, as many historians do, sum up the Europe of the nineteenth century under three names: Napoleon, Metternich and Bismarck. Yet it is true that this century can also be characterised—perhaps more adequately—by the one phenomenon which these three outstanding figures fought with only temporary success: the Revolution.

What was this Revolution, which was invincible until it was conquered by its own demon, and by that universal exhaustion, disillusion and fear in which the remainder of Europe still lives after the Second World War? Metternich can best define it. He does so in the following pages, in a memorandum written for the personal use of the Czar Alexander I in 1820, a copy of which the Austrian Chancellor communicated to his own sovereign, the Emperor Francis of Austria, as " a not very diplomatic document."

Metternich is less often remembered for what he wanted than for what he feared. As his English biographer, Algernon Cecil, remarks, he dominated his era " not by the sheer force of genius, but by the highest quality of understanding."

The tragedy of genius in action is a spectacular fall. The tragedy of intelligence and understanding is that it encounters a lasting misunderstanding. So lasting has been this misunderstanding of Metternich, that posterity is inclined to see him as the merely negative force of his age.

Metternich's life spans a long era of European history, which has often been described, and which will no doubt still be written about, for landscapes change with every move of the sun and with every step the spectator takes, and the history of an era provides just such a landscape. The light changes with the passing of time. After the First World War, the Vienna Congress, over which Metternich presided, became a popular subject for study. Harold Nicolson's book, and the *Talleyrand* of Duff Cooper, were the outstanding contributions in the inter-war years to the popular analogy between the statecraft of the peacemakers of the " post-war " which began in 1814, and that which began in 1919. Metternich's policy of peace and reconstruction contrasted very favourably for its elevation of thought, genuine concern for true civilisation, humanity and understanding, with the meanness, ignorance and hypocritical

formalism of the parliamentary democracies. The new appreciation
of the policy came from a very unexpected quarter: it was suggested
by the Italian statesman Francesco Nitti, in his *Europa senza Pace*.
An Italian and a Liberal was indeed the last man one would have
expected to stir up a historical controversy in favour of Metternich.
Memory connected the name of the Austrian Chancellor with the
persecution of the secret patriotic societies working for Italian
unity, and there was hardly a name which was more synonymous
with anti-Liberalism, or with the authoritarian theory of the State,
than Metternich's.

But after the First World War events moved quickly in Europe.
The outlook changed. Interest shifted from politics to society, to
culture and religion. Once the crisis was diagnosed as a lasting
phenomenon, and once it was diagnosed in its full context as the
crisis of moral and social values, politics and political economy
receded into the background, and once more the religious issue
became apparent. Before political or economic remedies could be
applied, politics needed to be re-defined, and so did economics.
The very principles of social life seem now to be at stake, just as
they seemed to be to Metternich. Thus from Metternich, the peace-
maker of 1814, and his colleagues and antagonists at the Congress
table of 1814-15, interest has shifted to Metternich, the European
statesman of a long period, in which he was almost alone in per-
ceiving the central importance of the revolutionary phenomenon,
and in observing it with deep misgivings.

Was it out of fear for the material possessions of the governing
class to which he belonged ? This primitive and over-simplified
interpretation must be left to a primitive school of thought, or rather
to the Marxist school of thoughtless repetition. The usual classification, into those who defend and those who attack an established
order of State and society, discloses little of the figures of a period.
Were they right or were they wrong to attack a fortress, the
strength of which is anyhow a fading memory ? Is a " governing
class " wrong in itself ? Are we bound to take it for granted, and
on whose authority, that the will to preserve—the most fundamental
of social facts, whether we are dealing with the initial social phenomenon of the family, or the more complex and broader phenomenon
of the State and the nation—is in itself an evil, and that upheavals
and radical changes are necessarily an improvement on the principle of preservation ?

These problems of political philosophy inevitably arise when we
deal with the judgements which are still current on the most sym-
bolical historic figure of the principle of preservation, or European
Conservatism. For Metternich was that figure, and neither praise
nor blame, nor any new historical interpretation, can turn him into
anything else.

What did Metternich see as the peril of the time and of the future,

K

and for what, and against what, did he struggle ? He gives the answer himself in the pages which follow. Society is governed, in his view, either by an eternally valid concept of God and Man, or it becomes a mere administration of ephemeral needs: worse still an ambitious scheme of " politics," conceived according to lights which are not more than human. Metternich always discriminates very strictly between " government " and " administration." He distrusts administration as such, " bureaucracy "—a word which he was possibly the first to coin in criticism of the administrative machinery of Austria. This arch-enemy of " doctrinaires " in politics delighted in formulating axioms, in bringing experimental wisdom to its highest theoretical expression. He gives the primacy always to the " social principle," which he interprets in the same way as Bonald; politics take second, and administration the third place only. The social principle is that of the family, the principle of preservation and continuity. Once political institutions or administration intrude upon the first principle, which is the preservation of personal rights and the rights of the family, there is no limit to further incursion by tyranny.

In the political testament which he composed after his resignation in 1848, Metternich strongly protests against a confusion of his principles with " Absolutism." He rejected, he says, both Absolutism and Democracy, two different names to describe the same evil, namely the placing of the human will and human judgement above the facts established by history, above fundamental laws such as that of inheritance, the Christian religion, the unwritten moral code. To recognise no limits to the power of a ruler, to admit his claim to make himself the supreme authority in matters of religion and conscience, to admit his right to confiscate inheritance, to interfere with autonomous institutions, such as academies, universities, professional bodies, is bad enough—as the short experience of the rule of Joseph II of Austria proved in Metternich's youth. It was bad enough to concede such rights to monarchs, who are at least bound, by the very principle which brought them to their thrones, to recognise the rights of the family, and by the religious character of their hereditary office to preserve some amount of Christian morality. But it was infinitely more dangerous to vest these powers in assemblies and elected authorities, not bound by the principle of their existence to respect any inheritance, spiritual or material. Metternich saw that Liberty could be safeguarded only by dogmatic authority of a spiritual nature. He believed, perhaps with some exaggeration, that movements of national independence were usually a pretext to establish a power which would remove all religious and spiritual safeguards, in order to institute political tyranny over the individual.

This vision of the problem set by the nineteenth century can hardly be said to be out of date, judging from our present perspective.

We have the same problem today, and the statesmen of our day quote Metternich's arguments more often than they realise—although few share his strong, somewhat unconditional condemnation of "democratism" and "parliamentarianism" as the potential source of arbitrary power and tyranny.

If Metternich opposed German unity, it was because he saw that the autonomous regional institutions offered the only safeguard to German liberty, to Germany's real, historically established constitution. A German confederation of autonomous states would be at liberty to participate in the political transactions of Europe, and have a permanent interest in preserving a European order. It would also, he thought, be the only means of avoiding either a bellicose Germany (which, in her isolated, central position, would conceive ideas of domination) or a Germany which, seceding from Europe, would unite all the other powers in alliance against her. Who could say that Metternich was a bad prophet, when we read such an analysis of Germany's position in the world ?

His opposition to Italian unity must be understood in its historical context. His reference to Italy as a " geographical expression,"[1] more often quoted than correctly understood, was a warning against the possible consequences of a secular and national power threatening the perfect independence of the Holy See. The latter, with the accession of Pius IX in 1846, repudiated any protection on the part of Austria (which Metternich was bound to defend in theory) and turned towards the concept of an independent confederation, under Papal leadership and with the participation of Austria, the natural ally of Italy in the political and economic field. Once more, could a retrospective history claim that Metternich was wrong ?

And are we not bound to recognise that his fear of Russian expansion, and a return to Russian barbarism was legitimate, unless those two factors which acted as a brake on Russia, Christianity and the Monarchy, brought Russia into a European system of alliances ? If he considered such an alliance as the only means of curbing Russia, he did not consider it to be a perfectly safe means, as we know from his correspondence with Ambassadors and Plenipotentiaries in Constantinople and Athens. He was fully aware of the dangerous tendencies existing in Russia, and attributed them, again not so wrongly, to circles which propagated innovations from the West.

Metternich's thought seldom reached the summits of Catholic theology. To prove the truth of theology by human tradition, as it

[1] Metternich: *Mémoires*, Vol. VII, p. 415. *Dépêche circulaire*, 6.8.1847, to Count Apponyi, Imperial Ambassador in Paris. N. 1610:
" *L'Italie est une expression géographique. La péninsule italienne est composée d'Etats souverains et indépendants les uns des autres. L'existence et la circonscription de ces états sont fondées sur des principes de droit public général et corroborées par les transactions politiques les moins sujettes à contestation. L'empereur, pour sa part, est décidé à respecter ces transactions et à contribuer autant qu'il est en son pouvoir à leur inaltérable maintien.*"

is seen in the law of nations, is one-sided, and, as the Spanish philosopher Menéndez y Pelayo remarks in his *Historia de los Hetero-doxos Españoles*, the Church only tolerated the traditionalism of Joseph de Maistre, Bonald and Donoso for the great merits of these thinkers, preferring St Thomas's proof of absolute truth to that of tradition alone. Yet, one-sided as this traditionalism may be, Metternich saw in it the source of political and social wisdom, as he says in his despatch to Count Lützow, his Ambassador to the Holy See:

" *Je suis, Monsieur l'Ambassadeur, un homme d'église, un franc et sévère catholique, et c'est pour cela même que je me crois à la fois un homme d'état pratique. La vérité est une et l'Eglise en est le premier dépositaire. Entre les vérités religieuses et les vérités sociales, il n'y a point de différence, car la société ne peut vivre que par la foi et la morale religieuse.*"[1]

MY POLITICAL PROFESSION OF FAITH[2]

" Europe," a celebrated writer said recently, " arouses pity in the heart of the thinking man and horror in the heart of the virtuous man."

It would be difficult to give in fewer words a more exact picture of the situation at the moment of writing these lines!

Kings have reached the stage of wondering how much longer they are going to last; passions are let loose and are in league to overthrow all that society has hitherto respected as the basis of its existence: religion, public morality, laws, customs, rights and duties; everything is attacked, confused, overthrown, or made a matter of doubt. The great mass of the people looks calmly on, in the face of so many attacks and upheavals, against which there is an utter lack of any sort of protection. Some of them are lost in vague dreams, whilst an overwhelming majority desire the maintenance of a public order which no longer exists, the very first elements of which seem to have been lost.

What is the cause of so many disorders ? By what means have they become established and by what means do they penetrate into all the veins of society ?

Are there any means of halting the growth of this disorder and in what do they consist ?

Such are doubtless the questions which are most worthy of the earnest attention of any man of good will, any true friend

---

[1] Metternich : *Mémoires*, Vol. VII, p. 427; N. 1614, Oct. 10, 1847.

[2] Taken from *Mémoires, Documents et Ecrits divers.* Edited by his son, Prince Richard Metternich (E. Plon et Cie. Paris, 1881).

of law and order, these two elements which are inseparable in their principles and which are the first necessity and at the same time the foremost good of humanity.

Has the world then not created any institution really worthy of this name ? Has truth then always been confused with error, ever since societies thought that they had the power of distinguishing one from the other ? Has all the experience bought at the price of so many sacrifices, and reiterated at so many different periods of history, and in so many different places, always proved wrong ? Has a torrent of light suddenly been shed over society ? Has knowledge in itself become an inspiration ? If a man could believe in such phenomena, he would still need to be first convinced of the reality of the fact. Nothing is as fatal as error, whatever the question at stake and it is our desire and intention never to abandon ourselves to it. Let us examine the situation.

THE CAUSES OF OUR DISORDERS

The nature of man is immutable. The first requirements of society always remain the same, and the differences we can see between them, when we reflect on the question, can be explained by the diversity of influences which natural causes exert on the race of men, such as diversity of climate, the barrenness or the richness of the soil, whether men live on an island or on the continent, etc., etc. These local differences no doubt produce effects which extend far beyond purely physical needs; they create and determine individual needs in a higher sphere; they finally settle types of legislation and their influence, even in the matter of religion, cannot be contested.

On the other hand, the same thing happens to institutions as to everything else. Uncertain in their origin, they go through periods of development and perfection, only to fall into decay, and conforming to the same laws which govern the nature of man, they have, like him, their infancy, their youth, their reasoned maturity and their old age.

Two elements alone remain at the height of their strength and constantly exercise their indestructible influence with a like authority. These are the precepts of morality, both religious and social, and the local needs of man. Once men begin to move away from these bases and to rebel against these sovereign arbiters of their destiny, society is in a state of unrest, which sooner or later will cause an upheaval. The history of every country can show blood-stained pages which tell the story of the consequences of such errors; but we dare to put forward this suggestion, without any fear of contradiction: that we should search in vain for a period when a disorder of this nature has spread its ravages over as vast a field as it has done in this present age. The causes underlying this state of affairs are natural ones.

History only embraces a very restricted lapse of time.

It only begins to deserve this name long after the fall of great empires. Where it appears to bring us to the cradle of civilisation, it leads us only to ruins.

We see republics come to birth and develop, fight and then suffer the rule of a fortunate soldier.

We see one of these republics pass through all the phases common to society and end in a Monarchy that was almost universal, that is to say that it conquered all the scattered parts of the then civilised world.

We see this Monarchy suffer the fate of every body politic; we see the original elasticity grow weak and bring about its own decay.

Centuries of darkness followed the barbarian invasions. The world however could not return to barbarism. The Christian religion had appeared on earth; imperishable in its essence, its mere existence was enough to dispel the darkness and re-establish civilisation on new bases, applicable to all times and all places, satisfying the needs of all on the basis of a pure and eternal law!

The Crusades followed the formation of new Christian states —a curious mixture of good and evil.

Three discoveries soon exercised a decisive influence on the fate of civilisation: the invention of printing, the invention of gunpowder and the discovery of the New World.

The Reformation then came, another event the consequences of which were incalculable, because of the moral effect it had on the world. From that time onwards, the face of the world was changed.

The communication of thought, facilitated by the invention of printing; the complete transformation of the means of attack and defence brought about by the invention of gunpowder; the sudden increase in the natural value of real estate produced by the great quantities of metal put into circulation following the discovery of America; the spirit of adventure which was encouraged by the opportunities of making a fortune in a new hemisphere; the modification which so many and so great changes had introduced into social intercourse—all this underwent still further development and in some measure was crowned by the revolution which the Reformation brought about in the moral order.

The march of the human spirit was therefore exceedingly rapid throughout the last three centuries. This march having progressed with a more rapid acceleration than the course of wisdom—the unique counterbalance to passion and error—had been able to take, a revolution, prepared by false systems of philosophy, and by fatal errors into which several sovereigns, the most illustrious of the second half of the eighteenth century, had fallen, at last broke out in that country which was one of the most advanced in intelligence, the most weakened by a love of pleasure, in a country inhabited by a race of people who can be considered the most frivolous in the world, considering the facility they have in understanding, and the difficulty they experience in judging an issue calmly.

We have glanced rapidly at the primary causes of the present state of society; now we must show in greater detail the nature of the disorder which threatens to disinherit it at one blow of a very real patrimony of benefits, the fruits of a real civilisation, and to disturb it in the enjoyment of these things. We can define this disorder quite simply in a single word: *presumption*, the natural result of such a rapid progress of the human mind in material improvements.

It is presumption which draws so many people today into the paths of error, for the sentiment has become widespread.

Religion, morality, legislation, economy, politics, administration, everything seems to have become common property, accessible to all. People think that they know everything; experience does not count for the *presumptuous man*; faith means nothing to him; he substitutes for it a so-called personal conviction and feels himself dispensed from any examination or course of study in order to arrive at this conviction, for these means seem too lowly to a mind which thinks itself powerful enough to take in at a glance a general review of problems and facts. *Laws* are of no value in his eyes because he did not help to make them and because it would be beneath the dignity of a man of his calibre to recognise the milestones traced by brutish and ignorant generations before him. *Authority* resides in himself; why should he subject himself to what is only of use to a man deprived of intelligence and knowledge ? What had formerly, in his view, been sufficient at a tender age no longer suits a man who has reached the age of reason and maturity, that degree of universal perfection which the German innovators designate by the idea, absurd by its very nature, of the *emancipation of the peoples*! *Morality* alone is not openly attacked, for without it he would not be sure of his own existence for a single moment; but he interprets it according to his own fancy and allows everybody else to do the same thing, provided that the other man neither kills nor robs him.

By sketching the character of the presumptuous man in this way, we think we have drawn a picture of the society of today which is composed of similar elements, if the name of society can be applied to an order of things which only tends in principle to *individualise* all the elements which compose society, and to make each man the head of his own dogma, the arbiter of laws according to which he can deign to govern himself, or allow others to govern him and his fellows, in a word, the only judge of his faith, of his actions and the principles according to which he means to regulate them.

Do we need to prove this last truth ? We think we furnish the proof by calling attention to the fact that one of the most natural sentiments in man—*nationality*—has been erased from the Liberal catechism, and that where the word continues to be used at all, it only serves as a pretext for the leaders of the party to fetter governments, or else as a lever to encourage upheavals. The true aim of the idealists of the party is religious and political fusion and, in the last analysis, is no other than to create in favour of each individual an existence which is entirely independent of all authority and all will, except his own—an absurd idea, which is contrary to the spirit of man and incompatible with the requirements of human society.

THE COURSE WHICH THE DISORDER HAS FOLLOWED AND STILL FOLLOWS

The reasons for which the disorder which weighs on society has acquired such a deplorable intensity appear to us to be of two kinds.

Some are so intimately bound up with the nature of things that no human foresight could have prevented them.

Others must themselves be sub-divided into two classes, however similar they may appear to be in their effects.

Some reasons are negative ones, others positive. We place

amongst the first the weakness and inertia of governments.

It is enough to cast a glance at the course governments have followed throughout the eighteenth century, in order to be convinced that none of them had any conception of the disease or the crisis towards which the body politic was moving.

It was quite otherwise with some men, unfortunately endowed with great talents, who were conscious of their own strength and who were not slow to appreciate the inroads of their influence, and to realise the weakness or the inertia of their opponents, and who knew the art of preparing and leading minds to the triumph of their hateful enterprise, an enterprise all the more odious because they pursued it without any thought for the consequences they would bring about, giving themselves up completely to the one sentiment which moved them: hatred of God and His immutable laws!

France was the country which was unfortunate enough to possess the greatest number of these men. It is within her bosom that religion, with all its most sacred associations, that morality and authority, with all their implied power to govern men, were attacked by them with systematic method and fury, and it is in that country that the weapon of ridicule was used with the greatest ease and success.

Drag the name of God in the mud and the authority instituted by His Divine decrees, and the road is open for revolution! Talk of a social contract and the revolution is a fact! It was in the palaces of kings, in the salons and the boudoirs of various towns that the Revolution was already a reality, while the way for it was still being prepared amongst the mass of the people.

It is not possible to omit here any reference to the influence which the example of England had exercised for so long on France—this country of England, placed in such a special geographical situation that we feel ourselves able to affirm boldly that no forms of government, no habits or institutions that are possible in this State, could ever suit a continental State, and that where it is taken for a model the result can only be defective and dangerous, without a single advantage accruing from it.

The intellectual atmosphere was such in France at the time of the convocation of the States General, and the influence on public opinion during the previous fifty years had been such— an influence which in the last instance had been reinforced, and in some measure made peculiar to France by the imprudent aid which the French Government had recently given to the American Revolution—that all reforms in France which touched upon the very foundation of the Monarchy were necessarily transformed into a revolution. What ought to have been foreseen, and what had in fact been foreseen by practically everybody, with the single exception of the Government, came to pass only too soon. The French Revolution broke out and went through a complete revolutionary cycle in a very short period of time, which only appeared long to its victims and its contemporaries.

The scenes of horror which marked the first phases of the French Revolution prevented the rapid propagation of its subversive principles beyond the frontiers of France, and the wars of conquest which succeeded them inclined public opinion abroad to view the progress of the revolutionary principle with disfavour. That is why the first criminal hopes of Jacobin propaganda failed.

The revolutionary germ however had penetrated every country and was more or less widespread. It developed still further during the period of the military despotism of Bonaparte.

His conquests changed a great number of sovereignties, institutions and customs, and broke all those links which are sacred for all peoples, and which resist the inroads of time even more surely than certain benefits do which innovators sometimes impose upon them. As a result of these disturbances, the revolutionary spirit in Germany, in Italy, and later on in Spain, was able to hide beneath the cloak of genuine patriotism.

Prussia made a serious mistake when she called to her aid weapons as dangerous as secret societies always prove to be; a mistake which cannot be justified by the deplorable situation in which that Power then found herself. It was she who first gave a vigorous impulse to the revolutionary spirit in her State and this spirit made rapid progress, supported as it was in the rest of Germany by the growth of a system of foreign despotism from 1806 onwards. Princes of the Rhenish Confederation in particular made themselves the auxiliaries and accomplices of this system, to which they sacrificed institutions in their countries which had from time immemorial served as safeguards against arbitrary action and the rule of the mob.

The War of the Alliance, by setting limits to the preponderance of France, was enthusiastically supported in Germany by the very men whose hatred for France was in reality nothing more than a hatred of the military despotism of Bonaparte, and who also hated the legitimate power of their own masters.

If only governments had shown wisdom and firmness in their principles, the end of the war in 1814 could still have assured a perfectly happy and peaceful future for the world. Much experience had been acquired and the great lessons which had been learnt could have been applied to some useful purpose. But fate decided otherwise.

The return of the usurper to France and the completely erroneous direction which the French Government took from 1815-1820 amassed for the whole of civilisation new dangers and immense disasters. It was to the first of these misfortunes that the critical state in which France and the whole of the body politic lie is in part due. In one hundred days Bonaparte wiped out the work of the fourteen years during which he had exercised power. He let loose the revolution which he had managed to hold in check in France; he rallied men's minds, not to the time of the 18th Brumaire, but to the principles which the Constituent Assembly had adopted in its lamentable blindness.

The harm which Bonaparte did in this way to France and to Europe, the serious errors which the French Government made and into which other governments fell later on in their turn— all these fatal influences lie heavy on the world today; they threaten with total ruin the work of restoration, the fruit of so many glorious efforts and of a union between the first Monarchs of the world which was without any precedent in the annals of history, and foreshadow incalculable disasters for society.

We have not yet in this present Memorandum touched on one of the most active and at the same time most dangerous instruments of which revolutionaries make use in every country, with a success that none can deny. These are the *secret societies*, which constitute a real power, all the more dangerous because it works in the dark and undermines all parts of the body politic, depositing everywhere the germs of a moral gangrene which will soon mature and bear its fruit. This scourge is one of the most real which governments who are the friends of public order and of their peoples should watch carefully and fight.

CAN THIS EVIL BE REMEDIED AND BY WHAT MEANS?

We regard it as a principle that every evil has its own remedy, and that a knowledge of the true nature of the one leads to the discovery of the other. Few men, however, take the trouble to make a deep study of the evil against which they propose to fight. Few men are exempt from the influence of various passions and nearly all are blinded by prejudice; a great number are guilty of a fault which is even more dangerous because of its flattering and often brilliant exterior; we mean those who are animated by *intellectual pride*; this pride, which is invariably in error, but which is indefatigable, audacious, insensitive to any rebuff, which satisfies the men who are imbued with it (for they inhabit and administer a world of their own), is all the more dangerous for the inhabitants of the real world, so different from the one created by intellectual pride.

There is another class of men who, seizing upon the outward form only of an evil, confuse the accessory manifestations with the evil thing itself, and who, instead of directing their efforts towards the source of the evil, are content to combat a few passing symptoms.

Our duty is to endeavour to avoid both of these two reefs.

The evil exists, and it is an immense one. We do not think we can give a better definition of it and the primary cause of it, which is perpetually at work everywhere and at all times, than we did when we used the word *presumption*, this inseparable companion of half-digested knowledge, this driving force of boundless ambition, which is easily satisfied at times of stress and upheaval.

The middle classes of society are the ones which are chiefly infected by this moral gangrene and the real *coryphées* of the party are only to be found in this section of society.

This gangrene is powerless against the great mass of the people and has no hold over them. The type of work to which this class—*the real people*—has to devote itself is too obvious and too positive for them to give themselves up to vague abstractions and the uncertain path of ambition. The people know that their greatest blessing is to be sure of the morrow, for it is only the morrow which brings them any reward for the troubles and the hard work of today. The laws which guarantee a just protection for the highest good of all, the security of individual families and the security of property, are simple in essence. The people distrust change, which is bad for trade and invariably brings in its train an increase of burdens.

Men of a higher class in society, who embrace the revolutionary career, are either ambitious hypocrites or perverted and lost minds in the widest sense of the word. Their career is for this reason usually short. They are the first victims of political reforms, and the part which the small number of survivors amongst them play is usually that of hangers-on, who are despised by their inferiors as soon as these latter have reached the highest dignities in the State.

France, Germany, Italy and Spain today offer many living examples of the theory we have just put forward.

We do not think that new upheavals of a directly revolutionary intention, other than palace revolutions and changes in the highest government posts, are to be feared today in France, if we take into account the profound aversion of the people to all that could disturb the tranquillity which it now enjoys, after so much suffering and so many disasters.

In Germany, as in Spain and Italy, the nations only ask for peace and law and order.

In these four countries, the dissatisfied classes comprise moneyed men who are really cosmopolitans, acquiring their profits at the expense of any existing order of things; civil servants, men of letters, lawyers and foolish professors.

The ambitious hypocrites belong also to these intermediary classes, few in number amongst the lower conditions of men, but more numerous amongst the higher ranks of society.

Furthermore, there is hardly a period in history when the various factions have not used some catchword.

Since 1815, the catchword has been *constitution*. But do not let us be under any illusion—this word, which lends itself to so wide a latitude in interpretation, is only imperfectly understood if we suppose that the various factions attach the same meaning indiscriminately to it under different forms of government. This then is not the case. Under autocratic Monarchies, it means *national representation*. In countries recently subjected to representative government, it calls itself development and guarantee of charters and fundamental laws.

In the one State which possesses an ancient national representation, it has *reform* for its objective.

Everywhere it means *change and disturbance*.

Paraphrased, it means under a despotic Monarchy: " Your heads too must suffer the levelling process of equality; your fortunes can pass into the hands of others; your ambitions, which have been satisfied for centuries, can give place to our impatient ambitions, which up to now have been denied."

In States subjected to a new régime: " Let ambitions which were satisfied yesterday give place to those of tomorrow, for we belong to tomorrow."

Finally, in England, the only country to be placed in the third class, the catchword—reform—combines the two meanings.

So Europe presents a deplorable and curious picture to the impartial observer.

We find peoples everywhere who desire only the maintenance of law and order, who are faithful to God and their Princes, and remain strangers to the increasing seductions and attempts made by factions who call themselves their friends and try to draw them into a movement against their will!

We see governments which have lost confidence in themselves, and are frightened, intimidated and routed by the catchword of this intermediate class of society, which is half-way between the kings and the peoples, which breaks the sceptres of the former and usurps the voice of the latter—seizing every avenue to the throne—of this same class which has so often been rejected by the people, when it presumes to speak in the people's name, yet is listened to, caressed and feared to excess by those who, with a single word, could drive them back to obscurity.

We see this intermediate class giving itself up with blind fury, and with a desperation which betrays its own fears far more than it reveals confidence in the success of its enterprises, to all the means which it thinks will assuage its thirst for power; applying itself to persuade kings that their rights do not go beyond sitting on a throne, while the caste has the right to administer and to attack all the sacred and positive things which the centuries have bequeathed for the respect of men; finally we see this class denying that the past is of any value and declaring that they are the masters and can create a future. We see them assuming any sort of a mask, uniting or forming splinter groups according to need, helping each other on the day of danger and tearing each other's throats on the morrow of each new conquest. That is the class which has seized control of the Press, which runs it and only uses it for the sole purpose of extolling impiety, disobedience to the laws of Religion and the State, and has even forgotten itself to such an extent that it preaches murder as a duty *for any man who is sure of what he wants.*

One of their leaders in Germany gave this definition of public opinion: " *The will of the strong man in the mind of the party*," a maxim which is put into practice all too often and is all too little understood by the men whose right and duty it is to save society from its own errors and weaknesses, and from the crimes which factions commit when they claim to act in its interest.

The presence of the evil is evident; the means used by the disruptive faction are so much to be condemned on principle, they are so criminal in their application, they even offer such a total of dangers for the faction itself, that what short-sighted men, whose heads and hearts are shattered by circumstances which are stronger than their own calculations or courage, look upon as the end of society, can become the first step towards a better order of things. These weak men will be proved to be right, unless men stronger than they come forward, close their ranks and make sure of victory.

We are convinced that society can be saved only by strong and vigorous determination on the part of governments which are still free in thought and action.

We think also that it can still be saved if these governments face the truth squarely, if they cast off their illusions, if they close their ranks and stand firm on a line of correct principles, from which all ambiguity is absent, and which are frankly upheld and stated.

By acting in this way, Monarchs will fulfil the first of the duties imposed upon them by Him who, by giving them power, charged them to uphold justice, the rights of each and all, to avoid the byways of error and to tread firmly the path of truth. Placed as they are outside the sphere of passions which rend society, it is above all during times of crisis that they are called upon to strip reality of all false appearances, and to show themselves for what they are, fathers invested with all the authority which rightly belongs to the head of the family, to prove that in times of disaster they can be just and wise and therefore strong, and that they do not abandon the people, whom it is their duty to govern, *to the sport* of factions, to error and its consequences, which inexorably bring about the ruin of society. The present moment, when we put down our thoughts in these pages, is one of those moments of crisis; the crisis is grave; it will be decisive according to the party-decisions we make, or refuse to make.

There is a rule of conduct common to individuals and to States, sanctioned by the experience of centuries, as well as by that of every day; this rule states: It is not in the stress of passion that we ought to think of *reform*; wisdom decrees that in such moments we should confine ourselves to *preserve*.

Let Monarchs adopt these principles whole-heartedly, and

let all their resolutions bear the imprint of them. Let their actions, the measures they take, and even the words they utter, state this determination to the world and prove it; they will find allies everywhere. When governments establish the principle of *stability*, they in no wise exclude the development of anything that is good, for stability does not mean immobility. It is, however, for those who are burdened with the heavy task of government to improve the wellbeing of their peoples! It is for the governments to decide the pace, according to needs and to circumstances. It is not by the concessions which the various factions think they can impose on the legitimate authority, and which they have neither the right to demand, nor the power to restrain within just limits, that wise reforms can be achieved! Our most ardent wish is that the utmost good should be done; but do not let what is not good be confused with what is good, and even let real good only be done by those who combine under the law authority and the means to do it. Such should also be the sincere desire of all peoples, who have learnt only too well at their own expense how to appreciate the worth of certain words, and the nature of certain caresses.

Respect for all existing things; liberty for every government to watch over the wellbeing of its own people; an alliance between all the governments to fight factions in every State; contempt for words devoid of meaning, which have become the catchwords of mischief-makers; respect for the progressive development of institutions according to the law; refusal on the part of every Monarchy to help or succour dissident elements, in whatever disguise they may appear: such are happily the thoughts of every great Monarch; the world can be saved if they are translated into action, it is lost if they are not.

Union between Monarchs is the fundamental basis of the policy which must be followed to save society from total ruin.

To what particular end should this policy be directed? The more important this question is, the more necessary it is to resolve it. A principle counts for much; it only acquires real worth when it is applied.

The primary causes of the evil which overwhelms the world have been summed up by us in this little work, which does not claim to be more than a sketch. The progressive causes of this evil are here indicated; if in its relation to *individuals* it was defined as *presumption*, we think that when we apply this word to society as a whole, it also describes the evil which exists in that *vagueness of thought which is due to an excess of generalisation*. Let us see what disturbs society today.

Principles which have hitherto been considered as fixed are now attacked and overthrown. In religious matters, *private judgement* and *examination* of the subject replace *faith*; *Christian morality* is to take the place of the *law of Christ*, such as it has always been interpreted by the relevant Christian authorities.

In the Catholic Church, Jansenists and a host of isolated sectarians who desire a *Religion without a Church* devote themselves to this enterprise with eager zeal; in the Protestant sects we have the Methodists, themselves subdivided into almost as many sects as there are persons, then the enlightened promoters of Bible Societies, and the Unitarians, or promoters of a fusion between the Lutherans and the Calvinists in an evangelical community.

The common aim of these men, irrespective of the sect to which they ostensibly belong, is no other than to *overthrow authority*. In the moral field, they want to *set souls free*, just as those men amongst the political revolutionaries, who do not abandon themselves exclusively to a calculating personal ambition, want to *set people free*.

If the same elements of destruction which today convulse society have existed in every century—for every age has seen the birth of unscrupulous and ambitious men, hypocrites, hotheads, pseudo-intellects and builders of castles in the air—our own age however, by the single fact of the licentiousness of the Press, possesses more possibilities of contact, of corruption and of influence, which are greater and more easily set in motion, and more susceptible of working upon this class of men, than any other age.

We are certainly not alone in wondering whether society can continue to exist when *the liberty of the Press* prevails, this scourge which was unknown in the world before the latter half of the seventeenth century, and only practised until the end of the eighteenth century, with few exceptions, in England, in this part of Europe separated from the Continent by the sea, as much as by its language and its individual customs.

The first principle which Monarchs, who are united in will as well as by the uniformity of their desires and their judgement, ought to proclaim is the stability of political institutions, in face of the disintegration which has taken hold of men's minds; the rigidity of certain principles, in face of the mania for

L

interpreting them; and *respect for existing laws*, instead of the *overthrow* of these laws.

The hostile section is divided into two very distinct groups. One consists of the levellers, the other of the doctrinaires.

United on the day of revolution, these men are divided when they play a merely passive rôle. It is the business of governments to know who they are, and to keep them in their place, in accordance with their real value.

Among the class of levellers, there are to be found strong-willed and determined men. The doctrinaires never count such men in their ranks. If the first category is more to be feared on the day of revolution, the second is more dangerous in those deceptively calm days which precede a storm in the social order, just as they do in the physical order. Constantly in the grip of abstract ideas which it would be impossible ever to apply to real issues, and which are ordinarily even in contradiction with those issues, it is men of this class who perpetually stir up the people with imaginary or simulated fears, and weaken governments in order to force them to deviate from the right path. Men want to be governed by facts and in accordance with justice, not with words and theories; society needs first and foremost to be upheld by a strong authority (any authority which lacks real strength is unworthy of the name), not to govern itself. If we calculated the number of disputes in which the various groups in mixed governments, and the number of just grievances to which an aberration of power in a Christian State can give rise, the result of this comparison would not be in favour of *modern theories*. The first and most important matter for the overwhelming majority of the nation is the stability of the laws, their continuity, and by no means their overthrow. Let governments govern then, let them maintain the fundamental bases of their institutions, ancient as well as modern; for if it is dangerous in any age to alter them, it is certainly not a propitious time to do so today, amidst the general unrest.

Let them acquaint their peoples openly with this determination and let them prove it by acts. Let them reduce the doctrinaires within their States to silence, and let them show their contempt for those who are beyond their frontiers. Let them not give colour by their demeanour, or by their acts, to the suspicion that they are either favourable to error, or indifferent to it; let them not give the impression that the lessons of experience go for nothing, and make way for experiments which, to say the least, are hazardous. Let each one of their words be precise and clear, and let them in no way try to win over by concessions those groups whose only aim is the destruction of all authority which is not in their own hands, who could not be won over by concessions, and who would become the more emboldened in their pretensions if they were granted concessions.

Let them be more cautious in troubled times than at any other time, in their approach to the questions of reforms which are genuine, and not demanded imperiously according to the exigencies of the moment, so that the very good that they do will not be turned against them—a contingency which can easily happen, if a government measure appears to have been granted out of fear.

Let them not confuse in this way concessions made to rival groups, with the good which they can confer on their peoples by modifying, according to *acknowledged* requirements, any particular branch of their administration which could benefit by such a measure.

Let them devote the most careful attention to the state of the finances of their country, so that their peoples may enjoy, by a reduction in taxation, the benefits of a period of real and not illusory peace.

Let them be just but firm; kind yet severe.

Let them uphold religion in all its purity, not suffering any attack upon dogma, or allowing morality to be interpreted according to the *Social Contract*, or the visions of simple sectarians.

Let them suppress secret societies, this gangrene which preys upon society.

Finally, let all the great Monarchs come closer together and prove to the world that if they are united, it can only be beneficial, for union between them will assure the political peace of Europe; that they are only firmly united in order to maintain public order at a time when it is menaced on all sides; that the principles they profess are as paternal and as much intended for the protection of good citizens, as they are repressive for dissident factions.

Governments of lesser Powers will see in such a projected union the anchor of their salvation and will hasten to associate themselves with it. Peoples will regain confidence and courage, and the deepest and most salutary pacification which the world has ever witnessed in all its long history could be established, for such a peace would first of all include all those States which are still left standing; it would not remain without a decisive influence on the fate of those which are threatened with imminent subversion, and even on the restoration of those which have already suffered the scourge of revolution.

Every great State which is determined to survive the turmoil of the time still has a good chance of salvation.

A firm union between States on the principles which we have just laid down will vanquish the turmoil itself.

VII. JUAN DONOSO CORTÉS

1809 - 1853

A FEW years before the European Revolution of 1848, which, in a very short time, had shown in a concentrated and spectacular form all those modern trends which for good or ill have dominated Europe ever since—Germanism and Slavism in the East and the social conflict in the West—one of the principal prophets of the Slav awakening, the romantic poet Kollar, who brought home to his Slovak mountains a somewhat rough, but still unadulterated, version of Hegel's philosophy from his Lutheran theological studies at Jena, wrote: " In the East, amongst the Slavs and for the Slavs, the sun is rising. Over the Germanic lands it is broad daylight. Over England it is high noon, over France and Italy the sun is already setting, over Spain and Portugal it is dark night."

The Slav poet, Lutheran in his religion, Hegelian in his philosophy, and Liberal in his politics, was not alone in considering the Spain of the post-Napoleonic era as the country of dark night. This opinion was general and most believers in the ingloriously, although somewhat slowly, expiring deity called the *Zeitgeist*, concurred in seeing in Spain nothing but a ruin and a past.

Few, far too few, eyes turned towards the " Far West," as some modern Spaniards like to call the Iberian peninsula and its transatlantic extension. The Spanish *ochocientos* presented a disturbed, almost chaotic picture of changing dynasties and ephemeral political régimes, of military upheavals and conspiracies, of a society near to disintegration, which the keenest observer was discouraged from penetrating and understanding. Yet, can we forget that Napoleon's first failure was in Spain, and that the whole historical and ideological trend symbolically summarised by the Battle of the Nations began on the Peninsula ? It was in Spain too that the conclusion of the great European crisis was summed up in terms of the philosophy of history, in terms of an eschatological interpretation of State and society, and above all in those deep accents of prophecy which only posterity appreciates at its full value. Two meteor-like figures of thinkers stand out in this post-Napoleonic generation in Spain: the philosopher-statesman Juan Donoso Cortés and the theologian and philosopher Jaime Balmes. Neither of them lived to be old. Donoso died when he was only forty-four, the great priest of Catalonia, Jaime Balmes, at the age of thirty-eight.

The Battle of the Nations at Leipzig in October 1813 was to some extent prepared and summarised by a philosophical movement in Germany which had an immense importance for the rest of Europe. Fichte and Hegel, and their common master Immanuel Kant, revolutionised European thought by the importance which they achieved as the ideological masters of their people during the national resistance to Napoleon. They educated Germany in the rôle she was to play from the time of the French Revolutionary wars to Napoleon. The great German innovation consisted of a new metaphysical approach to History, to art and human society, a new emphasis on the subjective, ethical conscience and on emotion, a neo-Platonic emphasis on the transcendental and symbolic significance of all earthly phenomena: " *Alles Vergängliche ist nur ein Gleichniss,*" as Goethe says in *Faust*—this line could almost stand as the device of the whole ideological movement of post-Napoleonic Germany.

Overwhelmed by German ideas, or rather by the new German emphasis, the European mind paid little attention to a philosophical movement which was hardly less intense, and which came from a different corner of Europe. This was the philosophical renaissance occurring in Spain, in the same context of a national awakening born out of resistance to Napoleon. Europe hardly noticed Spain in the nineteenth century. Power shifted to the East and to the North, as a result of the Napoleonic Wars. Almost every well-informed person considered in 1815, and in the years following, that the chief political factor of the present and the future was Russia, counter-balanced by Russia's only potential rival, England. The country producing new intellectual impulses was thought to be the Germany which emerged from the Battle of Leipzig, while France continued to dominate European civilisation by her language, and like a barometer registered the variations in pressure of the highly disturbed political, social and cultural atmosphere of the time.

The life-work of Donoso Cortés constitutes a spiritual link of considerable relevance between Spain, France and Germany. Born in 1809 in a convent of the Estramadura, where his mother was confined during the flight of the family from the French invaders, Juan María Donoso Cortés achieved a most brilliant literary, political and diplomatic career. As a child he was recognised to be an infant prodigy; at the age of twenty, he was a Lecturer at the University of Salamanca, where regulations had had to be waived in order that he might take his degree before the required age. Before he was thirty, he was elected by his native province to the Congress of Deputies, where he soon was called to a junior Cabinet post. Later on he held an important diplomatic post in Paris at the time of Louis Philippe and Guizot and was raised to the peerage with the title of Marquis of Valdegamas; in 1849 he was Ambassador Extraordinary and Minister Plenipotentiary to Prussia. He was again posted to Paris as Ambassador during the Presidency of Louis Napoleon and the beginning of the Second Empire. He died in Paris when, as we have seen, he was only forty-four.

Yet these external events of a short and brilliant career are but a feeble indication of the background to the pages which follow. More important in Donoso's life than his political career was his decision to renounce it early, for as he says in one of his letters to Louis Veuillot, he became convinced that prayers were more efficacious in good causes than anything politics had to offer.

As a young man, Donoso was a Catholic Liberal, attached to the service of Queen Isabella, as were all the Liberals—Moderados—during the years of the dynastic crisis, when Don Carlos rallied the party of the strict legitimists—Apostolicos—to the cause of the Salic Monarchy. His early writings, comprising a treatise on *The Law of the Nations*, an *Essay on Diplomacy*, a *History of the Eastern Question*, literary and political chronicles and comments on Spanish, French and world events of the 1830's and 1840's, do not show him yet in the light in which he stood after the European Revolution of 1848-49—a prophetic voice announcing with deep, mystical insight " the doom of the Kingdom of Philosophy " and the coming of the Kingdom of God amidst Revolutions of cosmic proportions and all the signs foretold in the Apocalypse. It was in Prussia—which under Frederick the Great had been the favourite country of foreign " philosophers " and again in 1813, the country of a German philosophy, the principal tenet of which is individual judgement, that spiritual and ethical inheritance of Protestantism—that Donoso became convinced of the impending " final dissolution of modern civilisation," the impending catastrophe which would overwhelm Europe, for some unrevealed, but certainly glorious, purpose of Providence.

In the history of post-revolutionary Christian thought and philosophy, Donoso represents a landmark of the greatest relevance, which few contemporary observers sensed, although their number is less important than their quality. Louis Veuillot, a close personal friend during his Paris years, was one of them; Barbey d'Aurevilly did not hesitate to place him beside Joseph de Maistre and Bonald as one of the " Lay Fathers of the Church "; Schelling, head of the German philosophers since the death of Hegel, greeted in him a new and unexpected luminary of the century; old Metternich did not hesitate to declare that " After Donoso Cortés, one has to put down one's pen, for nothing more and nothing better can be said on the historical transition we are witnessing."

Donoso Cortés says the final word on the Parliamentary Liberalism of the early part of the century—this political reflection, he says, of the Deist philosophy. He is, if not the first, certainly the most important Christian voice to comment on the deeper (and not merely political) Revolution through which Europe was, and still is, passing. The pantheist negation of God and authority has only one social expression, Communism—Donoso was the first to be fully aware of this—and when the belief in Divine privilege vanishes, the actual consequence of privilege, political and personal liberty, will also vanish. His *Essay on Catholicism* (1851), a masterly comment on the European Revolution of 1848-49, was perhaps the first, and at any rate for some time to come, the most elaborate and profound Catholic analysis of revolutionary Socialism and Communism. Time has also justified Donoso's vision of Russia and Germany as the two future centres of good and evil for Europe, as those quarters from which more deadly revolutions than the French one may come.

Prophecy has seldom been more conscious than in the speech on " Dictatorship " which Donoso delivered in Madrid in the Spanish Congress of Deputies on January 4, 1849, and which appeared in full soon afterwards in *L'Univers* and also as a brochure. We republish it here, omitting a few contemporary allusions which have now—especially outside Spain—lost their importance. Donoso's powerful and frightening image of a coming tyranny, on a scale yet unknown in the annals of mankind, which would come upon them in days not too far removed from their own, is the counterpart of the classic prophecy on the horrors of subversion to be found much later as an image of the future in Dostoievsky's *The Possessed*. Even without the *Ensayo*, it would raise Donoso from the level of the merely political theorists of his generation to that of the visionaries who saw spiritual doom in the age of material progress, such as Kierkegaard or Dostoievsky. Because of his Catholic vision, he uses better arguments concerning Authority and Faith and is a more systematic and more rational defender of spiritual truth than the other prophets of the modern Apocalypse.

1. THE CHURCH, THE STATE, AND REVOLUTION[1]

GENTLEMEN,

The long speech which Señor Cortina made yesterday, and to which I am going to reply by considering it from a certain angle, in spite of the vast implications it contains, forms but an epilogue: an epilogue to the errors of the Progressive party, which in their turn form but another epilogue: the epilogue to the errors which were invented three centuries ago and which rend in varying degrees every human society today.

At the beginning of his speech, Señor Cortina confessed, with

---

[1] Donoso Cortés' speech on Dictatorship to the Spanish Parliament, January 4, 1849 (*Obras Completas*, Tomo II, p. 187; *Biblioteca de Autores Christianos*, Madrid, 1946).

that good faith which distinguishes him and which enhances his talent to such a degree, that it has even occasionally happened that he wondered whether his principles might not be false and his ideas disastrous, when he saw them always in opposition but never in power. I will tell the honourable gentleman: if he reflects but a little, his doubts will become a certainty. His ideas are not in power, and are in the Opposition, precisely because they are the ideas of an opposition rather than of a government. They are barren ideas, Gentlemen, disastrous ideas which we must fight until they are laid to rest in their natural tomb, here beneath this dome, at the foot of the tribune.

Loyal to the traditions of the party which he leads and represents; loyal, I repeat, to the traditions of this party since the Revolution of February, Señor Cortina included three things in his speech which I shall term inevitable. The first is praise of his party, praise based on a recital of its past merits; the second is the dissertation on its present grievances; the third, the programme, or a statement, of the services it could render in the future.

Gentlemen of the majority, I come here to defend your principles; but do not expect the slightest praise from me: you are the victors, nothing is so becoming to the victor's brow as a crown of modesty.

Do not expect me either to speak of your grievances: your business is not to avenge personal insults, but those which traitors to their Queen and country have cast on society and the Throne. I shall not draw up an inventory of all the services you have rendered. What would be the object? To tell the nation about them? The nation does not forget.

It has not escaped your memory, Gentlemen, that Señor Cortina divided his speech into two parts. The Honourable Member dealt with the foreign policy of the Government and designated the events which have taken place in Paris, London and Rome as of great importance in the foreign policy of Spain. I, too, shall touch upon these questions.

The Honourable speaker then approached the question of domestic policy; and domestic policy, according to Señor Cortina, can be divided into a question of principles and a question of facts, a question of method and of application. By the voices of the Secretary of State for Foreign Affairs and the Home Secretary, who discharged their task with their accustomed eloquence, the Cabinet replied to the question of facts and of policy, as was fitting, considering that they have all the relevant data for this. The question of principle has been barely touched upon; I shall confine myself to dealing with that one question, and if the House gives me leave, I shall go into fundamentals.

What principle inspires Señor Cortina? This principle, if I have analysed his speech correctly. In home affairs, the form of the law; everything by the law, everything for the law, always the form of the law; the form of the law in every circumstance, the form of the law on every occasion. But I, who believe that laws are made for societies and not societies for the laws, I say: Society, everything through society for society; society always, society in every circumstance and on every occasion.

When the form of the law is sufficient to save society, the form of the law is best; when it is not, let us have dictatorship. This formidable word, Gentlemen—less formidable than the word Revolution, the most formidable of all—this formidable word has been pronounced by a man here, known to us all, and who assuredly is not of the stuff of which dictators are made. I myself understand them instinctively, but not in order to imitate them. I find two things impossible: to condemn dictatorship and to exercise it. Incapable, I recognise in all frankness, of governing with a lofty nobility, I could not in conscience accept the responsibility of government. I could not do so without setting one half of myself at war with the other half, my instincts with my faculty of reason, my reason with my instincts.

So, Gentlemen, all those who know me can bear witness: nobody, within or without these precincts, can say that they have rubbed shoulders with me along the crowded path of ambition. On the contrary, I shall always be found, and have always been found, in the modest path of the good citizen; and when my days are accomplished, I shall go down to my tomb without feeling remorse at having failed to defend society when it was barbarously attacked, or without feeling the bitter, and for me unbearable, sorrow of having done evil to any man.

I say, Gentlemen, that dictatorship, in certain circumstances, in given circumstances, such as those in which we find ourselves, for example, is a legitimate form of government, as good and as profitable as any other, a rational system of government, which can be defended in theory as well as in practice. Let us examine in what the life of society really consists.

The life of society, like human life, is composed of action and reaction, of the ebb and flow of certain forces which attack, and others which resist.

Such is the life of society and the life of man. Now the attacking forces, which we call disease in the human body, and by another name in the body politic, although in essence it is the same thing, appear in two forms. In one form they are spread here and there over society and are only seen in individuals; in the other, in the state of advanced disease, they take a more concentrated form and are seen in political associations. Very well, then, I say that the forces which resist, only present in the human body and in the body politic in order to repulse the attacking forces, must necessarily be in proportion to the actual strength of the latter. When the attacking forces are disseminated, the forces which resist must likewise be disseminated; they permeate the Government, the authorities, the Courts of Law, in a word, the whole body politic; but should the attacking forces be concentrated in political associations, then necessarily, without anyone being able to prevent it, without anyone having the right to prevent it, the forces which resist are concentrated into the hands of one man. This is the theory of dictatorship, clear, luminous and indestructible.

This theory, which is a truth in the rational order, is a constant factor in the historical order. Quote me one society which has never known a dictatorship, just one. See, on the contrary, what happened in democratic Athens, what happened in aristocratic Rome. In Athens, this sovereign authority was in the hands of the people and was called ostracism; in Rome, it was in the hands of the Senate, who delegated it to a prominent citizen bearing the rank of Consul, and that was called dictatorship, as it is in our own country. Look at modern societies; look at France amidst all her vicissitudes. I will not speak of the First Republic, which was a dictatorship of gigantic proportions, unbounded, full of blood and horror. I speak of a later time. In the Charter of the Restoration, dictatorship had taken refuge, or if you prefer it, had sought refuge, in Article 14; in the Charter of 1830, it was to be found in the Preamble. And where is it to be found in the present Republic? Do not let us talk of it: What is it, except a dictatorship disguised as a Republic?

Señor Galvez Cagnero quoted here, somewhat inappositely, the English Constitution. As it happens, Gentlemen, the English Constitution is the only one in the world (so wise are the English!) where dictatorship is not an exception in law, but is part of the common law. The matter is quite clear. In all circumstances, and at every period, Parliament possesses, when it likes, dictatorial powers, for in the exercise of its power it only recognises the one limit which bounds all human authority—that of prudence. It can do anything, and that is exactly what constitutes dictatorial powers; it can do anything except change a woman into a man, or a man into a woman, say its jurists. It has the power to suspend *habeas corpus*, to outlaw by a bill of *attainder*; it can change the constitution; it can even change the dynasty, and not only the dynasty but even the religion of the people; it has the right to oppress consciences; in a word it is all-powerful. Who has ever seen, Gentlemen, a more monstrous dictatorship ?

I have proved that dictatorship is a truth in the theoretical order and a fact in the historical order. Now I am going further: if I may say so without impropriety, dictatorship could be said to be a fact also in the divine order.

God has given the government of human societies into the hands of men, up to a certain point, and has reserved exclusively for Himself the government of the Universe. God governs the Universe, if I can so put it, and if I can use Parliamentary language for such an august subject—God governs the Universe constitutionally. Yes, Gentlemen. It is as clear as daylight and proved by evidence. The Universe is governed by certain precise and indispensable laws, which are called secondary causes. What are these laws, except laws analogous to those we call fundamental in human society ?

Now, Gentlemen, if God is the Legislator of the physical world, as certain men are legislators, although in a different way, of human societies, does God always govern according to the same laws which He has imposed upon Himself in His eternal wisdom and to which He has subjected us ? No, Gentlemen, for He sometimes manifests His sovereignty directly, clearly and explicitly by breaking those laws which He has imposed upon Himself and deflecting the natural course of events. Now, when God acts in this way, could we not say, if human language can be applied to divine things, that He acts dictatorially ?

That proves, Gentlemen, how great is the folly of a party which imagines that it can govern with less means of doing so than God, and refuses to use the means of dictatorship, which is sometimes necessary. That being so, the problem, reduced

to its real terms, does not consist in knowing whether dictatorship is justified or not, or whether in certain cases it is a good
thing, but whether such circumstances are present, or have
been present in Spain. This is the most important point and the
one on which I shall concentrate my attention exclusively. In
order to do so, and in this I shall but follow those speakers who
have preceded me in the tribune, I shall have to glance briefly
first at Europe and then at our own country.

The February Revolution, Gentlemen, like Death, came
unexpectedly. God had condemned the French Monarchy. In
vain had this institution undergone profound transformation,
in an attempt to adapt itself to circumstances and the times;
it was of no avail; it was irrevocably condemned, its fall was
inevitable. The monarchy of the Divine Right of Kings came
to an end with Louis XVI on the scaffold; the monarchy of
glory came to an end with Napoleon on an island; hereditary
monarchy came to an end with Charles X in exile; and with
Louis Philippe came to an end the last of all possible monarchies,
the monarchy of prudence. What a melancholy and pitiful
sight does an institution so venerable, ancient and glorious
present, when it cannot be preserved by divine right, legitimacy, prudence or glory!

When the startling news of this great Revolution reached
Spain, we were all plunged into consternation; we were all
terrified. Nothing could compare with our consternation and
our terror, unless it was the consternation and terror felt by the
defeated monarchy. Yet that is not all; a greater consternation
and a greater terror existed than that felt by the vanquished
monarchy—in the victorious Republic. Even today, ten months
after their triumph, ask them how they won, why and with what
forces they conquered, and they will be unable to tell you.
Why? Because it was not the Republic which conquered: the
Republic was only the instrument of victory in the hands of a
higher power.

This power, once its work was begun, destroyed the monarchy
with such a tiny thing as this Republic; do you doubt, Gentlemen, that if it was necessary, and in its own interest, it could
not overthrow the Republic in its turn with the shadow of an
empire or a monarchy? The cause and the effects of this
revolution have been the subject of wide comment in all the
Parliaments in Europe, and particularly in the Spanish Parliament, and I have marvelled at the deplorable frivolity with
which the deep-seated causes which bring about such upheavals

have been treated, here as elsewhere. Here as elsewhere, revolutions are always attributed to the mistakes of governments;
men forget that universal, unforeseen and simultaneous catastrophes are always providential; for such, Gentlemen, are the
characteristics which distinguish the works of God from the
works of man.

When revolutions betray these symptoms, be sure that they
come from Heaven and that they come as a result of our
mistakes and for the punishment of us all. Shall I tell you the
truth, Gentlemen, the whole truth concerning the causes of the
last French revolution ? The truth, then, is that the day came
last February of the great reckoning with Providence for all
classes of society, and that on that dread day all classes were
found to be bankrupt. I go further: the Republic itself, on
the day of its victory, confessed that it was bankrupt. The
Republic has said that it was going to establish in the world the
reign of liberty, equality and fraternity, three dogmas which
were born, not in the Republic, but on Calvary. What, Gentlemen, has it accomplished since then ? In the name of liberty,
it has made necessary, proclaimed and accepted dictatorship.
In the name of equality, in the name of the republicans of
yesterday and tomorrow, of men who were born republican, it
has invented a curious sort of aristocratic democracy bearing
ridiculous coats of arms. Finally, in the name of fraternity, it
has restored the fraternity of pagan antiquity, of Eteochus and
Polynices: and brother cut the throat of brother in the streets
of Paris, in the bloodiest battle the centuries have ever seen
within the walls of a city. I give the lie to this Republic which
calls itself the Republic of the three truths: it is the Republic
of the three blasphemies, the Republic of the three lies.

Let us now touch on the causes of this Revolution. The
progressive party always finds the same causes for everything.
Señor Cortina told us yesterday that revolutions occur because
of certain illegalities and because the instincts of the people
make them rise in a uniform and spontaneous way against
tyrants. Señor Ordax Avecilla told us previously: If you want
to avoid revolution, give the hungry bread. Here, in all its
subtlety, is the progressive theory: the causes of revolution lie,
on the one hand in poverty, and on the other in tyranny. This
theory, Gentlemen, is contrary, absolutely contrary, to historical fact. I challenge anybody to quote me one example of
a revolution which has been started and brought to a conclusion by men who were either slaves or hungry. Revolutions

are a disease of rich peoples, of free peoples. Slaves formed the greater part of the human race in antiquity: tell me one revolution these slaves ever made.

All that they could do was to foment a few slave wars: but deep-seated revolutions were always the work of wealthy aristocracies. No, Gentlemen, the germ of revolution is not to be found in slavery or in poverty; the germ of revolution lies in the desires of the mob, which are over-excited by leaders who exploit them for their own advantage. *You will be like the rich*— such is the formula of Socialist revolutions against the middle classes. *You will be like the nobles*—such is the formula of the revolutions made by the middle classes against the aristocracy. *You will be like Kings* is the formula of revolutions made by the aristocracy against Kings. Finally, Gentlemen, *You will be like gods*—such was the formula of the first revolt of the first man against God. From Adam, the first rebel, to Proudhon, the last blasphemer, such has been the formula of every revolution.

. . . I have always believed, Gentlemen, that in governments and peoples, as well as in individual cases, blindness is a sign of perdition. I believe that God always begins by making those He wishes to destroy blind, that He confuses their minds so that they do not see the abyss which stretches beneath their feet. Applying these ideas to the general policy pursued for some years by England and France, I can say here that I have long foretold great misfortunes and catastrophes.

It is a historical fact, recognised and incontrovertible, that the providential mission of France is to be the instrument of Providence for the propagation of new ideas, whether they be political, religious or social. In modern times, three great ideas have taken possession of Europe: the Catholic idea, the philosophical idea and the revolutionary idea. Now in these three periods, France was always made man in order to propagate these ideas. Charlemagne was France made man to propagate the Catholic idea; Voltaire was France made man to propagate the philosophical idea; Napoleon was France made man to propagate the revolutionary idea.

Similarly I believe the providential mission of England is to maintain a just moral equilibrium in the world by serving as a counterbalance to France. England is like the ebb and France the flow of the sea. Imagine for one moment the flow without the ebb and the seas would pour over all the continents; imagine the ebb without the flow, and the seas would disappear from the earth. Imagine France without England and you would see the world shaken only by convulsions; every day a new constitution and every hour a new form of government would appear. Imagine England without France and the world would vegetate indefinitely under the charter of John Lackland, that unchanging type of every British constitution. What is the significance then of the co-existence of these two powerful nations? It means progress within the bounds of stability, and stability quickened by progress.

For some years then, Gentlemen—I call contemporary history and your own memories to witness—these two great nations have lost all recollection of their traditions, all consciousness of their providential mission. France, instead of spreading new ideas in the world, has everywhere preached the *status quo*—the *status quo* in France, in Spain, in Italy, in the East. And England, instead of preaching stability, has everywhere preached revolt: in Spain, in Portugal, in France, in Italy and in Greece. What has been the result? The inevitable result has been that each of the two nations, playing a rôle which was never hers, has played it very badly. France has tried to transform herself from devil to preacher and England has tried to transform herself from preacher to devil.

Such, Gentlemen, is contemporary history; but to confine myself to England, for it is with her alone that I wish to deal at present, God forbid that the disasters she has invited by her mistakes should ever overwhelm her, as He has overwhelmed France! No mistake is of such magnitude as the one England has made by supporting revolutionary parties everywhere. Unhappy country! does she not realise that when danger comes, these parties, with a surer instinct than her own, will turn against her? Has it not already happened? And it had to happen, Gentlemen; for all the revolutionaries in the world know that when revolution becomes serious, when the clouds pile up, when the horizon grows dark and the waves grow higher, the vessel of Revolution has no other pilot than France.

This then has been the policy of England, or rather of her Government and her agents during the last few years. I have said, and I repeat, that I do not want to go into this question; grave considerations dissuade me. Consideration for the public good, first of all, for I solemnly declare: I desire the closest and the most complete union between the Spanish and the English nation. . . .

When he dealt with this question, Señor Cortina, if I may say so frankly, suffered from a kind of vertigo: he forgot who

he is, where he was and who we are. Although he spoke in
Parliament, he imagined himself to be a lawyer; speaking to
Members, he thought he was speaking to judges; addressing
a Consultative Assembly, he imagined he was addressing a
Court of Law; dealing with an important political and
national subject, he acted as though he were pleading a case;
a case there certainly is at stake, but two nations are the
interested parties. Now, Gentlemen, was it right of Señor
Cortina to constitute himself counsel for the prosecution
against the Spanish nation? Is that by any chance, Gentlemen, what we call patriotism? Is that the way to be a true
patriot? No indeed. Do you know what patriotism really is?
It means, Gentlemen, loving, hating, feeling as our country
loves, hates and feels.

Gentlemen, neither the state of home affairs, which was so
serious, nor that of foreign affairs which were so involved and
so full of peril, can soften the Opposition of the honourable
Members seated here. What about liberty? they say. What, is
liberty not to be prized above everything else? Should we not
respect individual liberty and has it not been sacrificed?
—Liberty, Gentlemen! Do those who pronounce this sacred
word understand the principle they proclaim and the name
they pronounce? Do they realise the times in which we live?
Have the reverberations of the recent disasters not yet reached
our ears, Gentlemen? Do you not know that Liberty is dead
now? Have you not followed its tragic passion in your mind's
eye, as I have? Have you not seen it persecuted, mocked,
treacherously struck down by all the demagogues in the world?
Have you not seen its long-drawn-out agony in the Swiss
mountains, on the banks of the Seine, beside the Rhine and the
Danube and alongside the Tiber? Have you not seen it mount
to its Calvary on the Quirinal?

This word makes us shudder, Gentlemen (but we ought not
to hesitate to pronounce such words when they express the
truth, and the truth I am determined to speak): liberty is dead.
It will not rise again, Gentlemen, on the third day, nor yet in
the third year, nor perhaps in three centuries' time! You are
alarmed at the tyranny we endure. You are alarmed by small
things: you will see far worse things. And now, Gentlemen,
I ask you to engrave my words in your memory, for what I am
going to tell you, the events which I am going to predict are
bound, in a future which cannot now be far distant from us,
to come to pass.

M

The cause of all your errors, Gentlemen, lies in your ignorance of the direction which civilisation and the world are taking. You believe that civilisation and the world are advancing, when civilisation and the world are regressing. The world is taking great strides towards the constitution of the most gigantic and destructive despotism which men have ever known. That is the trend of our world and civilisation. I do not need to be a prophet to predict these things; it is enough to consider the fearful picture of human events from the only true viewpoint, from the heights of Catholic philosophy.

There are only two possible forms of control: one internal and the other external; religious control and political control. They are of such a nature that when the religious barometer rises, the barometer of control falls and likewise, when the religious barometer falls, the political barometer, that is political control and tyranny, rises. That is a law of humanity, a law of history. If you want proof, Gentlemen, look at the state of the world, look at the state of society in the ages before the Cross; tell me what happened when there was no internal or religious control. Society in those days only comprised tyrants and slaves. Give me the name of a single people at this period which possessed no slaves and knew no tyrant. It is an incontrovertible and evident fact, which has never been questioned. Liberty, real liberty, the liberty of all and for all, only came into the world with the Saviour of the world; that again is an incontrovertible fact, recognised even by the Socialists. Yes, the Socialists admit it; they call Jesus divine, they go further, they say they continue the work of Jesus. Gracious Heaven! Continue His work! Those men of blood and vengeance continue the work of Him Who only lived to do good, Who only opened His lips to bless, Who only worked miracles to deliver sinners from their sins and the dead from death; Who in the space of three years accomplished the greatest revolution the world has ever witnessed and that without shedding any blood but His own.

Follow me carefully, I beg you; I am going to present you with the most marvellous parallel which history can offer us. You have seen that in antiquity, when religious control was at its lowest point, for it was non-existent, political control rose to the point of tyranny. Very well then, with Jesus Christ, where religious control is born, political control disappears. This is so true, that when Jesus Christ founded a society with His disciples, that society was the only one which has ever existed without a government. Between Jesus Christ and His disciples there was no other government than the love of the Master for His disciples and the love of the disciples for their Master. You see then, that when the internal control was complete, liberty was absolute.

Let us pursue the parallel. Now come the apostolic times, which I shall stretch, for the purposes of my plan, from the time of the Apostles, properly speaking, to the period when Christianity mounted the Capitol in the reign of Constantine the Great. At this time, Gentlemen, the Christian religion, that is, the internal, religious control, was at its zenith; but in spite of that, as always happens in human societies, a germ began to develop, a mere germ of protection and religious liberty. So, Gentlemen, observe the parallel: with this beginning of a fall in the religious barometer there corresponds the beginning of a rise in the political barometer. There is still no government yet, for government is not yet necessary; but it is already necessary to have the germ of government. In point of fact, in the Christian society of the time, there were no real magistrates, but there were adjudicators and arbitrators who form the germ of government. There was really nothing more than that; the Christians of apostolic times engaged in no lawsuits and never appealed to the Courts: their disputes were settled by the arbitrators. Notice, Gentlemen, how the scope of government is enlarged with the growth of corruption.

Then came feudal times. Religion was still at its zenith during this period, but was vitiated up to a point by human passions. What happened in the political sphere? A real and effective government was already essential; but the weakest kind was good enough. As a result, feudal monarchy was established, the weakest of all kinds of monarchy.

Still pursuing our parallel, we come to the sixteenth century. Then, with the great Lutheran Reformation, with this great scandal which was at the same time political, social and religious, with this act of the intellectual and moral emancipation of the peoples, we see simultaneously the growth of the following institutions. In the first place, and immediately, the feudal monarchies became absolute. You believe, Gentlemen, that a monarchy and a government cannot go beyond absolutism. However, the barometer of political control had to rise even higher, because the religious barometer continued to fall: and the political barometer did in fact rise higher. What did they create then? Standing armies. Do you know what standing armies are ? To answer that question, it is enough to know what a soldier is: a soldier is a slave in uniform. So you see once again, when religious control falls, political control rises, it rises as high as absolutism and even higher. It was not enough for governments to be absolute; they asked for and obtained the privilege of having a million arms at the service of their absolutism.

That is not all: the political barometer had to continue to rise because the religious barometer kept falling; it rose still higher. What new institution was created then ? The governments said: We have a million arms and it is not enough; we need something more, we need a million eyes: and they created the police. That was not the last word in progress: the political barometer and political control had to rise to a higher pitch still, because in spite of everything, the religious barometer kept falling; so they rose higher. It was not enough for the governments to have a million arms and a million eyes; they wanted to have a million ears: and so they created administrative centralisation, by means of which all claims and complaints finally reached the government.

Well, Gentlemen, that was not enough; the religious barometer continued to fall and so the political barometer had to rise higher. And it rose. Governments said: A million arms, a million eyes and a million ears are not sufficient to control people, we need something more; we must have the privilege of being simultaneously present in every corner of our empire. This privilege also they obtained: the telegraph was invented.

Such, Gentlemen, was the state of Europe and the world when the first rumblings of the most recent revolution intimated to us all that there is still not enough despotism on the earth, since the religious barometer remains below zero. And now the choice between two things lies before us.

I have promised to speak today with complete frankness and I shall keep my word. . . .

In a word, this is the choice we have to make: either a religious reaction will set in, or it will not. If there is a religious reaction, you will soon see that as the religious barometer rises, the political barometer will begin to fall, naturally, spontaneously, without the slightest effort on the part of peoples, governments, or men, until the tranquil day comes when the peoples of the world are free. But if, on the contrary, and this is a serious matter (it is not customary to call the attention of Consultative Assemblies to questions of this nature; but the gravity of events today is my excuse and I think I have your indulgence in this matter); I say again, Gentlemen, that if the religious barometer continues to fall, no man can see whither we are going. I cannot see, Gentlemen, and I cannot contemplate the future without terror. Consider the analogies I have put before you and weigh this question in your minds; if no government was necessary when religious control was at its zenith, and now that religious control is non-existent, what form of government is going to be strong enough to quell a revolt? Are not all despotisms equally powerless?

Have I not put my finger into the wound, Gentlemen? Yes, I have, and this is the problem which faces Spain, Europe, humanity and the world.

Notice one thing, Gentlemen. In the ancient world, tyranny was fierce and merciless; yet this tyranny was materially limited, since all States were small and formal relations between States were impossible from every point of view; consequently tyranny on the grand scale was impossible in antiquity, with one exception: Rome. But today, how greatly are things changed! The way is prepared for some gigantic and colossal tyrant, universal and immense; everything points to it. Observe that already moral and material resistance is at an end: all minds are divided, all patriotism is dead. Tell me now whether I am right or wrong to be preoccupied with the coming fate of the world; tell me whether, in dealing with this question, I am not touching upon the real problem.

One thing, and one alone, can avert the catastrophe: we shall not avert it by granting more liberty, more guarantees and new constitutions; we shall avert it if all of us, according to our strength, do our utmost to stimulate a salutary reaction —a religious reaction. Now is this possible, Gentlemen? Yes. But is it likely? I answer in deepest sorrow: I do not think it is likely. I have seen and known many men who returned to their faith after having separated themselves from it; unfortunately, I have never known any nation which returned to the Faith after once it was lost.

If any hope had remained in me, the recent events in Rome would have dispelled it. And now I am going to say a few words on the same subject on which Señor Cortina spoke.

No words can adequately describe what has happened in Rome. What word would you use, Gentlemen?—Deplorable?

All the events I have discussed are also deplorable. What has happened in Rome is worse than that. Would you use the word horrible? It surpasses even horror, Gentlemen.

There was—there no longer is—on the throne in Rome the most eminent, just and the most evangelical man on earth. What has Rome done to this just and evangelical man? What has this town, where once reigned heroes, Caesars, and Pontiffs, done? It has exchanged the throne of the Pontiffs for the throne of demagogues. Rebellious to God, it has fallen into the idolatry of the dagger. That is what it has done. The dagger, Gentlemen; the demagogic dagger, stained with blood, is today the idol of Rome. That is the idol which overthrew Pius IX. That is the idol which the Caribbean hordes are parading in the streets! Caribbeans? No: Caribbeans are fierce, but they are not ungrateful.

I have determined to speak frankly, Gentlemen. I say now that either the King of Rome must return to Rome, or, with all respect to Señor Cortina, no stone will remain standing in Rome.

The Catholic world cannot, and will not, consent to the virtual destruction of Christianity by a single town which has been delivered over to frenzy and madness. Civilised Europe cannot, and will not, consent to the ruin of the edifice of European civilisation, just because its cupola has been laid low. The world cannot, and will not, consent to the accession to the throne of a strange new dynasty, the dynasty of crime, in the Holy City. And let nobody say, Gentlemen, as Señor Cortina says and as the Members who sit on the left say in their newspapers and speeches, that two questions are at stake, one temporal and the other spiritual, and that the matter under dispute concerned the temporal Prince and his people; and that the Pontiff is still alive. Two words, two words only, will explain everything.

There can be no possible doubt that spiritual power is the principal attribute of the Pope: temporal power is accessory to it; and this accessory is essential. The Catholic world has the right to expect that the infallible mouthpiece of its dogmas should be free and independent; and the Catholic world can only be certain that its spiritual head is independent and free when this head is a Sovereign; only a Sovereign is dependent upon nobody. Consequently, Gentlemen, the question of sovereignty, which is universally a political question, is furthermore a religious question in Rome; the people, who can be sovereign everywhere else, cannot be sovereign in Rome; Constituent Assemblies, which can exist in every other country, cannot exist in Rome; in Rome there can be no other constituent power except the power already constituted there. Rome, Gentlemen, and the Papal States do not belong to Rome; they do not even belong to the Pope; they belong to the Catholic world. The Catholic world has recognised that they are an attribute of the Pope, so that he may be free and independent, and the Pope himself cannot divest himself of this sovereignty and this independence.

I will stop, Gentlemen, for the House must be tired and I am very tired too. I tell you frankly, I cannot go on any longer, because I am not well and it is a wonder that I have been able to speak at all; however, I have said most of what I wanted to say.

I have dealt with the three external problems touched upon by Señor Cortina and now I conclude with the internal problem. Ever since the beginning of the world until today, men have discussed the question as to which is the better course, in order that revolutions and upheavals may be averted—to grant concessions, or to offer resistance; but what had always been a problem from the year of Creation to the year of grace 1848 is no longer one today, it has been resolved; and if I felt strong enough, I would prove it to you by passing under review all the events which have occurred from last February up to today. I will limit myself to recalling two. In France—my first example —the monarchy offered no resistance and was conquered by the Republic, which scarcely had the vitality to set itself in motion: and the Republic, which scarcely had the vitality to set itself in motion, conquered Socialism, because Socialism offered no resistance.

In Rome—my second example—what happened ? Was not your model there ? Tell me, if you had been artists and wanted to paint the model of a king, would you not have chosen the features of Pius IX ? Pius IX tried to be magnificent and generous, like his Divine Master; he found outlaws, gave them his hand and returned them to their country; he found reformers, and granted them the reforms for which they asked; he found Liberals and granted them liberty: each word of his conferred some benefit. And now, Gentlemen, answer me this. Do the present ignominies he now suffers not equal in number the benefits he conferred, or do they not rather surpass them ?

Faced with this result, Gentlemen, is not the problem of a course of concession resolved ?

If it were a question here of choosing between liberty and dictatorship, we should all be agreed. Which man, in fact, possessing liberty, would prostrate himself before a dictatorship ? But that is not the problem. It is a fact that liberty does not exist in Europe: the constitutional governments which represented it in these last few years are today, in nearly every country, no more than structures lacking any solid foundation, bare bones deprived of life. Cast your minds back, Gentlemen, to Imperial Rome. Here in this Rome all the institutions of the Republic still survived: all-powerful dictators, inviolate tribunes, senatorial families, eminent consuls: all these people still existed; only one thing was lacking and only one thing was superfluous: what was superfluous was a man; what was lacking was the Republic.

Such, Gentlemen, is the state of nearly all the constitutional governments in Europe; and quite unconsciously Señor Cortina proved it to us the other day. Did he not say, and rightly so, that he prefers the example of history, rather than that of theory ? I call history to witness. What, Mr. Speaker, are these governments with their legal majorities, which are always conquered by turbulent minorities; with their responsible ministers, who have nothing to be responsible for; with their inviolable kings, who are always violated ? Thus, as I have said, Gentlemen, the choice does not lie between liberty and dictatorship; if that were so, I would vote for liberty, just as all of us here would do. The problem, and my conclusion, are as follows: we have to choose between the dictatorship of insurrection and the dictatorship of government; of these two alternatives I choose dictatorship on the part of the government, as being less onerous and less shameful.

We must choose between a dictatorship which comes from below or one which comes from above: I choose the one which comes from above, because it emanates from purer and more serene regions. Our choice must finally lie between the dictatorship of the dagger and that of the sword: I choose the dictatorship of the sword, because it is more noble. As we vote, Gentlemen, we shall divide on this question and in so doing we shall be true to ourselves. You, Gentlemen (*the Opposition*), will, as always, follow the most popular course and we (*the Government supporters*) will, as always, vote for what is most salutary.

2. SOCIALISM[1]

THE most consistent of modern Socialists appears to me to be Robert Owen. An open and cynical rebel, he breaks with all religions which are depositaries of religious and moral dogmas, rejects the idea of duty by his denial of collective responsibility (which constitutes the dogma of solidarity) and of individual responsibility, which rests on the dogma of the free-will of man. Then, having denied free-will, Robert Owen denies sin and the transmission of sin. So far, no one can doubt that these deductions are logical and consistent; but the contradiction and the extravagances begin when Owen, having denied sin and free-will, makes a distinction between moral good and evil, as if there could be any good or evil where free-will is non-existent and as if evil and sin were not synonymous. Furthermore, he differentiates between good and evil, while denying the penalty which is the necessary consequence of evil.

Man, according to Robert Owen, acts in consequence of certain deep-rooted convictions. These convictions come to him in part from his peculiar heredity and in part from his environment; and as he is the author of neither his heredity nor his environment, it follows that both have a fatal and an inevitable effect upon him.

All this is logical and consistent, but it is completely illogical, contradictory and absurd to postulate good and evil, when human liberty is denied. Absurdity reaches grotesque proportions when our author attempts to found a society and a government in conjunction with men who are irresponsible: the idea of government and the idea of society have no meaning apart from the idea of human liberty; denial of the one follows from the denial of the others and if you deny or affirm them all, you deny or affirm one and the same thing. I do not know whether the annals of mankind show a more striking proof of blindness, inconsistency and madness than that which Owen gives, when, not satisfied with the extravagance of affirming the existence of society and government, after having denied individual responsibility and liberty, he goes still further and falls into the inconceivable extravagance of recommending benevolence, justice and charity to those who, being neither responsible nor free, can neither love, nor be just, nor be benevolent.

[1] Donoso Cortés, *Essays on Catholicism, Liberalism and Socialism.* Wm. B. Kelly. 1874. Translation by Rev. William M'Donald, Rector of the Irish College, Salamanca, *revised.* Pp. 279 *et seq.*

. . . This shameful contradiction in terms which is the essence of Socialism is so palpable that it will be easy to set it in relief, even on those points on which all these sectarians appear to be united in agreement. If one single negation is common to them all, it is assuredly the denial of the solidarity of the family and of the nobility. All revolutionary and socialistic masters of doctrine are unanimous in their rejection of this communion of glories and misfortunes, of merits and demerits in generation after generation, which mankind has recognised as a fact throughout the ages.

Now these same revolutionaries and Socialists affirm quite unconsciously by their practice the very thing they deny in theory in other people. When the French Revolution in its frenzy and blood-lust had trampled all the national glories underfoot; when, intoxicated with its triumphs, it believed final victory certain, a mysterious aristocratic pride of race took hold of it, which was in direct contradiction to all its dogmas. Then we saw the most famous of the revolutionaries, as proudly as any feudal baron of old, behave with great circumspection, so that the privilege of entering their family was only accorded with reserve and at the cost of many scruples. My readers will remember that famous question put by the doctors of the new law to those who presented themselves as candidates—" What crime have you committed ? " Who could not but sympathise with the unfortunate man who had committed no crime, for never would the gates of the Capitol, where sat the demi-gods of the Revolution, terrible in their majesty, be opened to him. Mankind had instituted the aristocracy of virtue, the revolution instituted the aristocracy of crime.

. . . Examine all the revolutionary schools one by one and you will see that they all vie with each other in an effort to constitute themselves into a family and to claim a noble descent: Saint-Simon the aristocrat is the ancestor of one group; the illustrious Fourier of another, and Babeuf the patriot of a third group. In each one you will find a common leader, a common patrimony, a common glory, a common mission; each group is distinct from the other, then breaks away from the others to form a splinter group, all the members of which are linked together by a narrow solidarity and seek out of the depths of the past some famous name as a rallying cry. Some have chosen Plato, the glorious personification of the wisdom of the ancients; others, and they are numerous, carrying their mad ambition to the heights of blasphemy, do not fear to profane the sacred name of the Redeemer! Poor and abandoned, they would perhaps have forgotten Him; humble they would have scorned Him; but in their insolent pride they do not forget that poor, wretched, and humble as He was, He was a King and that royal blood flowed in His veins. As for M. Proudhon, that perfect type of Socialist pride, which in its turn is the prototype of human pride—carried away by his vanity, he goes as far back as he can to the remotest ages, in an attempt to seek his ancestry in those times which bordered upon Creation, when the Mosaic institutions flourished amongst the Hebrews. As a matter of fact, his lineage and his name are still more ancient and illustrious than he thinks; to discover their origin, we must go back still further, to times beyond the pale of history, to beings who in perfection and dignity are incomparably higher than men. At present, suffice it to say that the Socialist schools of thought tend inevitably towards contradiction and absurdity; that each one of their principles contradicts those which precede or follow; and that their conduct is a complete condemnation of their theories, as their theories are a radical condemnation of their conduct.

. . . The fundamental negation of Socialism is the negation of sin, that grand affirmation which is, as it were, the focal point of the Catholic affirmation. This denial logically implies a whole series of further negations, some of them relating to the Divine Person, others to the human person, others still to man in society.

The most fundamental of them all is this: that the Socialists not only deny the fact of sin, but the possibility of sinning; from this double negation follows the negation of human liberty, which is meaningless if we ignore the power given to mankind to choose between good and evil and to fall from the state of innocence into a state of sin.

The denial of free-will leads to a disclaimer of human responsibility; the responsibility of man being denied, penalties for sin are also denied, from which follows on the one hand the negation of divine government, and on the other, the negation of human governments. Therefore, as far as the question of government is concerned, the negation of sin ends in nihilism.

To deny the responsibility of the individual in the domestic, political and human spheres is to deny the solidarity of the individual in the family and in the State; it is to deny unity in the species, in the State, in the family and in man himself, since there is such complete identity between the principles of solidarity and unity that one thing cannot be conceived in isolation without reference to the principle of solidarity and vice-versa. Therefore, as regards the question of unity, the negation of sin ends in nihilism.

Unity being denied absolutely, the following negations are implied—that of humanity, of the family, of society and of man. The fact is that nothing exists at all except on condition of being " one," so that the existence of the family, of society and of humanity can only be postulated on condition that domestic, political and human unity is affirmed. If these unities are denied, the negation of these three things must follow; to affirm that they exist, and to deny unity between them, is a contradiction in terms. Each of these things is necessarily " one," or it cannot exist at all; therefore if they are not " *one* " they do not exist; their very name is absurd, for it is a name which does not describe or designate anything.

The negation of individualism also follows from the negation of the principle of unity, although by a different process. Only individual man can, up to a certain point, exist without being " one " and without having any solidarity with his fellows: what is denied in this case, if his unity and solidarity with mankind is denied, is that he is always the same person at different moments of his life. If there is no bond of union between the past and the present and between the present and the future, it follows that man exists only in the present moment. But in this hypothesis, it is clear that his existence is more phenomenal than real. If I do not live in the past, because it is past, and because there is no unity between the present and the past; if I do not live in the future, because the future does not exist and because when it will exist it will not be future; if I only live in the present and the present does not exist, because when I am about to affirm that it exists, it has already passed, my existence is manifestly more theoretical than practical; for in reality, if I do not exist at all times, I do not exist at any time. I conceive time only in the union of its three forms and I cannot conceive it when I separate them. What is the past, unless it is something which no longer is ? What is the future, unless it is something which does not yet exist ? Who can halt the present long enough to affirm that it is here, once it has escaped from the future, and before it relapses into the past ? To affirm the existence of man, denying the unity of time, amounts to giving man the speculative existence of a mathematical point. Therefore the negation of sin ends in nihilism, as regards both the

existence of individual man, of the family, of the body politic
and of humanity. Therefore, in every sphere, all Socialist doctrines, or to be accurate, all rationalist doctrines must end
inevitably in nihilism. Nothing is more natural and logical
than that those who separate themselves from God should end
in nothing, since there is nothing outside God.

Having established this much, I have the right to accuse
present-day Socialism of being timid and contradictory. To
deny the Christian God in order to affirm another god; to
deny humanity from one point of view in order to affirm it from
another; to deny society in certain of its forms in order to
affirm it in different forms; to deny the family on one hand and
to affirm it on the other; to deny man in one of his aspects in
order to affirm him in other and contradictory ones—is not all
this to enter upon the path of conflicting actions, the consequence of timidity and irresolution ?

. . . Present-day Socialism is a kind of semi-Catholicism and
nothing more. In the work of the most advanced of its doctors,
there is a greater number of Catholic affirmations than
Socialist negations; with the result that we have a Catholicism
which is absurd and a Socialism which is contradictory. If we
affirm the existence of God, we fall into the hands of the God
of the Catholics; if we affirm the existence of humanity, we
must accept the humanity one and indivisible of the Christian
dogma; if we affirm the existence of society, we must come
sooner or later to the Catholic teaching on social institutions;
if we affirm the existence of the family, we are bound to affirm
everything which Catholicism lays down and Socialism denies
on the subject; in a word, that every affirmation concerning
man, whatever it may be, is finally resolved into an affirmation
of Adam, the man of Genesis. Catholicism can be compared to
those huge cylinders through which the whole must pass, if a
part has done so. Unless it changes its course, Socialism with all
its pontiffs and doctors will pass through this cylinder, without
leaving any trace.

. . . Catholicism is not a thesis, consequently it cannot be
combated by an antithesis; it is a synthesis which embraces
all things, contains all things and explains all things, which
cannot be—I will not say conquered—but even combated,
except by a synthesis of the same kind, which like it should
embrace, contain and explain all things. All human theses and
antitheses find their place in the Catholic synthesis: it attracts
and resolves all things into itself by the invincible force of an

incommunicable virtue. Those who imagine that they live outside Catholicism really live within its orbit, because it is as it were their intellectual climate. The Socialists have met the same fate as the others: in spite of the gigantic efforts they have made to separate themselves from Catholicism, they have done no more than to become bad Catholics.

VIII. JAIME BALMES

1810 - 1848

IN Jaime Balmes, whom Donoso considered to be the master of his mind, we miss the poetic note and the prophetic vision. He was, above all, a theologian. His mind was of a more scholastic formation, and he lived to see only the beginning of those events in Europe which raised Donoso's thought to its highest level. Though less striking as a literary personality, and less of an original thinker than Donoso, the importance of Balmes in the history of apologetics cannot be, and indeed never has been, overlooked.

It had been usual, ever since Montesquieu's day, to postulate the social good in the political theory of Europe, and to relegate theological truth, not only to a secondary plane, but to deny that dogma had any justification at all. Montesquieu and his successors still recognised Christian morality as the best foundation for society. Yet he protested at the same time that a definite system of Christian dogma was not necessary to produce that moral good which society derives from Christian beliefs. According to him, that religion is best which fully meets the circumstances and requirements of the time and the place: Catholicism is best for Monarchies, Protestantism for Republics and even Islam for the East, although in his view Islam is less promising as a religion when we consider " our welfare in this world and the next " (*Esprit des Lois*).

The historical schools of the early nineteenth century—Guizot, Michelet and Quinet in France, and especially Macaulay in England—went much further, and saw the Protestant Reformation as a step forward on the road of the inevitable and salutary progress, a phase in the " emancipation " of mankind. Macaulay identified material progress with Protestantism and thought that such progress was incompatible with Catholic civilisation.

During the three decades following the Napoleonic Wars, two political influences were at work in Spain, the country which had played such a tremendous part in frustrating Napoleon's plan to dominate and conquer Europe. Both Britain and France attempted to make the Peninsula an outpost and an extension of their own power: Britain almost in the spirit which we know from George Borrow's *Bible in Spain*, and France in the spirit of Guizot, who was not only the foremost ideological influence in the reign of Louis Philippe, but for some years was also a leading statesman, especially

at the moment of the treaty of 1846,[1] which seemed to establish
French influence in Spain for some time to come, to the dissatisfac-
tion of Palmerston. The Spanish supporters of the British and
French influence in Spain hoped to bring material prosperity to
Spain and to " emancipate " the " backward " Spanish masses
through Liberal institutions.

Balmes wrote his *Protestantism* as a reply to these widespread arguments, which were found in the 1840's in the Spanish Press and
Parliament. He went part of the way with Bossuet, who in his
History of Variations showed that every " variation " from the unity
of dogma is bound to lead, sooner or later, to the vague and hardly
Christian doctrine of the " Unitarians " of Socinius, and he wrote
his monumental book to establish the necessity of a precise and
authoritative dogma.

Balmes accepts discussion with his opponents, on ground of their
own choosing, not in the field of dogmatic truth, but in that of
history and culture, which they consider to be of primary importance. He proves with historical arguments that Luther's break
with the Church was, far from being an act of progress and emancipation, a great retrogressive step. Denying as it does any other
basis for theological truth except individual judgement and personal
interpretation of a text, Protestantism rules out spiritual authority.
This way leads either to anarchy or to despotism, to an undue
buttressing of the secular and temporal authority, which Luther
called to his aid when some of his followers attempted to push his
doctrine to its extreme, although logical, consequences. Deprived
of the consecration which the Church conferred on temporal power,
and limited to temporal purposes by the very nature of its own legitimacy, Protestantism had to find some other grounds for the justification of the authority of the law and for social order. Thus we
find Calvin justifying the inheritance of wealth through the doctrine
of Grace, and Luther proclaiming Adam, and not Christ, to be the
father of the temporal order, which therefore is bound to remain
under the stain of original sin, and the despotic excesses of which
—as Hobbes, developing Luther's argument later on in a more
systematic way, explains—are bound to be the punishment for
original sin.

Anarchy or despotism is the Protestant alternative to the Catholic
synthesis of Authority and Liberty. Balmes is naturally ready to
recognise that a great deal of the Catholic inheritance survived the
Reformation of the sixteenth century, and extenuated Protestant
practice, just as he is ready to admit that the Catholic political
order often fell short of the ideal. But with his critical analysis of
Protestantism as the religious origin of spiritual anarchy and temporal tyranny, he brought a new and immensely important element

---

[1] This treaty arranged the marriage of the Duc de Montpensier, youngest son
of Louis Philippe, to the Infanta sister of Queen Isabel II.

into the historical and political controversy of the time. It is enough to recall the sociological school of the German Liberal Protestant scholars, such as Max Weber and Ernst Troeltzsch, in the first two decades of the present century to show that Balmes' analysis of Luther and Protestantism fell on fertile soil in Luther's own country, Germany.

Almost everybody who has tried to analyse seriously the causes which led Germany to the virulent crisis of the First World War and to the diabolical rule of Hitler has seen the origin of the German tendency to anarchy and despotism in Luther's attitude to temporal authority—more often than not in unconscious imitation of Balmes.

Balmes is the teacher of the Church on Order and Liberty, a master in the controversy against political and social Protestantism, as Bossuet was the master in the controversy against theological Protestantism. Thus he stands—with Donoso Cortés—at the threshold of the new, glorious and historical rôle which fell once again in the post-revolutionary age to the Christian and national genius of Spain.

FAITH AND LIBERTY[1]

THE supposed incompatibility of unity in faith with political liberty is an invention of the irreligious philosophy of the last century. Whichever political opinions we adopt, it is extremely important for us to be on our guard against such a doctrine. We must not forget that the Catholic religion stands high above all forms of government—she does not reject from her bosom either the citizen of the United States, or the inhabitants of Russia, but embraces all men with equal tenderness, commanding all men to obey the legitimate governments of their respective countries. She considers them all to be children of the same Father, participators in the same Redemption, heirs to the same glory. It is very important to bear in mind that irreligion allies itself to liberty, or to despotism, according to its own interests; it applauds unstintingly when an infuriated populace burns churches, and massacres the priests at the altar, but it is always ready to flatter monarchs, to give an exaggerated importance to their power whenever they win the favour of this power by despoiling the clergy, subverting discipline and insulting the Pope. It cares little what instruments it employs, provided it accomplishes its work: it is Royalist when it is in

---

[1] Taken from *European Civilisation, Protestantism and Catholicity*, John Murphy & Co., Baltimore, 1868. Translated by Messrs. Hanford and Kershaw (*revised*).

a position to influence the minds of kings and expel the Jesuits from France, from Spain and from Portugal, and to pursue them to the four corners of the earth without giving them any respite or peace; it is Liberal when it shows itself inside popular Assemblies, which exact sacrilegious oaths from the clergy and send into exile, or execute, those priests who remain faithful to their duty.

The man who cannot see the strict truth of my argument must have forgotten history and paid little attention to very recent events. When religion and morality are present, all forms of government are good; without them, none can be good. An absolute monarch, imbued with religious ideas, surrounded by counsellors whose doctrines are sound and reigning over a people who share the same doctrines, can make his subjects happy and is bound to do so, as far as circumstances of time and place permit. A wicked monarch, or one surrounded by wicked advisers, will do harm according to the extent of his power; he is even more to be dreaded than revolution itself, because he has better opportunities for laying his plans and carrying them out more rapidly, he is faced with fewer obstacles, can assume a semblance of legality and can claim to serve the public interest, so that he has a far greater chance of success and of achieving permanent results. Revolutions have undoubtedly done great injury to the Church; but persecuting monarchs have done her as great injury. A whim of Henry VIII established Protestantism in England; the cupidity of certain other princes produced a like result in the nations of the North; and in our own days, a decree of the Autocrat of Russia drives millions of souls into schism. It follows that an absolute monarchy is not desirable unless it is a religious one; for irreligion, which is immoral by nature, naturally tends to injustice and consequently to tyranny. If irreligion is seated on an absolute throne, or if it takes possession of the mind of the occupant of that throne, its powers are unlimited; and for my part, I know nothing more horrible than the omnipotence of wickedness.

In recent times, European democracy has been lamentably conspicuous for its attacks upon religion; a state of affairs which, far from furthering the cause of democracy, has injured it considerably. We can indeed form an idea of a government which is more or less free, when society is virtuous, moral and religious; but not when these prerequisites are lacking. In the latter case, the only possible form of government is despotism,

the rule of force, for force alone can govern men who are without
conscience and without God. If we compare the American and
the French Revolutions carefully, we find that one of the principal differences between them is that the American Revolution
was essentially democratic and the French was essentially
impious. In the manifestoes which inaugurated the former revolution, the name of God and of Providence appears everywhere;
the men engaged in the perilous enterprise of shaking off the
yoke of Great Britain, far from uttering blasphemies against the
Almighty, invoke His assistance, convinced that the cause of
independence was also the cause of reason and justice. The
French began by deifying the leaders of irreligion, over-
throwing altars, watering churches, streets and scaffolds with
the blood of priests—the only revolutionary sign recognised by
the people is Atheism hand in hand with liberty. This folly
has borne its fruits—it spread its fatal contagion in other
countries which have recently experienced revolutions—the
new order of things has been inaugurated with sacrilegious
crimes; and the proclamation of the rights of man was
preceded by the profanation of the churches of Him from whom
all rights come.

Modern demagogues, it is true, have only imitated their
predecessors the Protestants, the Hussites and the Albigenses;
with this difference, however, that in our day irreligion has
manifested itself openly, side by side with its companion the
democracy of blood and baseness; while the democracy of
former times was allied with sectarian fanaticism. The dis-
solving doctrines of Protestantism rendered a stronger power
necessary, precipitated the overthrow of ancient liberties and
obliged authority to hold itself continually on the alert, and
to be ready to strike. When the influence of Catholicism had
been weakened, the void had to be filled by a system of espion-
age and compulsion. Do not forget this, you who make war
on religion in the name of liberty; do not forget that like causes
produce like effects. Where no moral influence exists, its
absence must be supplied by physical force: if you deprive
people of the sweet yoke of religion, you leave governments no
other resource than the vigilance of the police and the force of
bayonets. Think of these things and make your choice. Before
the advent of Protestantism, European civilisation, under the
aegis of the Catholic religion, was evidently tending towards
that general harmony, the absence of which has rendered an
excessive use of force necessary. Unity of faith disappeared,

leaving the way open to an unrestrained liberty of opinion and religious discord: the influence of the clergy was destroyed in some countries and weakened in others: thus an equilibrium between the different classes no longer existed and the class which was destined by nature to fulfil the rôle of mediator was deprived of any influence. By curtailing the power of the Popes, both people and governments were loosed from that gentle curb which restrained without oppressing, and corrected without degrading; kings and peoples were set at variance one with the other, without any body of men possessed of authority being able to mediate between them in case of conflict; governments lacking a single judge who, as the friend of both parties and with no personal interest in the quarrel, could have settled their differences impartially, began to rely upon standing armies, and the people began to rely on insurrection.

It is no use alleging that in Catholic countries a political phenomenon was seen familiar to the one we see in Protestant nations; for I maintain that amongst Catholics themselves, events did not follow the course which they would naturally have followed if the fatal Reformation had not intervened. In order to reach its full fruition, European civilisation required that unity from which it had sprung; it could not establish harmony between the diverse elements which it sheltered within its bosom by any other means. Its homogeneity was lost immediately the unity of faith disappeared. From that hour, no nation could organise itself adequately without taking into account, not only its own internal needs, but also the principles that prevailed in other countries, against the influence of which it had to be on its guard. Do you imagine, for instance, that the policy of the Spanish Government, constituted as it was the protector of the Catholic religion against powerful Protestant nations, was not powerfully influenced by the peculiar and very dangerous position of the country?

I think I have shown that the Church has never opposed the legitimate development of any form of government; that she has taken them all under her protection and consequently that to assert that she is the enemy of popular institutions is a calumny. I have likewise placed it beyond doubt that the sects hostile to the Catholic Church, by their encouragement of a democracy which is either irreligious, or blinded by fanaticism, have, in fact, far from helping on the establishment of just and rational liberty, left the people no alternative between un-bridled licentiousness and unrestrained despotism. The lesson with which history thus furnishes us is confirmed by experience and the future will but corroborate the truth of this lesson. The more religious and moral men are, the more they deserve liberty; for they need less external restraints in that case, having a most powerful one in their own consciences. An irreligious and immoral people stand in need of authority of some sort, to keep them in order, otherwise they will constantly abuse their rights and so will deserve to lose them. St Augustine understood these truths perfectly and explains in a brief and beautiful way the conditions which are necessary for all forms of government. The holy Doctor shows that popular forms of government are good where the people are moral and conscientious; where they are corrupt, they require either an oligarchy or an autocratic monarchy.

I have no doubt that an interesting passage in dialogue form that we find in his first book on Free Will, Chapter vi, will be read with pleasure.

Augustine: You would not maintain, for instance, that men or people are so constituted by nature as to be absolutely eternal, subject neither to destruction nor change?

Evodius: Who can doubt that they are changeable and subject to the influence of time?

Augustine: If the people are serious and temperate; and if moreover they have such a concern for the public good that each one would prefer the public interest to his own, *is it not true that it would be advisable to decree that such a nation should choose its own authorities to administer their affairs?*

Evodius: Certainly.

Augustine: But imagine that these people become so corrupt that *the citizens prefer their own good to the public good; supposing they sell their votes, that corrupted by ambitious men they entrust the government of the State to men as criminal and as corrupt as themselves;* is it not true that in such a case if there should be a man of integrity amongst them, who possesses sufficient power for the purpose, he would do well to take away from these people their power of conferring honours, and concentrate it in the hands of a small number of upright men, or even in the hands of one man?

Evodius: Undoubtedly.

Augustine: Yet since these laws appear very contradictory, the one granting the right of conferring honours and the

other depriving them of that right; since moreover they cannot both be in force at once, *are we to affirm that one of these laws is unjust, or that it should not have been made ?*
Evodius: By no means.

The whole question is contained here in a few words: Can monarchy, aristocracy and democracy all be legitimate and proper ? Yes. By what considerations are we to be guided when we wish to decide which of these forms is legitimate and proper in any given case ? By considering existing rights and the condition of the people to whom such a form is to be applied. Can a form of government, once good, become bad ? Certainly it may; for all human things are subject to change. These reflections, as solid as they are simple, will prevent all excessive enthusiasm in favour of any particular form of government. This is not a question of theory only, but one of prudence. Now prudence does not decide before having considered the subject carefully and weighed all the circumstances. But there is one predominant idea in the doctrine of St Augustine: the idea, which I have already indicated, that great virtue and disinterestedness are required under free government. Those who hope to build political liberty on the ruins of religious belief would do well to meditate on the words of this illustrious Doctor of the Church.

How do you think people could exercise extensive rights, if you prevent them from doing so by perverting their ideas and corrupting their morals ?

You say that under representative forms of government, reason and justice are secured by means of elections; and yet you strive to banish this reason and justice from the bosom of that society in which you talk of securing them. You sow the wind and reap the whirlwind; instead of models of wisdom and prudence, you offer the people scandalous scenes. Do not say that we are condemning the age and that it progresses in spite of us: we reject nothing that is good, but perversity and corruption we must condemn. The age is making progress, it is true. But neither you, nor we, know which direction it is taking. Catholics know only one thing on this subject and that is that good social conditions cannot be formed out of bad men. They know that immoral men are bad, and that where there is no religion, morality cannot take root. Firm in our faith, we shall leave you to try, if you so desire, a thousand forms of government. Apply your palliatives to your own social patient;

impose it upon him with deceitful words. His frequent convulsions, his continued restlessness, are sufficient evidence of your lack of skill. It proves that you have not succeeded so well in securing his confidence. If ever you do secure it, if ever he fell asleep in your arms, " All flesh will then have corrupted its way " and we may fear that God will have resolved to sweep man from the face of the earth.

IX. LOUIS VEUILLOT

1813 - 1878

THE following pages, which comprise the Foreword to Louis Veuillot's *The Freethinkers*, published amidst the upheavals of the Revolution of 1848, tell us almost all there is to know about the author and about the part played by him in his time. Veuillot appears here at his best.

The Freethinkers is a monumental image of a period, and is a landmark in the history of post-Revolutionary apologetics, just as the year which saw its publication was a landmark in the post-Revolutionary history of France and of Europe. What La Bruyère's *Characters* was for the seventeenth century, Veuillot's *Freethinkers* might deserve to be for the nineteenth century. The first is a grandiose satirical panorama of human weaknesses in an age of social and national splendour; the second a polemical and satirical dissection of human stupidity disguised as intellectual pride, in an age of social crisis and national decadence. And La Bruyère may be said to have outlined the principal theme of *The Freethinkers* in the final chapter of his *Characters*, when he describes the *Esprits Forts*:

" Do strong minds realise that this name is bestowed upon them ironically ? What greater weakness is there, than for a man to be uncertain as to the principle which guides his existence, his life, his senses and his attainments, and to what it all leads ! What greater discouragement can there be for a man, than to doubt whether his soul is not as much matter as a stone or a reptile, or whether it is not as easily corrupted as these vile things of clay ? Do we not show more strength and greatness by accepting in our minds the idea of a Being, superior to all other beings, Who has made them all, and to Whom all must return; of a Being Who is sovereignly perfect and pure, Who has neither beginning nor end, in Whose image our souls are created, and if I may so express it, a part of which is, as it were, spiritual and immortal ?

" The docile mind and the weak mind are both impressionable; the one receives good impressions, the other bad ones; in other words, the first is convinced and faithful, while the second is obstinate and corrupted. Hence the docile mind accepts the true religion, and the weak mind does not accept any religion, or else accepts a false one: now the strong mind has no religion, or else invents one for itself; therefore the strong mind is really the weak one."

These " strong minds," just numerous enough to be noticed in the century of Louis XIV, invaded the French scene a hundred years later, and became the masters. After the great Revolution and the Napoleonic epic, Victor Hugo and the Romantics brought down to the level of the profane crowds the majestic mysteries of the language of Pascal and Bossuet, and by an often cheap and vulgar melodrama, the precursor of the cinema, and by their easy rhetoric, precursor of the Press and modern propaganda, they became the symbol of an age which it is the lasting merit of Veuillot to expose and reject.

Veuillot was a man of the people, son of a poor, working-class family, grandson and great-great-grandson of peasants. This gave him the right to reject with indignation and horror the sugary spiritual poison which was offered as food for the " people " by those who claimed to be the people's friends. Veuillot was a son of the poor. He had an incontestable right therefore to reject the unwanted advocates of the people who schemed to detach the poor from the protection of Christ the King, to withdraw from the poor their right to persevere in their allegiance to Christ and His Vicar on earth. There is hardly a writer more at war with the authorities of his time than was Louis Veuillot. Hardly ever has a writer said worse things about authorities than this untiring defender of Authority, not of course because constitutional monarchs, royal ministers, Parliaments, academies and universities, and last, but not least, bishops of the Church, were autocratic in his eyes, but because they did not always have the courage of their authority, and courted popular favour by bribing the anti-Christian forces and pseudo-ideas of the age with cowardly concessions.

Balzac knew the Holy Ghost mainly under His aspect of Prudence. Veuillot derived from Him mainly the virtue of Fortitude. Both are one-sided, of course, just as Bonald, who saw God mainly as the author of Law and Order, and Joseph de Maistre, who saw Him mainly as Providence in action, moving History through events which seem a chaos to uninformed human eyes, were one-sided before them. Yet fully enlightened wisdom on the workings of God—which is not yet full knowledge—is the privilege of the Church, guardian of God's name among men. Her lay defenders have done enough for the salvation of their time, and possibly enough for their own salvation, if they proclaimed loudly enough the inseparability of any particular human virtue or understanding from the Creator of all fortitude and all knowledge.

Joseph de Maistre—and especially Bonald—are still near to the Cartesian method. They are still trained in Descartes' school; in their meditations on the State and its upheavals, on nations and their destinies, their chief concern is to find a law and a rule, and in the great Revolution they mainly see aberration and deviation from Truth and from Law. Veuillot, at first sight merely a chronicler who found his subjects for meditation in the futile and ephemeral events of the town, inaugurates a different and a new approach. Bonald and de Maistre fight false ideas, errors and aberrations; for Veuillot, the principles and forces of evil appear in their personal incarnations, in their human forms. Veuillot is the chronicler of a society at a period of crisis.

Bonald and de Maistre saw the nations in error and tried to restore the Law. Veuillot knows—for he lived to see it—that restorations do not help much, and when they were tried, proved to be ephemeral. Society itself is in dissolution, the people themselves are cast out—perhaps for centuries—into the desert, where they will have no kings, no prophets and no sacrifices, as Nehemias said of the Jews; the fall of Crowns, once given to crown the glory of Christian nations, was but a beginning. Veuillot sees his time as the beginning of the Rejection. In this prophetic vision, which is no more Cartesian, in this vision which is formed and inspired by the Old Testament and the Apocalypse alone, and not by any method of reasoning derived from Descartes or Leibnitz, Veuillot was confirmed by a great Christian visionary, who began as a philosopher and a political thinker, but who was changed into a mystic and prophet by the first European Revolution—by Donoso Cortés. From a simple chronicler of Parisian characters and events, Veuillot reaches the much higher sphere of the Absolute, after the Revolution of 1848 and the years spent in Donoso's company, until the death of this latter in 1853.

Perhaps he never fully reached this sphere. We do not need to defend Veuillot against the opponents of his day. Most of them were the enemies of the Church and of Christ, or, worse still, they were those modern Pharisees who, like the sweet-tongued and benevolent Renan, were prepared to recognise a moralist and a poet in the Lord and Redeemer. But he had Catholic opponents too: not only politicians like Falloux, Berryer or Montalembert, but Liberal and slightly Gallican bishops, Mgr. Sibour or Mgr. Dupanloup, who would have preferred L'Univers to be an organ of day-to-day politics in the interest of the Church in France, and complained that Veuillot spoilt chances of Parliamentary compromise on practical matters such as legislation for the schools. Veuillot considered himself to be the Pope's soldier, and the direct personal approach which Pius IX always readily granted him was sometimes the object of complaint or objection by the French hierarchy.

We do not need to defend Veuillot from Victor Hugo's biting rhymes in Les Châtiments, which made him out to be the defender of all tyrannies because he was prepared to accept the protection of any legal order against revolutionary terror and disorder. Victor Hugo was perhaps the only temperament and the only master of style who could treat Veuillot with a polemical talent worthy of his own, but as Veuillot answered Hugo with a series of replies which

he collected into a whole volume—which has the merit of re-
vindicating the best of Victor Hugo for Christian inspiration and
makes good fun of the rest—we may consider this debate as closed.
We can dismiss as much below the level of literary debate such
opponents of Louis Veuillot who thought fit to assert that he was
personally employed by Pius IX to spy upon the bishops who were
opposed to the Bull of Infallibility!

Nevertheless, we must try to find an explanation of the disappointment Veuillot caused to men like Barbey d'Aurevilly, Ernest Hello,
and Léon Bloy; for it was Veuillot's fate to disappoint those whom
he inspired and for whom he was in a certain sense a precursor and
a master. He wrote from day to day for some forty-five years, of
which he asked posterity to discount the first fifteen. Before being
overwhelmed by the *Soirées de St Pétersbourg*, and " before being
moved by Joseph de Maistre to seek his peace in the Church through
confession to a Jesuit," Veuillot was, as he says, a " condottiere of
the pen " at the service of the Liberalism of Louis-Philippe and
Guizot. He asks us to consider all that he wrote in his early years
for other reasons than the glory of God and the truth of the Church
as unwritten. In fairness to him we may do so, although he probably
judged himself more severely than we may do. Even before his
irrevocable engagement in the cause of the Church, Veuillot was
not an enemy of God's cause, any more than was King Louis-
Philippe, or the Protestant statesman and historian Guizot. But a
life of daily polemics in the turbulent, revolutionary street life of
Paris did not allow him to show God in His glory, consoling the
solitude of sad hearts. A good soldier in all battles for God's honour,
he was not—like Léon Bloy—a poet of God's glory.

As we said in the Introduction the history of apologetics is a history
of answers; it begins with the Redeemer's own answer to the Rabbis
and Pharisees, whose reasonings on the Scriptures He has for ever
defeated. In France, Pascal was a reply to Montaigne. The great
humanist's aphorisms on the relativity of everything human was
defeated by a greater humanist, who, through a more masterly
exposition of human relativities, concluded that *Jesus Christ will
suffer agony to the end of the world; we must keep watch until then*. Joseph
de Maistre was a reply to Voltaire; to Voltaire's paradoxical wit,
the Church riposted with a more brilliantly paradoxical wit. To
oppose Montesquieu's wise and stoic search for harmony and
equilibrium in human institutions, the Church found Bonald, a
greater teacher of harmony, order and perfect equilibrium.

Mazzini's and Proudhon's burning desire for justice and for the
" People " found its reply in Louis Veuillot.

Then, a little later, when the idol of " the People " was replaced
by the aesthetic idol of artistic perfection and inventive genius, the
Church found her reply in Barbey d'Aurevilly, Léon Bloy, Ernest
Hello and Charles Péguy, as it found her doctors of objective science,

this other idol of the age, in Cardinal Newman and Lord Acton, and as the eternal agony of Christ found its voice, amidst the pleasant and shallow declamations of the aestheticism of a prosperous age, in Kierkegaard and Dostoievsky. *Opportet ut fiat scandala.* Louis Veuillot—this is his immense merit, while it is perhaps also his limitation—was the Christian scandal for the strong minds of popular " Enlightenment."

THE TRUE FREEDOM OF THOUGHT[1]

I UNDERSTAND by " free-thinkers," as they call themselves, those men of letters (or people who imagine themselves to be such) who, in their writings, their speeches and their daily lives, cunningly endeavour to destroy revealed religion and its divine system of morality in France. Professors, writers, legis-lators, bankers, gentlemen of the Bar, industrialists and business-men—they are ubiquitous, they have a hand in every-thing, they are our masters; it is they who have placed us in our present position, which they exploit and aggravate.

I have tried to paint their portrait in this book, not, I confess, in admiration. A Catholic and a son of the people, I am doubly their enemy, from the time when I began to *think* too, that is to say from the time when, by the grace of God, my mind was freed from the yoke which they had placed upon it for so long. " Free-thinkers " sounds as unpleasant to my ears as " Jesuit " does to theirs. But being a Catholic meant that I had to con-form to certain obligations. It would have been wrong of me to *burlesque* a single portrait. I have copied from life; yet if I have not allowed myself to embellish anything, I have not drawn a veil over much. If a character seems to be far-fetched, he has been taken from an original which was even more brazen. The way in which these gentlemen present us on their side is a matter of common knowledge. The reader will judge whether the Jesuit's pencil is nearer to the truth than the free-thinker's paint-brush.

I began this book several years ago, laid it aside and picked it up again many times, until finally I had it ready for the printer, when the adventure of last February[2] intervened, so that publication was postponed. I publish it now without altering anything; I only omit a few chapters whose argument

---

[1] Foreword to Louis Veuillot's *Libres Penseurs*, Paris, Jacques et Cie, 1850.
[2] The February Revolution of 1848, which replaced the Constitutional Monarchy of Louis-Philippe with the Second Republic.

was riddled by the bullets which overthrew Charter,[1] Throne and Parliament. If only it had enabled me to tear up the whole book! The anger, the sorrow, and the fears which filled my heart when I wrote it would have vanished. I should have lost my misgivings over the terrible dangers I tried to foretell. But these dangers are still present in our principles and the Revolution at most has only changed our laws.

. . . I expect to have one reproach levelled at me. Nearly all the free-thinkers belong to that class of well-dressed people of formal education which is known as *bourgeois*; and I have not been able to deal with them without bespattering the *bourgeoisie* with mud. I shall be told that this is not the time to stir up criticism against the middle classes, when their very existence is threatened.

Granted that their very existence is threatened. But when I wrote my book they seemed to be flourishing; and I wanted to give a warning that, on the contrary, they were running a great risk.

Who spoilt everything for them ? Neither I nor my brethren. Exceedingly badly treated by the Government, the Administration, Literature, Philosophy, Legislation and *bourgeois* predominance; cavilled at, insulted, oppressed, imprisoned, fined, we have rendered good for evil. We have never failed to raise our voices to point out the dangers which we were incurring; we have never asked for anything but justice and liberty; nobody can quote a single word or action of ours that has been seditious.

Others did not observe such self-restraint. Nevertheless, the *bourgeoisie*, and only the *bourgeoisie*, is responsible for the danger in which they stand. The plots which have finally overthrown the middle classes were either hatched in their midst, or only achieved anything because of their support; the *bourgeoisie* loaded the muskets and sharpened the sword which struck them down; they undermined the ground on which they stood, so that now they have lost their grip and are breaking up. I think I am doing the *bourgeoisie* a particular service by trying to make them understand these facts, which they seem deliberately to refuse to recognise, and which it is high time that they should know. If they do not understand what I am trying to say, I am confident that their enemies will understand me even less. I speak a language which is not current in the red

---

[1] The Charter granted by Louis XVIII, on his restoration in 1814 after Napoleon's fall, which formed the constitutional basis of the new Monarchy.

suburbs; I have not the smallest fear that any workman will spend three francs on my book, in order to find arguments which popular hatred no longer finds useful, alas, and those which it would find in it are hardly suitable for its purpose. I will add that few *bourgeois* have gone on as many patrols as I have since February 26th, or mounted guard more often. I served with the National Guard during the latest riots. I shall go to the barricades as often as it is necessary. I think I have done my duty; in any case, I could not do more. I shall go to the barricades with an aching heart, to save the State from a present and very real danger; not in the least to bear witness that I think all is well, and will go well, within the State. Thanks to the recent painful victories, something is still left standing; the vessel has not foundered, there is a ray of hope, a miracle may happen: God is so good! I fight sorrowfully therefore against the misguided workers, because of all the misfortunes which threatens them, the greatest and the most irreparable of all would be their own triumph. If the sacrifice of my life could postpone by one day this fatal triumph, I would gladly give it; but with my dying breath I should say to my companions in the fight: Do not wrap my body in your flag! I came amongst you with very different aspirations from yours. It is your doctrines which have fermented these frightful passions. You must take your share of the blame for this impious warfare.

Pray do not confuse me with those flatterers of the people, those depraved men, who assert that intelligence and virtue are only to be found in the ranks of those who are corrupt and ignorant enough to follow them! All my life I have fought the ambition of these so-called democrats, devoid as it is of talent and above all, of conscience; they represent in my eyes *bourgeois* vice at its worst. Since I first began to study them, I never remember discerning in them any noble or sincere impulse; I have always found them to be violent, lying, deceitful and insolent; the only argument they know how to use is the Moloch of steel, the triangular axe, which they call *liberty, equality and fraternity*.

But if I am not on the side of the revolutionaries and cutthroats, neither do I belong to the ranks of polite sceptics, blasphemous men of letters and swindlers, whose folly and greed have dug the abyss confronting us. There is one thing which is as intolerable as the vile unscrupulousness of men who flatter the populace: it is the imperturbable flow of words with which the multitude of advocates pleads the complete innocence of the *bourgeoisie*, asking: " What crime have they committed ? "

Free-thinkers, and free-doers (a man cannot be one without the other)—I accuse the free-thinking *bourgeoisie* of having hated God and, as a logical and premeditated result, of having despised Man. This is their crime, if they really want to know. They propagated and imposed this crime—yes IMPOSED it by example, by cunning and by the laws they made—on a section of the people; that is the danger which confronts them, and at the same time, it is their retribution.

Men of letters, statesmen, learned gentlemen of the middle classes, what is your achievement since you came to power ? You found the Church to be superfluous in this world. Not only did you steal its wealth, destroy its institutions and reject its laws; but we have seen you tireless in preaching, teaching and commanding a like scorn and a like revolt amongst the poorer classes; certainly they never wanted you to take away their religion, for irreligion strips them bare and kills them. You wrote books and newspapers; you supported black-hearted pedants and obscene mountebanks, so that they could help your laws to loosen the remaining hold which Catholicism still had over the masses; madmen that you were, you did not realise that each victory they achieved was one more stone torn from the frail bulwark of your treasure and your power. When low murmurs coming from the hearts of the multitudes, like gusts of wind, precursor of the storms already brewing in those innermost depths, brought before your very eyes some fragment of the new dogmas, which were still being propagated in whispers, you burst out laughing and said: " It is madness." And if somebody called out to you: " Take care! It is madness; but you are dealing with barbarians and God alone can save you! "—then you paraded your police, your soldiers, your penal codes, your subservient law courts and you answered: " What is God ? "

There were several apostles of this gospel of revenge and frenzy amongst you, wearing moreover your own livery. You crowded round them, applauded them, cherished them. " He is a poet, he is saying something new; he rants, but his anger is amusing; he is a sophist, but he is eloquent! "—And you loaded them with almost as many favours as you give to a clever dancer.

You welcomed everything that these buffoons said, prophets several degrees lower down the social scale than yourselves.

They indicted you, they called curses down upon you, they even calumniated you. . . . But while they cursed you, they cast insults at the eternal Christ; that was enough, you recognised your own kind. If a priest said the same things to you, inspired by faith and the promptings of charity, you stoned him. Combalot, servant of God, missionary of the people, who spent his whole life preaching forgiveness, reconciliation and hope; Combalot was fined and imprisoned because he gave a true description of University teaching. Who condemned him ? This same *bourgeoisie*, in the name of whom, and for the benefit of whom, a newspaper proprietor paid Eugène Süe 100,000 francs a year to teach Communist doctrines.

Is all this true, or am I accusing people falsely ? Have the " thinkers," from Voltaire to M. Süe[1]; the statesmen from M. de Choiseul to M. de Thiers; the legislators and administrators from the last Judicial Courts and the last Provincial Assemblies of Royal Absolutism, down to the last Chamber of Deputies and the last Prefects of Departments of the Constitutional Monarchy (I say nothing of the rest), been anything else but *bourgeois*, or faithful supporters of the *bourgeoisie* ? Did they not hate the Church, impede her action, misrepresent her doctrine and pour scepticism in full measure into the hearts of the people ?

Well, they succeeded! The people—not the whole of the people, through the grace of God, but an appreciable section of them, the workmen, the townsfolk, those who read and discuss politics—this part of the people lost their faith. They are only a minority. They would have liked to win over more, and had hoped to do so; but nevertheless, there are still one and a half million able-bodied men who have arrived at " free thought "—in other words, who have ceased to believe in God.

The Church, deprived of her institutions and her liberty, cannot teach them any more; deprived of her wealth, she cannot succour them any more; dishonoured in their consciences by the calumnies of the " philosophers," made ridiculous in their minds by the gibes of Voltaire, she can no longer bring them back within her fold. Hence all Christian links have been broken; every Christian habit has been lost. The people are outside the bosom of the Mother of all charity; they have ceased to drink from her breasts, from which they used to draw faith and hope. That is exactly what was wanted.

---

[1] Eugène Süe, 1804-1857, fashionable French novelist of the time, of naturalistic tendencies and style.

Unfortunately, other, unforeseen phenomena have developed, parallel with the successful issue of the *bourgeois* plot. The people are suffering, they are becoming a nuisance and are getting out of hand. Their lowly station, which they once accepted as a dispensation of Providence, in return for alleviations which this same Providence had designed for them, and which were distributed by the Church, they no longer accept with resignation, now that it is dependent upon inexorable chance, which brings no attendant alleviations. They begin to ask dreadful questions: they wonder if all men were born equal or no, and why some men are rich and others poor. They are told that they are sovereign, they point to their masters; they are told that their condition is improving, they reply that they are hungry; books full of fine reasoning and beautiful statistics on the inevitable inequality of the human State are cast at them, they do not bother to read them. They prefer to listen to the insane doctrines which are ventilated in the darkest recesses of their infinite poverty. Instead of the Gospel of God, which used to be their consolation, and of which they have been robbed, they accept other doctrines which drive them to frenzy. Like a dog which has gone mad, because it was tied too long to its leash, they threaten to destroy the material order, to hurl themselves upon society and loot it. What an uproar they make, more alarming than peals of thunder! What strength there is in those bare arms, more relentless than a hurricane! All the brilliance, all the glory, all the authority of the body politic is vanquished within an hour. These straws which take flight in the wind and disappear—they are the King, the Charter, Parliament, the Judiciary and the Army. The victors stop short in their progress, themselves amazed at their conquest. They had not realised there would be a battle: they had merely been giving vent to their impatience.

Terror (a legitimate terror!) rises in the hearts of the mighty of the earth; they ask: What shall we do? What is going to happen to us? With perspiring brows and white faces they hastily construct a new government. They try a thousand different means to push the people aside, those frightening actors who had appeared prematurely on the stage; but the people themselves are determined to play the rôle for which the *bourgeoisie* had long trained them. In vain do the *bourgeoisie* try to throw them off. With unrelenting rage, they lay siege to a bulwark which they know is too weak to withstand them. In vain are promises, decrees, millions of francs thrown out to them from within the

O

gates; they shout for the *bourgeoisie* and repulse the sops which are offered them in panic and fear: *What I am after is your life's blood*, they jeer. They are still with us, their eyes haggard, their hearts full of hatred, their hands threatening fire and destruction, brooding over the bitter memories of their wrongs.

Their wrongs! Have they suffered then so cruelly? Some there are who deny it. Well-written books and eloquent speeches testify to perfection that the people are freer, more respected, better paid, better fed, than at the time when they had no grievances. Granted; but all the same, the people are discontented.

The truth is that they are under a delusion, vile flatterers have led them astray; the truth is that they have given themselves up to absurd dreams and a savage pride. . . . Alas, who has brought them to this pass, and what remedy can you suggest?

My father died at the age of fifty. He was a simple workman, without any education or pride. Countless obscure and cruel misfortunes had marked his days, which were spent in toil; amongst so many trials, only the joy he took in his virtues, unshakable though quite unconscious, brought him some slight consolation. For the space of fifty years, nobody had paid any attention to his soul; never, except in his last moments, had his heart, ravaged by anxiety, rested in God. He had always known masters who were ready to sell him water, salt and air, to claim a tithe of the sweat of his brow, and to require the lives of his sons in war; never had he known a protector who could defend and succour him; never a guide who could enlighten him, or pray with him, or teach him how to hope. At bottom, what had society said to him? What had all these rights, which are written so pompously into charters, meant in his case? " Work hard, be obedient and honest; for if you rebel, you will be killed; if you steal and are found out, you will go to prison. But if you suffer, weep alone, we cannot help you; if you have no bread to eat, go to the workhouse, or starve; it is none of our business." That is what society had said to him and nothing more; and whatever promises are written into constitutions, it cannot do or say anything else. It only provides bread for the poor in the workhouse; it cannot offer consolation and self-respect anywhere. Heavens! what good does it do to deceive ourselves and follow a will-o'-the-wisp? Every day I listen to the speeches deputies make, and I have just followed most carefully the debate on the right to public assistance and to work; not a single legislator who does not look on the poorest citizen as his brother, I am sure; but what lies at the end of all these homilies ? Nurses at the workhouse and the bolted doors of the asylum of Bicêtre!

So my father had worked, suffered and died. Standing at his open grave, I conjured up in my mind's eye the long-drawn-out trials of his life, every one of them, and I thought of all the joys his heart, which was truly created to love God, in spite of the state of servitude in which he lived, ought to have known: pure and celestial joys, which cannot be told in words, and of which he had been cruelly and criminally deprived by society. Then from the tomb of that poor workman there came to me as it were a glimmer of truth from the grave, which made me understand, and call down a curse . . . not on work, on poverty, or on suffering, but on the great social crime, the crime of irreligion, which robs the disinherited of this world of the compensations by which God has offset their lowly fate; I felt a malediction rise up from the depths of my grief.

Yes, it was at that precise moment that I began to understand and judge this society, this civilisation, these so-called wise men who had denied God, and by denying God had rejected the poor and took no further interest in their bodies and their souls. I said to myself: This social structure is iniquitous, it will crumble and perish.

I was a Christian by that time: if I had not been, from thenceforth I should have joined the various secret societies. I should have reasoned, like so many others to whom the light from on high has not been transmitted: Why should other people be well-housed, well-clothed and well-fed, while we are covered with rags, huddled together in garrets, forced to work in sunshine or in rain to earn scarcely enough to die on ? This dangerous problem would have made my head reel; for if God gives no answer to it, no man can do so. When I was a child and one of my father's employers would come along and roughly give him his orders, without bothering to remove his hat, my heart would thump as I felt a frantic longing to humble this insolent creature, to humiliate him and crush him. I would say to myself: Who made him the master and my father the slave ? My father, who is good, decent and strong, and who never did harm to a soul; while this man is puny, evil, dishonest and leads a scandalous life! My father and this man represented the whole of society in my eyes. Now if I had remained as ignorant as working people usually do, does anybody imagine that the *Short Treatises of the Academy of Moral and Political Science* would have meant anything to me, and that I would have accepted as inevitable that unequal division of the world's goods of which I was fated to have such a small part? The logic of passion works differently. Either I would have done my utmost to seize a larger portion or I should have shouted with the crowd: Let us break up the lion's share, so that at least there will be equality of poverty! Perhaps I shan't get any benefit out of it, but I can't lose anything by it either— at least I shall have the satisfaction of taking my revenge and I shan't be insulted any more.

There lies the wound in the people; it is in their soul; it is a deep one, septic and fearful to behold. Constitutions will not help much, guns not at all. Society is threatened with complete ruin if it does not spit out the poison which it has been imbibing for the last century, a poison which traitors and fools are still offering it, even in these crucial days when everything seems to be breaking up.

Let society lose no more time! Perhaps it only needs one last dose, one last law against Christ and His Church, before it is utterly destroyed.

I point out in my book, as well as I can in my weakness and obscurity, some of the men who are trying to poison society, in order to give the public a warning. They are the same today as they were seven months ago: revolutionaries wearing the Republican cap, just as once they wore the livery of the king.

Liberty, equality, fraternity! Vain words, even fatal ones, now that they have acquired a political sense; for politics have changed them into three lies. Liberty really means justice; equality is humility and fraternity is another word for charity. We shall have liberty when we dispense justice; we shall accept equality, when we have all bowed our heads to the level of the Cross; we shall practise fraternity when we adore OUR Father Who is in Heaven, and when we have asked Him to give us the grace to love our brothers with the same love which He gives to His children. Until that time there will be nothing in our souls but selfishness, covetousness and pride; and the Republican device will only mean, as in the past, a bullet in our guns or the blade of the guillotine in the hands of triumphant factions.

I end with the words which the universal Church in her faith sings on this very day (The Feast of the Exaltation of the Cross):

*Dominus ostendit Moysi lignum: quod cum insisset in aquas, in dulcetu-
dinem versae sunt.* This wood which the Lord shows to the leader
of the people, and which, cast into the waters, makes them sweet
where once they were bitter, is a figure of the Cross. Only the
Cross can save the world.